# Scots Who Made America

*Rick Wilson*

BIRLINN

This edition published in 2016 by
Birlinn Ltd
West Newington House
10 Newington Road
Edinburgh
EH9 1QS

www.birlinn.co.uk

First published in 2006

ISBN 978 1 78027 380 8

British Library Cataloguing-in-Publication Data
A catalogue record for this book is available
from the British Library

Typesetting and origination by Brinnoven, Livingston
and Hewer Text UK Ltd, Edinburgh
Printed and bound by Grafica Veneta (www.graficaveneta.com)

# Contents

Introduction                                                        vii

AMERICA'S GREAT SCOTS
Henry St Clair (1398)                                                  1
Captain Kidd (1645–1701)                                              6
John Witherspoon (1723–94)                                          12
James Craik (1730–1814)                                             17
James Wilson (1742–98)                                              21
John Paul Jones (1747–90)                                           25
Alexander Wilson (1766–1813)                                        32
'Uncle' Sam Wilson (1766–1854)                                      36
Archibald Binny (?–1838) and
James Ronaldson (1768–1842)                                         39
James Gordon Bennett (1795–1872)                                    42
Allan Pinkerton (1819–84)                                           46
Andrew Carnegie (1835–1919)                                         54
Andrew Smith Hallidie (1836–1900)                                   63
John Muir (1838–1914)                                               67
Robert Dollar (1844–1932)                                           75
Alexander Graham Bell (1847–1922)                                   80
David Dunbar Buick (1854–1929)                                      89
Bertie C. Forbes (1880–1954)                                        95
Tommy Armour (1895–1968)                                           103
Harry Benson (1930–  )                                             107
Hugh Grant (1958–  )                                               113

THE SCOTTISH INFLUENCE
Alexander Selkirk (1676–1723)                                      119
William Cullen (1710–90)                                           124
Adam Smith (1723–90)                                               129

James Small (1740–93)                          135
John McAdam (1756–1836)                         137
Robert Burns (1759–96)                          140
Charles Macintosh (1765–1843)                   146
Walter Scott (1770–1832)                        149
Johnnie Walker (1800–59)                        152
Alexander Bain (1811–77)                        155
James Dewar (1842–1923)                         159
Robert Louis Stevenson  (1850–94)               161
Arthur Conan Doyle (1859–1930)                  165
James Matthew Barrie (1860–1937)                169
Harry Lauder (1870–1950)                        173
Alexander Fleming (1881–1955)                   177
John Logie Baird (1888–1946)                    181
Robert Watson-Watt (1892–1973)                  184
Sean Connery (1930–   )                         187
Jim Clark (1936–68)                             193
Tom Farmer (1940–   )                           197
Tony Blair (1953–   )                           204

# Introduction

I could try to put this modestly, but that would be simply disingenuous. While I wish to avoid the impression of 'wha's like us' chest thumping, this book is an unashamed celebration of home-born Scots who have had an incalculable effect on the life and culture of the United States. Most of them ended up on those western shores, though some performed their magic from afar. Most are gone now, but a few are happily still with us.

I have not tried to be particularly objective – one person's objectivity often being quite different from another's – but have elected to profile especially colourful, imagination-capturing personalities in the fields of science, culture, engineering, publishing, literature, business and medicine. Neither have I felt limited by this or that period, in covering notable achievements from the (alleged) discovery of America by Scots nobleman Henry St Clair in the fourteenth century to the photographing of no fewer than ten American presidents by Harry Benson, a New York-based cameraman who often flies home to walk along his native Scottish beaches with old pals from his childhood.

I have, however, employed some criteria that have precluded our dwelling on the already much-covered impact of second, third and succeeding generations of Scottish-Americans. With that remit, the sky would have been the limit. I could have mentioned multi-millionaire John D. Rockefeller, who inherited Scottish blood from his mother; James Naismith, who invented baseball; James Monroe, the US president and great-grandson of a Scots Covenanter who arrived in the USA in chains; President Lyndon Johnson, whose family came from Dumfriesshire; Neil Armstrong, the first man on the moon, also descended from a Dumfriesshire family; Davy Crockett, the legendary adventurer of Scots descent; Walter, Arthur and William A. Davidson, co-founders of the Harley Davidson motorbike group, whose family hailed from Angus; billionaire tycoon Donald Trump, whose mother was born on the Isle of Lewis; Robert Barclay of Aberdeenshire roots, who was founding governor of New Jersey; and even Elvis Presley, also rooted in Aberdeenshire via a Presley who went to America in the early 1700s. So, in visiting the shores of Britain only once – en route to America from his army unit in Germany – Elvis did so aptly at Scotland's Prestwick Airport in 1960.

But from the McDonalds hamburger chain to the McDonnell Douglas aircraft company, Scottish blood runs through every vein of America, and the little land at the top corner of Europe can lay claim to having indirectly bred some of the most symbolic contributors to US society – sharp-suited entrepreneurs such as IBM builder Thomas Watson and Microsoft founder Bill Gates – as well as some of the more leathery and controversial Wild West figures, like Wyatt Earp, Jesse James and James Wilson Marshall, who started the Californian gold rush.

Indeed, 61 per cent of US presidents have had Scottish origins, and nine of the thirteen governors of the newly created United States of America were Scots. Everywhere you look in America there are fascinating traces of tartan – even on the dollar bill itself: the Scots typefounders Archbald Binny and James Ronaldson designed the dollar sign, while Scots-descended James Pollock became Director of the Mint at Philadelphia and was responsible for putting the phrase 'In God We Trust' on US money.

But it is not American-born Scots on whom I have focused this exercise, and neither have I insisted on US residency as a qualification for inclusion. Some big Scots names have impacted on America without being on the spot. Some have just spent some time there. So a fair part of the book focuses on 'influencers from afar', people such as movie star Sir Sean Connery, who have been much in demand, though not resident, in America. I have noted the magical effects of certain stay-at-home figures, such as Peter Pan creator J.M. Barrie and Crusoe-inspiring Scots sailor Alexander Selkirk. I have examined the life-changing temptations that emigration presented to Scotland's famous writers like Robert Louis Stevenson and Robert Burns, who, despite their subsequent impact on American culture, never quite made the break. I have acknowledged the significant impact that Scots-resident groundbreakers in radar, penicillin, television and refrigeration made on both sides of the Atlantic. And I have noted that other developments, such as the ever-popular mac raincoat and tarmac road surfacing, have been successfully exported into US life without the accompanying presence of their Scots inventors. I have even paid due heed to the regard with which Edinburgh-born Tony Blair is held in America.

But the bulk of this volume is devoted to the men who gave not just their talents but also their whole physical selves to America; whose work made them famous after their arrival on its shores. Obvious names like Andrew Carnegie, the weaver's son from Dunfermline who became the richest man in the world, and Alexander Graham Bell, well-named inventor of the telephone; as well as lesser-known characters like Andrew Hallidie, who invented the San Francisco cable car, or Alexander Wilson, the Paisley-born father of American ornithology.

Such human stars of the American element of the Scottish diaspora provide a clear illustration of just how actively creative immigrants can be. Indeed, Andrew Carnegie himself said: 'Without the Scots America would have been a poor show.' I would not go that far, but – particularly in the days of the Highland Clearances, when people were forced to make way for sheep (1790–1845) – there was a mutual enthusiasm for what each party had to offer. The Scots sought new opportunities and the Americans welcomed their industry, application and high standard of education. One American observer wrote: 'Of all immigrants to our country, the Scotch are always the most welcome. They bring us muscle and brain and tried skill and trustworthiness in many of our great industries, of which they are managers of the most successful.'

Women readers may be disappointed that all the personalities covered in the book are men. This is largely because at the point of the biggest explosion of Scottish emigration to the USA – after the 1707 Act of Union between Scotland and England and before female rights began being properly asserted in the late twentieth century – it was, like it or not, a man's world. A few names of enterprising women were considered but they were so few that I suspect the charge against me then would have been 'tokenism'. Let's trust that, a century from now, there will be opportunities aplenty for the publishing of such a book focused on the exported achievements of Scottish women.

But for the moment, I celebrate the Tartan Titans, the Scotsmen who shaped America.

I am grateful to friends and colleagues who have helped with this project, particularly journalists Jack Webster and Jim Gilchrist, and my eagle-eyed wife Alison, who can spot an errant comma from a mile away.

# America's Great Scots

# Henry St Clair (1358–1400)

*He led, Columbus followed*

Could it possibly be true that America was discovered by a Scots nobleman almost a century before Christopher Columbus? It is a beguiling proposition that captivates a growing number of today's natives of Caledonia, the more familiar they become with the story and evidence of Sir Henry St Clair and his medieval meanderings.

One compelling piece of evidence is to be found on Edinburgh's doorstep today, in a fascinating ancient place redolent of medieval intrigue and mystery just south of the city: a finely hewn building like a miniature cathedral where pagan and Christian traditions live a little uneasily side by side.

This is the well-preserved fifteenth-century Rosslyn Chapel – described by its caretakers as a 'jewel in stone' – whose elevated but secluded position near the rolling foothills of the Pentlands is not only beautiful but dramatically illustrative of the difference between Scotland then and now. Why? Simply and mundanely because of its proximity to the hugely popular Edinburgh outlet of the Swedish IKEA furniture group.

Only a few miles apart, both powerful symbols taken together show just how ages and ever-evolving cultures have radically changed the Scots. But they have one thing in common: they can really pull in the crowds – albeit of acutely different kinds of people. The chic-but-cheap store daily attracts hundreds of materialistic home-improvers happily absorbed into the Scandinavian furnishing trend that has flooded almost every corner of every household in the land; the chapel is a magnet for more spiritual and cerebral types like historians, students of religion and mystics . . . joined relatively recently by the Hollywood actor Tom Hanks and waves of international book and movie fans keen to take in and sense the denouement scene of Dan Brown's blockbuster novel and film, *The Da Vinci Code*.

What they behold is a compact, filigreed masterpiece of the stonemason's art that defies description – at least by some, such as a lost-for-words author called Britton who, in his 1812 *Architectural Antiquities of Britain,* said the chapel would be found 'curious, elaborate and singularly interesting, impossible to designate by any given or familiar term', its 'variety and eccentricity not to be defined by any words of common acceptation'.

But should they start to study the detail of the elaborately carved interior, a visitor's already dazzled eye might settle on the pattern of repeated bulbous shapes that make a sweeping lower border to the arch over one of the chapel windows. These have been identified as American maize, which should not have been known in Britain when the chapel was founded in 1446 by William Sinclair, the third earl of Orkney.

If the American continent was only found by Columbus in 1492, and even if the chapel took another forty years to complete, how did these representations manage to appear in Scotland? It is only logical to conclude that someone with a connection to Rosslyn must have made the transatlantic voyage before that date; and the common assumption is that that person was William's grandfather, Sir Henry St Clair, sometimes described as 'Prince' Henry because of his royal connection. The current earl of Rosslyn, who has written an informative introductory book about the chapel for visitors, simply asks: 'Is it possible that knowledge [of the plants] brought home by Prince Henry passed to his grandson?'

But for many Scots who look askance at the annual celebration of the Genoese navigator's 'discovery' of America, there is very little doubt that, having crossed the Atlantic at the head of an impressive fleet, the Scottish knight set foot on the rugged shores of Nova Scotia, near to what is now Guysborough, on the Feast of the Trinity in 1398. And they see it as quite natural that his grandson William should have immortalised that early transatlantic voyage in stone at the chapel in the family estate of which he was the baron.

But Henry St Clair was not just the baron of Rosslyn. He was known by many other grand titles: knight, of course, and Lord Chief Justice of Scotland, Admiral of the Seas, and First Prince [or Earl] of Orkney – the last bestowed upon him by King Haakon of Norway, who endowed him with 200 strategically located Scottish islands over which he reigned all-powerful, more like a king than a prince. But he is also thought to have been the legendary figure known as 'Glooscap' among the Micmac Native American Indians whose folklore is said to describe his ships as 'islands with trees growing on them'.

To begin, however, at the beginning . . .

What we know of the story is largely thanks to chronicles of a sixteenth-century Venetian, whose namesake and forebear, Nicolò Zeno, was sailing round the north coast of Scotland when, after being shipwrecked off the Faroe islands, he was rescued and befriended by a local chieftain. Was this St Clair? That point is not clear, but gratefully wishing to help the chief in his endeavours, the Italian summoned his brother Antonio from Venice and together, in 1393, the two skilled shipbuilders led a successful mapping expedition to Greenland. Nicolò died the following year, but Antonio stayed on to make another expedition in 1398, this time almost certainly with Sir Henry.

Known as the *Zeno Narrative*, the story of St Clair's voyage to North America was written by the 'new' Nicolò Zeno a historian and prominent citizen, in 1558. His claimed sources were letters written by the original Nicolò, and his brother Antonio. Antonio's letters (as given in the *Narrative*) also refer to a book he had written that described in detail the lands they visited, and they included a map of the islands and countries of the North Atlantic.

But why was such an ambitious expedition mounted? The St Clairs were linked to the once-powerful Knights Templar, some of whom had fled to Scotland after they were outlawed, and it is speculated that the journey was intended to find and found a Templar colony far from their hunters' eyes. Formed during the Crusades, the Knights Templar were a wealthy band of warrior-monks who had become the most feared soldiers of Christendom – until, after two centuries of unrivalled power in Europe and the Holy Land, they were abruptly suppressed by King Philip IV of France and proclaimed open to arrest over most of Europe on charges of heresy, blasphemy and obscenity. Scotland was one of only two European countries – the other was Portugal – where the order was not proscribed by the Pope. It was seen as their last refuge from persecution; but was it far enough away from the rest of Europe?

In any case, some records say bluntly that Sir Henry sailed from Orkney 'with Templar funding', and it was certainly with a big and well-equipped force that he did so. No fewer than twelve ships set off with what seemed indeed remarkably like a colonising 300-strong company – of Templar knights, soldiers, sailmakers, armourers, carpenters and farming monks – complete with Venetian Pietro cannon.

Sailing via Shetland, they first reached Newfoundland from where, after making an unsuccessful attempt to land, they pushed on south through vicious seas – losing no fewer than five ships – to Nova Scotia. The remaining ships must have been struggling by the time they got there, and readers can surely draw their own conclusions from the fact that, in 1849, two brass Venetian naval cannon of the late fourteenth century were dredged up off the shore of Louisburg harbour on Nova Scotia's Cape Breton Island.

In any case, perhaps in an attempt to cut his losses, it was in Nova Scotia that Sir Henry is said to have sent most of his fleet back to Orkney while he and his shore party spent more then a year exploring the new land and making the acquaintance of the Micmac Indians.

So the story goes. But what evidence is there? It is largely anecdotal, but it is intriguing nonetheless. Along with other tribes in the surrounding regions, the Micmacs have a legend of a white 'prince' who came from across the sea and met their people at Pictou, which has been identified as the second landfall of the expedition. Said to have been wise and kindly, he apparently showed the Indians the European styles of fishing, hunting and plant cultivation. The lore also records that the white prince travelled in 'a great stone canoe', also described as 'a floating island with trees growing out of it', which surely evokes the picture of a European sailing ship with high masts.

These and other native American peoples are also said to have referred in their folklore to the landfall of a vessel 'like a bird with a broken wing' and still act out the arrival of a foreign hero called 'Glooscap', a name reckoned by some to be the Indians' version of Earl Sinclair. And according to Jim Gilchrist, a Scots writer who has done considerable research into the subject, 'ethnologists say that it was around this period that the natives of the area started fishing with nets, European-style, rather than with lines, while others point to Gaelic and Norse words assimilated into the vocabulary of the Algonquin and other native peoples'.

It is also told that when Sir Henry took his leave of his new-found admirers after his mutually enriching year among them, his intention was to be heading for home. A sudden storm blew up, however, and drove him south to Massachusetts, which was the catalytic moment that meant he was to set foot in what we now know as America almost a century before Columbus. Shortly after his landing there, it is recorded in the *Zeno Narrative*, they climbed a hill where his close companion and cousin, the Templar Knight Sir James Gunn of Clyth, suddenly died – either from heat exhaustion or by being beaten in a fight. And it is here that further compelling evidence of the landfall begins to emerge.

There has since been discovered, roughly scratched out of a rock at Prospect Hill in Westford, Massachusetts, the unmistakable effigy of a fourteenth-century knight holding a sword – dated between 1375 and 1400 – and a shield which was identified by a former Lord Lyon, the Scottish authority on crests, as being from the Gunn family.

Sir Henry may even have reached as far south as Rhode Island, where some evidence suggests that he and his men could have built Newport Tower, a two-storey circular stone needle which, say researchers, is definitely European – rather than native American – and has architectural features that owe something to the medieval church towers of Scotland's northern isles.

If all this is true (and it has to be said that there are many dissenters, even in Scotland), it would be touching and apt for Sir Henry to have left such an impact over the centuries; for he was undoubtedly a man of great courage, achievement and presence. Indeed, his Venetian companion Antonio Zeno is recorded as saying that 'if ever there was a man worthy of immortal memory, it is this man'.

While the time and place of Sir Henry's death remain a mystery – some say his remains were brought to Rosslyn Chapel to be buried among the other St Clair knights who lie there – those words would surely have made a suitable epitaph for the enterprising Scot who (probably) 'discovered' America for the Europeans.

*Note.* 'The whole business of "discovering" countries is, of course, somewhat subjective,' says Jim Gilchrist. 'High-profile explorers get recorded in the history text books, others "discover" places without posterity noting the fact. Thus, ten years after his "discovery" of America, Christopher Columbus received a letter from some English merchants alleging that he knew perfectly well that they had already been there for fish.'

# Captain Kidd (1645–1701)

*The reluctant pirate*

When we talk of pirates and their dastardly deeds, the name Captain Kidd is sure to come quickly to mind. How does the image go again? An evil-looking, lank-haired man with knife gripped between rotting teeth, a red headscarf roughly stained with skull-and-crossbones, the quick flash of evil in the one eye not covered by a patch, and a less-than-pleasant bodily odour. Those who don't see Captain Kidd as the archetypal bad guy of the seven seas are rare, for he was so successfully demonised in a propaganda exercise that, over the three centuries since his body was trussed up to rot on the oak gibbet at Tilbury after his hanging in London, succeeding generations of readers have swallowed the story. Right up to the present day. And the story's essence is that, in the days of mean ship-raiding swashbucklers, he was the meanest of them all.

Interesting idea, pity it's not the truth.

There are, admittedly, many things that we don't know about Captain William Kidd, such as his age when he was so crudely dispatched to meet his maker in 1701 – many accounts of his life say he was born in 1655, others say his birth year was 1645. All are agreed that he was born in Scotland, but there is considerable disagreement about where.

Several accounts say he came from Greenock, the west coast port near Glasgow, but others suggest that he was in fact from the east coast, and that his place of birth was actually Carnock 'near Dundee'. It depends what is meant by 'near', of course, for there is no Carnock in the immediate vicinity of Dundee, though there is one very close to Dunfermline in Fife – the county south of the River Tay, on whose northern bank Dundee sits.

The distance between Carnock and Dundee is some fifty miles, and as Kidd lived much of his life in New York and often referred to Dundee as his provenance, perhaps that was just his shorthand for the convenience of others who may have heard of the city but not the village. From that faraway standpoint, they would not have considered the city-to-village distance so great.

There is more in favour of the east. At a hearing in the High Court of the Admiralty in 1695 he gave his age as forty-one and his place of birth as Dundee. The surname Kidd is popular in Fife but relatively rare on Scotland's west coast. His father is listed as a seaman, which explains why one of the chronicles of the day (the *Newgate Calendar*) called him a man 'born to sea'. The exhaustively researched book *The Pirate Hunter* by Richard Zacks simply calls him 'Captain Kidd of New York City and Dundee'. But the clinching fact for this writer is that Kidd affectionately named his black cabin boy 'Dundee'. Anyone who knows the Scots and their little geographic loyalties knows that no one from the west coast would be inclined to put sentimental store on anywhere in the east, or vice versa.

The west coast author Sandra Macdougall, who claims William Kidd for Greenock – 'although there are no local records confirming this fact' – in her book on famous people from Inverclyde's past, will no doubt take issue with this conclusion, especially as my own attempts at finding evidence of his birth in pretty little Carnock also drew a blank. Neither the local church minister nor the nearest library at Oakley had heard of the link. But both were intrigued and, as you read this, might still be burrowing excitedly into their records. So might Lizz Mogg, senior teacher at Carnock School who has chronicled the village's history. 'Captain Kidd came from here?' she exclaimed. 'That really would be something to update my book with. The children would love that.'

Carnock is certainly near enough to big water – the Firth of Forth is visible four miles away – to have weaned a famous sailor. And it is old enough to feel like his cradle. A handful of simple cottage-style buildings, it nestles in the dale of the Carnock Burn three miles north-west of Dunfermline. Said to have been named after St Caranoc, a disciple of St Ninian, it has a parish church built in 1840; but nearby in the old kirkyard stand the ruins of the original twelfth-century parish church and the fine gravestone of John Row, minister of the parish and the Church of Scotland's first historian, who died in 1646. Thus would two famous lifelines have crossed in the village – if William Kidd was indeed born in Carnock in 1645.

It can't be denied that his early career was obscure, and all accounts of his colourful life are plain on that point. But what they all also agree on is that, however he spent his early years at sea – buccaneering

or privateering – by the time he surfaced on the record in 1689 as
a legitimate privateer for Great Britain against the French, he had
learned how to cultivate important people and was himself something
of a gentleman.

In other words, he was nothing like the clichéd wild man still
pictured by so many people. Indeed, it is questionable whether
William Kidd was ever a pirate at all, so much of his fate resting as
it did on the sometimes-difficult distinction between that word and
the word privateer (having government permission to attack enemy
ships on the understanding that the spoils will be shared).

In any event, he was as much a well-to-do merchant as he was either
of these. While the sea was in his blood and he always felt drawn back
to it, he owned considerable property in New York, married a rich
widow there, was very well connected in the city all the way up to the
governor, and wore – in his only known contemporary portrait – a
gentleman's fashionable long wig.

There is, though, a decidedly sharp adventurer's glint in his eye,
and there is no doubt about the fact that he was something of a
magnet for trouble. A Scot who lorded it over Dutch, English and
American crew members was never going to be popular and when he
captained a privateer ship, *Blessed William*, commissioned in 1689 to
protect the English colonies in the Caribbean against French attacks,
his crew mutinied and left him stranded on the island of Antigua.

Not a bad place to be stranded, some might argue, but he made
his way back to New York where he could have settled quietly into an
elite business life. Adventure still called, however, and by 1695 he was
on his way to London to take a contract as a privateer commanding
the 237-ton, 34-cannon *Adventure Galley* with orders to attack and
loot any (then enemy) French ships.

The *Adventure Galley* had not gone far on her journey to New
York and then on to the Red Sea – to capture any ship belonging
to a country at war with England – when she was relieved of much
of her crew by a Royal Navy squadron desperate to replace sailors
lost to scurvy: a right that it had by law against any ship flying an
English flag.

Scraping the bottom of the barrel in New York, a frustrated Captain
Kidd added more crew – probably with piratical tendencies – then
set sail for the Indian Ocean on his mission to clear the sea there
of pirates, though there was probably an unspoken understanding
between him and his scheming backers, who included Richard

Coote, the earl of Bellomont and other nobles (such as the king), that he would also consider any enemy ships with valuable cargo fair game.

Mutinous muttering began again as months went by and Kidd's failure to take a prize ship meant that, under the terms of the privateer's contract, there would be no pay for the crew. They pressured Kidd to turn pirate and attack anything, and after he refused to plunder a becalmed Dutch ship they had sighted, a row broke out in which he killed gunner William Moore by hitting him violently over the head with a bucket.

Then, finally, in February 1698, Kidd took his most valuable prize – an Indian-owned ship, the *Quedah Merchant,* which carried a treasure trove of a cargo worth some £710,000 and had French papers making her a legal target under Kidd's privateer terms. She was renamed *Adventure Prize* and her cargo of silk, muslins, sugar, calico, iron and saltpetre seemed set to enrich her captors and their backers. But there was a snag . . . or two.

It did not look like it, but luck was turning against Kidd just as abruptly as politics in London. He had been away from there for nearly two years and in that time there had been a dramatic change in attitude towards piracy and privateering. Officialdom now wanted to pursue only legal trading procedures. And complicating things further was the fact that the *Quedah Merchant* belonged to an influential Armenian merchant who demanded that the East India Company, the English trading company in the East Indies, make restitution.

Having thus offended England's commercial establishment, William Kidd was denounced as an 'obnoxious pirate' and murderer. All the circumstances were crowding against him, as they had done from the moment his crew had forced him over the privateering edge. He had become very bad news, as the enemies of his backers used him to discredit the Whig party to which many of his powerful friends belonged. Soon, his friends distanced themselves from him too.

When Kidd got full appreciation of his plight, he ran for New York where he thought his influential friends, including the governor, would attest to his innocence. He made his way to Block Island, where he began negotiations through his contacts in New York to gain a pardon for his actions, claiming he had been forced into piracy by his crew. But it didn't work. He was captured in July 1699, jailed, then sent to England aboard the frigate *Advice,* to stand trial and incidentally become a political pawn to bring down powerful men in the government.

The trial started on 8 May 1701, and despite his protests that he was not prepared for it and could prove, given time 'to get my evidence ready', that he was only a privateer, it was completed the next day. He was not a man of particular guile and his bluntness could grate in a well-oiled courtroom, but he fought hard and straightforwardly for himself. A small exchange from the trial went like this:

Kidd to character witness Colonel Hewetson: 'Do you think I was a pirate?'

Hewetson to the court: 'I know his men would a gone a-pirateering and he refused it, and his men seized upon his ship.'

And in a letter protesting his innocence he wrote: 'I must be sacrificed as a pirate to salve the Hon'r of some men who employed me . . .'

William Kidd was nonetheless found guilty of multiple piracies and murder (ironically committed when trying to stamp down piracy in his crew) and sentenced to hang on the gallows on 23 May 1701. But he did not do so in total sobriety – 'he was inflam'd with Drink', said his attending priest – or with convenient good grace. The rope broke on the first attempt, granting him another ten minutes of life before it was replaced. At that moment, it was later reported, Kidd sobered up and asked those around him to send his love to his wife and daughter back in New York and said his greatest regret 'was the thought of my wife's sorrow at my shameful death'.

An accurate report? Why should he have felt shamed if he was not guilty, as he had protested? William Kidd may not have been an angel but he was a victim of heavy politics, rich men's plotting and a set of cruel circumstances. If he was a pirate, he was probably an unwilling one. Certain items could have helped his case. But strangely, his logbook was burned and the papers that might have proved his innocence disappeared in Lord Bellomont's hands.

During his career, at least the recorded part of it, Kidd had never seen the need to return to his native Scotland. But that he remained a proud Scot was evidenced by his disparaging reference in one letter to 'their' justice. Then, as now, England and Scotland had distinctly different justice systems.

Certainly, he had no reason to hold the English Establishment in high regard. All his life he had been used as a scapegoat by those more politically powerful than he, and now, even in death, there was no mercy – only humiliation. The Scottish captain's corpse was tarred and suspended and displayed to rot in an iron cage on the dock at Thames estuary for several years as a warning to would-be pirates, and a grim welcome to seafarers arriving in England's main port.

For him, every strategy of self-defence had failed; even the letter to the Tory speaker of the House of Commons in which he offered the government £100,000 worth of his 'lodged goods' if he were allowed to lead a ship to them. His offer fell foul of more pressing business that day, but it has never been forgotten since.

Captain Kidd is believed to have buried much of his treasure from the *Adventure Prize* in several places, and while some of it was found during his life or shortly after his death, the largest deposit is thought to be still for finding, and even today, as author Richard Zacks reminds us, that promise prompts 'treasure hunters to dig holes all over New England, the Caribbean and Madagascar'.

Imagine if the cards had fallen more fortunately for William Kidd. He could have made his way back to his 'lodged goods' and bellowed out a last laugh to reverberate all the way back to Carnock. But it was not to be.

# John Witherspoon (1723–94)

*Princeton president, freedom fighter*

Yester is not a bad name for the East Lothian parish where John Witherspoon was born, in the manse of the little towered kirk that sits neatly atop the rise of pretty Gifford village. Not a bad name – evocative as it is of 'yesterday' – because at first glance almost everything here seems to have stood still for centuries. Many of the venerable gravestones clustered about the white-walled church are infirm, weather-worn and leaning, adding to the general feeling that, on entering the village, you have entered another, earlier age.

Save for the occasional modern shop nestled between them, the modest sandstone houses that line the village's few streets would seem to have changed little since the young Witherspoon grew up here, where his father preached in the early 1700s. But appearances can be deceptive. Unexpectedly elegant interiors and the occasional fine car parked outside betray a 21st-century reality: that such precious olde worlde village atmosphere now comes at a price, making this special place on the River Gifford – a tributary of the Tyne – one of the hottest property spots in the general vicinity of the hottest of them all, Edinburgh.

John Witherspoon has to be its other claim to fame.

Having learned that the church's exterior boasted a plate to the memory of this Scots minister who found fame by becoming president of Princeton University and a signatory of America's Declaration of Independence, this writer repeatedly circled the old churchyard getting steadily more puzzled while failing to find the tribute supposedly erected in 1955 by the St Andrew's Society of the State of New York.

But just as I stepped into the body of the village to seek help from the locals, a reflected sun-ray sparkled into my eye, as if to say, 'I'm here' and, thus pulled back almost magnetically, I saw, behind a small expanse of grass, the head-high bronze plate on an old stone wall across the Haddington road from the church. And as I read the inscription, the image of the old minister seemed to look on approvingly . . .

In honoured memory of the Reverend
JOHN WITHERSPOON, D.D., LL.D.

Only clergyman to sign the American Declaration of
Independence. The first Moderator of the Presbyterian General
Assembly in America, and President of Princeton University. Born
in the manse of Yester, Gifford, Feb 5th, 1723

'. . . The States of America may hand down the blessings of peace
and public order to many generations.'

Property values would not have much interested the self-denying Witherspoons. As minister of Yester parish, the father passed on to the son not just his piety and fluent literacy but also a love of simple tastes. Which was probably already in the genes, for they were lineally descended from the formidable ascetic reformer John Knox, whose prayers made Mary Queen of Scots – she once said – 'more afraid than of an army of ten thousand men'.

Like that ancestor and his own father, John Witherspoon was also to become a renowned preacher whose reputation would carry his career to great heights. After initially exercising his keen mind in his schooling at Haddington, he went to Edinburgh University at fourteen and made a big impression in the theological hall before completing his studies at twenty-one and going straight into preaching in the parish of Beith, in the west of Scotland, where he was held in high regard by his congregation. From there, he went to Paisley, near Glasgow, where he won over the affections of a new and larger congregation.

By all accounts, Dr Witherspoon was a compelling preacher. But he was not just a pulpit thumper; his merits as an author were much appreciated, and an admirer said of his writings that 'to every serious and intelligent reader, they discover an uncommon knowledge of human nature, and a deep and intimate acquaintance with the holy scriptures'.

Somehow, this tall, dignified gentleman managed to combine duties as a devoted pastor with his increasingly ambitious literary efforts – one of which really set the heather on fire in 1753. 'Anonymous' it may have claimed to be, but his was suspected to be the pen behind the satire, *Ecclesiastical Characteristics,* which stung the Church of

Scotland as it identified the shortcomings of some of its ministers. It was the talk of the coffee houses – as was its follow-up, *A Serious Apology* [for the *Characteristics*] in which Dr Witherspoon admitted writing the *Characteristics*.

Three years later he published, from Glasgow, his acclaimed essay *Connexion Between the Doctrine of Justification by the Imputed Righteousness of Christ, and Holiness of Life*. This was followed by a still more celebrated work, *A Serious Inquiry into the Nature and Effects of the Stage*, and in 1764 he went to London to oversee publication of his *Essays on Important Subjects* – a three-volume collection of essays already sporadically published in Scotland.

Unsurprisingly, all this publishing activity spread his reputation far and wide, and soon he was fighting off 'please join us' invitations from congregations in Dublin, Dundee and even the Scottish church in Rotterdam. His attachment to Paisley was too strong to break for any of these, but – with his fame having even crossed the Atlantic – something completely different soon came along which was sufficiently appealing for him to leave not just Paisley but his beloved Scotland.

This was an invitation from the trustees of the College of Princeton, New Jersey (now Princeton University), to become their president. Sympathising with his wife's fear of sailing and of leaving friends and family behind, he at first declined, and indeed he could well have profited from sticking to that decision, for a rich relation offered to make him his heir if the call were ignored. On rethinking things, however, Mrs Witherspoon steeled herself and Dr Witherspoon changed his mind, leaving behind not just great sadness among his Paisley people but, according to one chronicler, 'a sphere of great respectability, comfort, and usefulness'.

He and his family – three sons and two daughters – landed safely in America in August 1768, and in the same month he was inaugurated as the sixth president of the College of Princeton. The excitement of having acquired a man of such erudite reputation to be an intellectual leader in this corner of America caused an immediate fillip not just to the number of students but to the college's funds, which had not been overly healthy at a time when it depended upon contributions rather than state support. And as its finances began to flourish, with new contributions recorded from Virginia to Massachusetts, so did the college's reflected reputation. And the early faith in Dr Witherspoon proved not to have been misplaced. Soon, he had wrought a total revolution in the instruction system practised before his arrival, boosting the study of mathematical science and natural philosophy, bringing in 'all the most liberal and modern improvements of Europe', and making changes in every department of instruction, from history to law, while personally passing on many of the principles of good taste and good writing.

Said to be 'the most companionable of men' with a good sense of humour, his natural facility for governing was a bonus much admired by many of his students who sought to copy, and even emulate, such leadership skills. During his administration the college achieved a national reputation that it has preserved to this day. The number of high achievers who studied under him during his twenty-six-year tenure at Princeton is impressive. They included: US President James Madison, Vice-President Aaron Burr, nine cabinet officers, twenty-one United States senators, thirty-nine members of the House of Representatives, twelve governors, six members of the Continental Congress, three Supreme Court Justices, thirty-three state and federal judges and thirteen college presidents.

But there was another, high-achieving John Witherspoon. It was when the start of the American Revolutionary War caused the college's officers and students to be broken up and dispersed in 1776 that he appeared in a new and surprising public guise – not so much the divine philosopher as the thinking civilian. Incurring the severe displeasure of his friends back home in Scotland, where he was called a 'rebel and a traitor', he embraced and expounded America's case for independence and, receiving a totally different reaction from his American friends, was sent by them as a representative of the people of New Jersey, to the Congress of the United States.

His opinion on all the great issues was valued and he was a true and outspoken champion of his new country's right to independence. Those who opposed his viewpoint were liable to feel – at least – the sharpness of his wit. When one claimed the land was not yet ripe for independence, Dr Witherspoon replied scathingly: 'Sir, in my judgement the country is not only ripe, but rotting.'

Another example of his quick wit was seen in the tale of the rather slow messenger sent to convey the news of the British Army's surrender to General Gates at Saratoga. The aide took so long to reach Philadelphia to impart the vital intelligence, that when he finally arrived, he was told that it had reached the city three days before. As it was customary to offer such a messenger a gift from

Congress, a fine sword was proposed – at which point Dr Witherspoon rose to amend the motion by substituting a pair of spurs.

Amusing or not, the six-foot Scot never forgot that first and foremost he was a solemn clergyman – the only one, indeed, to sign the Declaration of Independence; and a month before doing so, he preached regretfully of 'all the disorderly passions of man' and asserted that only God could turn conflict to good.

When the question of American independence was settled in early 1783, Dr Witherspoon resumed his college duties for a couple of years before paying a short visit to Britain to refresh old friendships. Feelings about his loyalties were still running high, however, and the trip was not a great success. After some preaching sessions in Paisley he said his final fond farewells and returned to America to wind down into retirement. But not before he contributed significantly to the organisation of a newly independent and national Presbyterian Church, opening its first General Assembly in 1789 with a sermon, and presiding until the election of its first moderator.

In domestic life, Dr Witherspoon was an affectionate father and husband, having been married twice – latterly when he was seventy and the young lady only twenty-three. This did not mean, however, that he was particularly young for his age; indeed, his health was fragile and, after losing his sight for the last few years of his life, he died on 15 November 1794.

His spirit lived on at Princeton, however, and in the following century another learned Scot – James McCosh, from Ayrshire – took over the baton as the college's eleventh president. The latter's impact was also impressive during his twenty-year tenure, and in what was (almost) a remarkable conjunction of dates, he died on 16 November 1894, exactly a century and a day after Dr Witherspoon.

# James Craik (1730–1814)

*The first president's doctor*

They were born not far apart in years, and even less so in geography, where we are talking mere metres. Indeed, if their age difference had been a bit smaller than seventeen years, they might have grown up as young friends playing among the same woods and gentle coastal hills. And they had more than the same root in common. Both famously 'went native' on making acquaintance with America, both also shipped out of Scotland in the mid-1700s, and neither ever looked back, each writing himself indelibly into the history of the new United States. The rather more famous one – John Paul Jones – became the celebrated father of the American navy (see page 25); but the other well-known emigrant son of Kirkbean was also a man of remarkable achievement.

James Craik was the son of Robert Craik, a British MP and laird of Arbigland – a sizeable family estate on the north bank of the Solway Firth in placid, low-lying Dumfriesshire – where John Paul Jones' father was the gardener.

Born in 1730, Dr Craik was educated to be a surgeon in the British Army, taking a medical degree from the University of Edinburgh, but ended up as Physician General of the United States Army and as the personal physician to George Washington, first president of the United States, by whom he was called 'my old and intimate friend'.

The Scots doctor even had the debatable honour of being on duty at the deathbed as he and a colleague strove to save the president's life in 1799. But to arrive at this trusted position in the eyes of such a great statesman had not been so long and challenging a journey as one would imagine. They were firm friends within a few years of Craik's arrival on American soil.

He had set off for the Caribbean to work as an army surgeon in 1751 but, intrigued by the lure of a nascent America, soon moved on to that land to set up a medical practice at the frontier village and military base of Winchester, Virginia. From there he was drawn – as surgeon of the Virginia Provincial Regiment, latterly commanded by Washington – into the American phase of the French and Indian war between France and Britain, and it was during this campaign that the lifelong friendship between him and Washington took root.

On duty in the ill-fated advance against Fort Duquesne in 1755, Craik found himself in the thick of the battle in which the British were routed by the French and their Indian allies; indeed, he dressed the wounds of the doomed General Edward Braddock on the field and tended him until his death the next day, when the then 23-year-old Washington, as senior surviving officer, read a funeral tribute over his body.

Craik then went with Washington to Winchester, where, between 1755 and 1758, the latter was in command of provincial forces charged with protection of the Virginia and Maryland frontier from hostile Indian forces until the final fall of Fort Duquesne on 25 November 1758, in which the bold young leader played a glorious part.

The Indians' faith in the invincibility of the French thus punctured, their raids ceased and Dr Craik resigned from the army, moving to Maryland, where he bought a plantation at Port Tobacco, set up a medical practice, and built an impressive home for his new bride, Marianne Ewell, great-aunt of General Richard S. Ewell of the Confederate army.

But the Scot and Washington remained steadfast friends. And it was around this time that the two men's loyalty to Britain began to come under severe strain as domestic peace proved less promising than they had hoped.

Washington's peace plan was to manage his Mount Vernon lands well and build a happy home life within his marriage to the attractive widow Martha Dandridge Custis; but along with other planters, he began to feel frustrated, exploited and infuriated by British merchants and British regulations.

Then suddenly, while so volubly resisting the mother country's trading restrictions, he was catapulted into the role of Commander-in-Chief of the Continental Army when attending the Second Continental Congress as a Virginia delegate in Philadelphia in May 1775.

Meanwhile, Dr Craik had been taking an active part in a meeting of Charles County citizens at Port Tobacco in which resolutions were adopted protesting against the blockade of Boston and pledging aid in commercial reprisals against the British.

It looked inevitable that the two friends would soon be back on the warpath, both having come to similar conclusions about revised political allegiances.

Dr Craik joined the American army in 1777 when Washington offered him a position as a medical officer, and he rose rapidly through the ranks during the Revolutionary War. In 1780 a reorganisation of the medical department made him the senior of four, holding the title of Chief Hospital Physician and Surgeon. He was active in disclosing the conspiracy of 1777 to remove the commander-in-chief, and in 1781, as director-general of the hospital at Yorktown, he was present at the surrender of Cornwallis after the siege there, when Cornwallis's entire army marched out with its band playing 'The World Turned Upside Down'.

But the Scot's elevation to the US army's very top medical position was not to be – until after the war. Having left in 1783, he had returned to private practice, this time in Alexandria, Virginia, and looked settled for life – until in 1798 Washington, now the former first president, was summoned from retirement to command the army in a threatened war with France. Now in a strong position to have all of his conditions accepted, he named Dr Craik for his chief medical officer, and the Scot was appointed Physician General on 19 July of that year.

In the event, the feared war never materialised but Dr Craik's association with George Washington continued quite literally to the end – when, as the ex-president's private physician, he was called to Mount Vernon to diagnose the old man's final illness and treat him till his last hours on 14 December 1799.

Dr Craik, still the army medical chief, found the 68-year-old Washington to be suffering from 'cynanche trachealis', a throat-restricting infection now called streptococci cellulitis.

As attending physician, the doctor's account of the death read:

> He was fully impressed at the beginning of his complaint, as well as through every succeeding stage of it, that its conclusion would be mortal; submitting to the several exertions made for his recovery, rather as a duty, than from any expectation of their efficacy. He considered the operations of death upon his system as coeval with the disease; and several hours before his death, after repeated efforts to be understood, succeeded in expressing a desire that he might be permitted to die without further interruption.

But the president had not forgotten his old friend. A great honour was paid to the Scot in Washington's will, when he wrote: 'To my compatriot in arms, and old and intimate friend, Dr Craik, I give my bureau (or, as the cabinet makers call it, tambour secretary), and the cabinet chair, an appendage of my study.'

Dr Craik himself died in Fairfax County, Virginia, on 6 February 1814.

# James Wilson (1742–98)

*Creator of the US presidency*

Few people in his native land have heard of James Wilson, but he was one of the most important Scots ever to settle in America. For when the new nation was being moulded, he was instrumental in shaping the still-enduring structure of its presidency. A big achievement without doubt, so why so little recognition for it?

While he was conspicuously intelligent and a brilliant speaker deserving of a significant place in history on both sides of the Atlantic, could his reputation have fallen foul of his undoubted character flaws? His abundance of brainpower and personal ambition were matched only by his lack of personal control in matters of investment risk-taking and/or gambling. Enough to have him airbrushed out? It's debatable, so he was probably the least understood and most underrated of America's founding fathers.

One of seven children, born in 1742 to a Presbyterian farming family in Fife, Wilson was always a clever man, having attended no fewer than three Scottish universities – Glasgow, Edinburgh and St Andrews – the last being nearest to his home village of Carskerdo. The plan was that he would join the Church of Scotland ministry, but the death of his father forced him to abandon his studies and rethink his intended trajectory.

Like many of his countrymen at the time, he was less than enamoured of Scotland's relatively recent surrender of its free nationhood to 'the union' and couldn't wait to take off to another place where independence was rising against that force rather than yielding to it. So, resolved to add his undoubted promise to the promised land, he sailed for America in 1765, but confident as he was, even he could not have guessed at the catalytic role he was to play, as a signatory of the Declaration of Independence and member of the Constitutional Convention of 1787, in the new country's foundation.

With the help of letters of introduction, he soon became a

tutor – and recipient of an honorary MA degree – at the College of Philadelphia, Pennsylvania, and was hailed as the best classical scholar ever to hold such a position; yet he did not hold it long. Taking a sudden interest in the study of law, he was admitted to the bar within two years of his arrival. Soon, he was practising in a couple of smaller towns before settling back in Philadelphia.

Meanwhile, he had truly 'gone native', supporting the revolutionary struggle for American liberty with an impressive zeal. Indeed, it was said that he had become American at the moment he landed on the western shore, and a powerful tract he published – *Considerations on the Nature and Extent of the Legislative Authority of the British Government* – bluntly challenged British parliamentary authority over America, asserting that, as the colonies had no representation within it, parliament could have no power over the colonies.

As an increasingly prominent lawyer, he signed the Declaration of Independence in 1775 as a member of the Second Continental Congress – after some weeks' hesitation, caused by the fact that he represented the Middle States, where opinions differed on the crucial matter of independence. But his eventual signing committed Pennsylvania to an independence vote.

He reached the pinnacle of his career as a member of the celebrated convention of 1787, which gathered in Philadelphia for no less a task than forming the Constitution of the United States. There, his influence on the Committee of Detail was formidable and his powers of oration and passion of delivery were much commented upon.

Being such a fluent and compelling speaker, he helped define great points of principle in the formation of the new government when, for instance, delegates considered important points such as the amount of power the executive should have or the best means by which to elect the executive. And when they discussed whether presidential power should be in the hands of a single individual or shared by several people, Wilson moved it should consist of the former. After he had put his case with his usual fluency, arguing that conflicts would be more easily avoided if there were only one executive, who could be carefully watched by Congress and answerable to it, a lengthy silence ensued. But the other framers finally yielded to his view and decided upon a single president.

Wilson, who was practically alone among the Founding Fathers in advocating direct election of the single-person executive, later said: 'The president is the dignified, but accountable magistrate of a free and great people. The tenure of his office, it is true, is not hereditary; nor is it for life: but still it is a tenure of the noblest kind.'

Though the president would enjoy many powers, the framers were anxious to avoid the reign of a tyrannical one – and so proposed a system of checks and balances. Such as: the 'chief' would be ineligible for re-election, could be impeached and convicted by the Supreme Court, and could have his/her actions checked by two-thirds of both Congressional houses. Several adjustments were made to the proposals in the final days of the Convention, and the executive office evolved into its current form.

Was Wilson happy with that? When the state convention of Pennsylvania assembled to ratify the federal constitution, he confessed to it:

> I am not a blind admirer of this plan of government, and there are some parts of it which, if my wish had prevailed, would certainly have been altered. But, when I reflect how widely men differ in their opinions, and that every man (and the observation applies likewise to every state) has an equal pretension to assert his own, I am satisfied that any thing nearer to perfection could not have been accomplished.
>
> If there are errors, it should be remembered that the seeds of reformation are sown in the work itself, and a concurrence of two-thirds of the Congress may, at any time, introduce alterations and amendments. Regarding it, then, in every point of view, with a candid and disinterested mind, I am bold to assert, that it is the best form of government which has ever been offered to the world.

Among the powers granted to his single-person executive were commander-in-chief of the armed forces, the authority to grant pardons and reprieves, the ability to veto legislation, the power to make treaties with other nations, and the power to appoint judges.

There was a certain irony in the last point, as Wilson had high hopes of being appointed Chief Justice of the Supreme Court as a reward for his service in the formation of the federal government. But in the event, the first president, George Washington, appointed him only an associate justice in 1789.

Wilson was tall, dignified and graceful, but he was no paragon. He had borrowed heavily and gambled aggressively throughout his life. And after his wife died in 1786, he fell into an ill-advised land speculation deal, which so financially compromised him that he spent some time in a debtors' prison while still serving as a judge. Indeed, he continued in that role until his death in 1798, while on circuit duty at Edenton, North Carolina.

He was fifty-six and left six children from the first of his two marriages.

# John Paul Jones (1747–90)

*US naval hero, British pirate*

Down by the sandy shore at Carsethorn, all you can see today that evokes the tears and fears of the busy, long-gone era of the sailing ship are a few posts of black, rotting wood that once supported a great jetty jutting out into the Solway Firth. Sit beside them for a while and you can almost hear the excited chatter of ghosts; the ghosts of thousands of Scots who took their families and their dreams this way out to the New World.

The high-masted ships came in the other way too, of course, bringing exotic cargoes from far-off lands, so that the great triangle of water that cleaves its western way between Scotland and England was for many years a bustling, fascinating thoroughfare of water-borne traffic.

In the mid-1700s, when lands and alien cultures were still being discovered in a great adventure even more intriguing than today's exploration of space, the romantic lure of the sea and its mysteries must have been hard to resist, especially if you enjoyed a view of the Firth like that of the young John Paul (who added the Jones later). As he looked at it in wonder from the south-facing windows of his parents' cottage at the nearby Arbigland estate – where his Fife-born father was the gardener – the water and its promising passport to an exciting future seemed almost to lap at the door; in fact, it was barely a mile off. Indeed, Carsethorn was near to him in more ways than one, being literally central to his life, almost equidistant from his home and his school at Kirkbean; so he spent much of his time around the port and its traffic in a form of play that was to have a significant influence on his life.

William Craik, the Arbigland estate owner's son, once recalled how John Paul 'would run to Carsethorn whenever his father would let him off, talk to the sailors and clamber over the ships' and would teach his playmates to manoeuvre their little boats 'to mimic a naval battle, while he – taking his stand on the tiny cliff overlooking the roadstead – shouted shrill commands at his imaginary fleet'.

It was his grooming for the adult responsibilities that were to come sooner than even he had hoped or imagined. It was not surprising that the romantic pull of the sea seduced the boy, but who could have guessed that he would have risen to become a captain by the tender age of twenty-one . . . and eventually, the victorious Admiral John Paul Jones of the American Revolution, often called the founding father of the American Navy (though marked down as a fearful pirate in the land of his birth). Yet his early, formative days left an indelible mark on him. He was famed in later life not just for his achievement of rank and swashbuckling deeds of daring but also for dramatic pronouncements that had a ring of playground bravado about them. Such as . . .

'I wish to have no connection with any ship that does not go fast, for I intend to go in harm's way' – when responding in 1779 to a French invitation to buy a captured British ship in Brest harbour.

'I have not yet begun to fight' – at the vicious Battle of Flamborough Head, when it initially looked as if superior British firepower would prevail and he was thus invited to 'strike' (lower his flag in surrender).

Facing out across the Solway Firth to the English Lake District, the flat curve of coastal land at Arbigland is sandy, with sparse vegetation. Inland a little, dropping away from the wings of the old Georgian house, azaleas and rhododendrons flourish alongside the gardens. This is where, in the still-standing white-painted small cottage at the end of an avenue of pines, John Paul was born in 1747. It has changed little on the exterior, apart from bearing a wall plaque that reads:

> Commodore John Paul Jones, Illustrious Naval Hero of the American Revolution, Born here July 6, 1747. This tablet was placed in his memory by the Naval Historical Foundation and the Army and Navy Chapter of the Daughters of the American Revolution both of Washington DC, United States of America. AD 1953.

But changes have taken place in and around the cottage since Jack and Primrose Dougan – last of the estate workers to live there – left in 1990.

Primrose used to receive spontaneous visitors who made the pilgrimage to the remote cottage. Interviewed in the 1980s, she said: 'Most of them are American or ex-navy and most of them don't have a clue what they are coming to see. So it's often a disappointment when they discover it's still just a private cottage instead of a museum.'

That state of affairs was attended to in 1993 when the cottage became the centrepiece of the John Paul Jones Museum (with an outbuilding as a supporting shop), established with the help of private donations. Although some might argue for keeping such a house lived in, the glossed-up concept tunes in well with modern thinking – on audio headsets, visitors can hear the story of life in the cottage as told by the great man's 'mother' – while still evoking the atmosphere of John Paul Jones' time there, as the middle child of a family of seven.

The two-roomed cottage is furnished in the style of the 1700s, and in an extension built in 1831 by an admiring US navy lieutenant there is a reconstruction of the great cabin of the *Bonhomme Richard*, the ship John Paul Jones led into the blazing Flamborough Head engagement in 1779. But it is the cottage's small windows to the water that fascinate above all.

'If you stand at these windows, you can see why John Paul got the call,' said last resident Primrose. 'He was bound to go down to the shore and watch the ships going by. No wonder he didn't want to stay.'

In fact, he was thirteen when he crossed the firth to the English port of Whitehaven, signed up for a seven-year seaman's apprenticeship, and set off on the Barbados–Virginia run in a ship called the *Friendship*. He was a quick and willing learner, picking up skills and sophistication wherever he could. While that first ship was in port at Fredericksburg, Virginia, he spent much of his time learning navigation, and no doubt took on board (literally) some sartorial tips and creations from his older brother William, who had emigrated there to thrive as a tailor.

Despite being less than tall, John Paul had a handsome, well-defined face with strong nose and high cheekbones, and he always took pains to be well turned out. No one could have better personified the saying that 'clothes make the man'. It was perhaps another of his romantic views of the seafaring life: that the captain should have some theatrical flair and look good in his uniform. And he expected similar standards from his officers. 'When we went to dine with him, we were obliged to appear in the great cabin with our best clothes on,' one wrote, 'otherwise we were sure not to meet a favourable reception from him.'

When it came to career and love life, this philosophy certainly did him no harm. He was blessed with robust health too, and when fever gripped a ship on which he was serving, killing its captain and mate, he was forced to take command, bringing it safely home and so launching his career as a captain at the remarkably tender age of twenty-one.

But despite the fact that he had just washed his hands of the 'abominable' slave trade after serving as mate on two 'blackbirders', this developing gentleman was not always a gentle soul, and his quick temper – while giving him the necessary edge as a leader – would often get him into unfortunate scrapes. Two of these involved deaths of seamen, the first – of which he was acquitted – alleging excessive punishment with the cat-o'-nine-tails; and although suspicion would stick to him like a limpet, the second was more serious and prompted him to change not only his name but also his country of residence – and, probably in consequence, his sense of national loyalty.

It was in 1773, after having been in command of the West Indian ship *Betsy*, that he was accused in the West Indies of having put fatally to the sword the ringleader of a mutinous dispute over wages ('a brute of thrice my size'). Sensing local feeling against him and reckoning the chances of a fair trial remote, John Paul made his escape to Virginia, using first the name of John Jones and later John Paul Jones, probably to set him apart from the many Welshmen of that name in the area. As the American Revolution began to boil up and his letters revealed growing loyalty to the colonists, he surfaced again a couple of years later when – as a Scot and no great believer in Great Britain anyway – he offered his services to the Continental Navy being formed by Congress, and was appointed a first lieutenant.

The ragbag American Navy was beginning with but six extant ships and thirteen frigates on the drawing board, and soon – as he distinguished himself as lieutenant of the *Alfred* and later captain of the *Providence* – his professional advice on the drafting of naval regulations became highly valued. With a direct clash between Britain and her colony looming, his skills as a seaman were at a premium. But he preferred practice to theory.

A life of action was what this wiry swashbuckler wanted, and while enjoying the burgeoning executive role his growing reputation was giving him, he was soon out at sea again, getting 'in harm's way'.

Jones believed that any navy formed by the colonists could be most effective by avoiding head-to-head confrontation and seeking and striking the Royal Navy's weak spots. In June 1777 he was appointed captain of the *Ranger* and sailed for France – where he forced the

French to salute the American flag in a harbour for the first time – before embarking on an audacious direct attack on a British town.

Because he knew it so well – and also knew response to such an action would be exaggerated by the British – he decided to raid the port of Whitehaven, from which he had sailed as a ship's boy in 1760. After taking and capturing some small ships in the Irish Sea, the assault turned out to be a messy, half-hearted affair – while he knocked out the port and set fire to some colliers, a number of his men chose to go to the pub, having won no loot to speak of. But the psychological impact was immense. Had the Royal Navy been asleep? This was the first raid on an English port since the Dutch Admiral de Ruyter raided the Thames and Medway in 1667. Britain was plunged into turmoil and, as some locals had recognised the commander, his name hit the headlines and his demonisation grew some more.

Operationally, John Paul Jones was proving to be a painful thorn in old Albion's side. Pledged to destroy British commerce in the North Sea, as captain of the *Bonhomme Richard* – a French East Indiaman he had converted into a warship – he led a squadron of seven ships into Edinburgh's Leith harbour in August 1779, intending to capture the port and extract a £50,000 ransom. The ill-prepared defenders were quaking with fear, but the American attackers were foiled by a gale that blew them back out to sea.

Not much more than a week later, however, the *Bonhomme Richard* was making big trouble again – this time by engaging in the bloody confrontation for which John Paul Jones is most remembered: the Battle of Flamborough Head.

Circling south of Newcastle with the intention of cutting off London's winter coal supply, Jones' squadron – trailing a string of captured vessels – sighted off Scarborough a forty-one-strong convoy protected by the fifty-gun *Serapis* and the sloop-o'-war *Countess of Scarborough*. Seriously outgunned, John Paul Jones nevertheless calculated that he would have to deal with the warships to get his hands on the merchantmen, and so fearlessly lashed his ship alongside the *Serapis* and simply began to slug it out for four hours, watched by crowds of fascinated onlookers lining Flamborough Head.

It was early in this battle that he was invited to surrender but famously replied: 'I have not yet begun to fight.'

Fearing damage to itself, the *Serapis* could not use its superior fire power at such close quarters to best effect, and slowly but surely the muskets and hand grenades of the *Bonhomme Richard* cut down the *Serapis'* crew.

A witness aboard Jones' ship, Midshipman Nathaniel Fanning, recalled the captain's impressive demeanour in the heat of the boarding action:

> Captain Jones ordered the sailing master, a true-blooded yankee whose name was Stacy, to run our jib boom into *Serapis*. Jones at the same time cried out 'Well done, my brave lads, we have got her now; throw on board the grappling irons and stand by for boarding.' Jones assisted Mr Stacy fasten the end of the enemy's jib stay to our mizzen mast, where he checked him for swearing by saying 'Mister Stacy, it is no time for swearing, you may by the next moment be in eternity'.

Though great losses were sustained on both sides – over half of the two ships' crew members died or suffered dreadful burns – in the end, it was the British captain, Pearson, who surrendered to the American ship – ironically, just before it sank like 'a battered raft', according to one chronicler.

And Fanning recalled:

> The captain of the *Serapis* gave repeated orders for one of his crew to ascend the quarter deck and haul down the English flag, but no one would stir to do it. They told the Captain they were afraid of our riflemen . . . the Captain therefore ascended the quarter-deck and hauled down the very flag which he had nailed to the flag staff little before the commencement of the battle; and which flag he had at that time, in the presence of his principal officers, swore he would never strike to that infamous pirate John Paul Jones. Thus ended this ever memorable battle, after a continuance of a few minutes more than four hours.

It was indeed a memorable battle. It has been described as 'a naval combat the like of which has never been fought before or since', and Jones' dramatic victory was the high point of a career that made a spectacular contribution to the American War of Independence, while also making him a feared and hated pirate figure in his own land.

From then on, however, his career slipped slowly downhill. Though in 1781 Congress passed a vote of thanks to him for 'sustaining the honour of the American fleet' and he spent the last years of the war advising on the establishment of the navy and the training of naval officers, oddly he seemed to be more honoured by other countries as he grew older. He became the toast of Paris, being awarded the Order of Military Merit by Louis XVI, and, in a political secondment recommended by Thomas Jefferson, he was made a rear admiral in the Russian navy by Empress Catherine II. After prevailing in a battle against the Turks, he wrote: 'I am delighted with the courage of the Russians, which is more glorious because it is without show off'.

After returning to Paris in 1790, he was struck by pneumonia and died at the age of forty-five, before he could learn that he had been appointed US Consul in Algiers. He was buried in an unmarked grave in a cemetery for foreign Protestants and forgotten about.

Better late than never, however, the USA eventually came to recognise fully the little Scot's significant influence in founding its navy, and in the early summer of 1905 four American cruisers, *Brooklyn*, *Tacoma*, *Chattanooga* and *Galveston*, crossed the Atlantic to France on a special mission – to bring back for President Theodore Roosevelt the American hero's body that had been buried outside the walls of Paris more than a century before. In 1913, he was laid to rest in a grand Napoleon-style sarcophagus in the crypt of Annapolis Naval Academy.

And forty years later another great warship crossed the Atlantic on his behalf – the one that carried the plaque to grace the wall of his birth-cottage. The name of the vessel? The USS *Paul Jones*. The ghost of the little ship-watcher of Arbigland would have been inordinately proud of that.

# Alexander Wilson (1766–1813)

*Ornithologist extraordinary*

During his twenty-eight early years in Scotland Alexander Wilson revealed only slight shadows of the driving curiosity and drawing talent that would one day make him – through his classic nine-volume *American Ornithology*, published from 1808 – the recognised father of American ornithology.

Born in 1766 and growing up in the weaving town of Paisley, not far from Glasgow, he displayed no particular interest in his Scottish feathered friends, although he was conspicuously creative, trying desperately to emulate the rampant poetic success of Robert Burns, seven years his senior. Indeed, what little success as a poet 'Sandy' Wilson did have was registered by a comic ballad titled 'Watty and Meg', which was published anonymously but ironically thought by many to have been written by Burns – who, equally ironically, is said to have praised it.

The son of an illiterate but intelligent distiller who encouraged his education, Wilson was apprenticed as a weaver but did not pursue that trade with any enthusiasm, opting instead to produce a veritable mountain of verse, which – according to one critic – needed assiduous gold-panning to find 'the few pieces that are really good . . . like modest little poppies that have caught the bright colours of the sunlight and the freshness of the dewdrop, but are overlooked in the great field of dry stubble'.

Like Burns, the slight but handsome Wilson was also given to writing satire, but perhaps could not command the required forgiving elegance, for in 1792 some of his poetic comments on the unfair treatment of weavers by their bosses landed him in trouble with local manufacturers, and led to a fine, the enforced burning of his offending poems, and a short term in jail.

Generally speaking, life in Scotland did not promise much for Sandy Wilson as he approached thirty, and he knew it. Never financially successful at publishing his own verse, which he vainly peddled around, and unwilling to commit his artist's heart and soul to the weaver's sedentary existence, he was virtually penniless and almost hopeless when he heard the siren call of the young United States and reckoned he had nothing to lose by answering it. In July 1794, he raked up enough money to buy deck space for himself and a nephew on an American ship bound for Delaware from Belfast.

It was an inspired move. While his nephew set off in search of a farm to develop, the heady freedom of America immediately became the wind beneath the wings of Sandy's creativity. His well-practised writing skill was more appreciated in Pennsylvania where, after dabbling in copperplate printing, he became a weaving teacher with a regular wage and decided to take drawing lessons. At first, he struggled, but when he attempted the delineation of birds, he soon acquired a technique that not only impressed his teachers but overtook them. His success in this prompted a sudden enthusiasm for ornithological work, and with encouragement from the naturalist William Bartram, whom he had befriended, he first mentioned 'making a collection of all our finest birds' in letters to friends in 1803.

So fired was he by this inspiration that he decided to release himself again – to draw, research and write on birds, with the highly ambitious aim of depicting every species in North America. The decision was truly the start of something big: an obsession that was to make him, but also literally to kill him, at the cruelly young age of forty-seven.

After setting up a dollar-a-day page-engraving deal with a publisher, in 1804 Wilson armed himself with sketching materials, notebooks, guns, a horse, a parrot and a messianic sense of mission, then plunged into the swamps and undergrowth to travel over 10,000 miles through the eastern USA observing and recording the previously unrecorded.

He published his first volume of *American Ornithology* in 1808. Enthused by the acclaim it received, he said he was now 'fixing correspondents in every corner of these northern regions, like so many pickets and outposts, so that scarcely a wren or a tit shall be able to pass along, from York to Canada, but I shall get intelligence of it'.

But Sandy Wilson drew most of the birds himself, and for the rest of his life wore himself down by rough-travelling widely, bird-spotting, note-taking, drawing and collecting subscribers for his book's successive volumes. He found travels over treacherous terrain often arduous, once recalling a 'howling wilderness' where he was challenged not just with dysentery but with

> the most horrid swamps I had ever seen . . . covered with a prodigious growth of canes and high woods, which together, shut out almost the whole light of day for miles. The banks of the deep and sluggish creeks, that occupy the centre, are precipitous, where I often had to plunge my horse seven feet down, into a bed of deep clay up to his belly; from which nothing but great strength and exertion could have rescued him; the opposite shore was equally bad, and beggars all description.

And he wrote to his brother David:

> Since February 1810, I have slept for several weeks in the wilderness alone, in an Indian country, with my gun and my pistols in my bosom; and have found myself so reduced by sickness as to be scarcely able to stand, when not within 300 miles of a white settlement, and under the burning latitude of 25 degrees. I have, by resolution, surmounted all these and other obstacles, in my way to my object, and now begin to see the blue sky of independence open around me.

His second *Ornithology* volume was published by late 1810, and Wilson – now celebrated as an important American ornithologist, naturalist and illustrator – then dedicated himself to publication of the third and fourth volumes in 1811, the fifth and sixth in 1812 (when he became a member of the Society of Artists of the United States) and the seventh in 1813.

It was in that year that things became particularly difficult, as volumes eight and nine made exceptional demands on his body and soul. Planning now to focus on water birds, Wilson and his friend George Ord made a four-week journey into New Jersey's Great Egg Harbour, a trip that plainly weakened him, and when he returned to find himself (after a workers' dispute) doing much illustration-colouring alone, by mid-August he was exhausted and stricken again by dysentery. He died ten days later, during the writing of his ninth volume, and some accounts say he drowned in pursuit of a rare bird.

Wilson's short life was nevertheless a fulfilled one, despite its unpromising beginnings. Not only were several species of bird named after him – Wilson's Plover, Wilson's Phalarope, Wilson's Warbler and Wilson's Storm-petrel – but he garnered many an honour to be proud of. He was elected a member of the American Philosophical Society and other learned bodies. His reputation spread not only in America, but throughout Europe, and few crowned heads did not subscribe to the *American Ornithology*. He is now regarded as the greatest American ornithologist prior to Audubon.

As a driven perfectionist, he would have been eternally grateful to know that volumes eight and nine were still published, thanks to the hard finishing work of George Ord, who saw them both completed by May 1814. And although the whole work fell short of Wilson's original plan to document every American feathered thing, it illustrated 268 species of birds, 39 of which had not previously been described, and was highly respected throughout the whole of thinking society – though it never made him rich. Wilson nonetheless achieved his own American dream by realising his pledge to himself – 'to raise some beacon to show that such a man had lived'.

Yet he felt he owed it all to the encouragement of his father. In February 1811, he wrote:

> The publication of my *Ornithology*, though it has swallowed up all the little I had saved, has procured me the honour of many friends, eminent in this country, and the esteem of the public at large; for which I have to thank the goodness of a kind father, whose attention to my education in early life, as well as the books then put into my hands, first gave my mind a bias towards relishing the paths of literature, and the charms and magnificence of nature. These, it is true, particularly the latter, have made me a wanderer in life; but they have also enabled me to support an honest and respectable situation in the world, and have been the sources of almost all my enjoyments.

Wilson's mother died when he was ten but his father survived him by three years.

# 'Uncle' Sam Wilson (1766–1854)

*The United States personified*

For many Americans the ideals encompassed in his name give him an almost god-like status. Soldiers die for him, athletes run for him, and families metaphorically embrace him as a kind of permanent, if abstract, super-president. But even in Europe and many other parts of the world the image of Uncle Sam – essentially as portrayed in Flagg's famous portrait on the 'I Want YOU' army recruiting poster from the First World War – is the ultimate symbol of US conscience and culture. So much so that in some faraway places with extreme views it is not uncommon to see his effigy being carried shoulder high or consumed in flames, depending on the point of view being expressed about America.

But what were the origins of this revered badge of American-ness? We know that they were human, and even Scottish, just as we know too that the man himself was never a caricature like the one we now know – a tall, white-goatee-bearded figure with intense eyes, top hat, striped pants and red, white and blue star-spangled suit – thanks to the inventiveness of artists and cartoonists.

No, it is safe to believe that Samuel Wilson looked nothing like that universal image of Uncle Sam. But how did a clean-shaven man with Scottish roots come to be the provenance of the universal symbol of America in general and the US federal government in particular?

It is here that we have to come clean. An essential criterion for selection of the names featured in this book has been that they were born in Scotland. We know that Sam Wilson was born of parents from the south-western Scottish port of Greenock – Edward Wilson and Lucy Francis – and that he was the sixth of their thirteen children. Not being certain of when they got on the boat for the New World, however, we are tempted to believe that Sam might have been conceived in Scotland. In this exceptional case, I respectfully ask the benefit of the doubt!

In any case, Samuel was born on 13 September 1766, in Menotomy (now Arlington), Massachusetts, and at fourteen moved with his family to Mason, New Hampshire, where he was eventually to meet his young sweetheart Betsy – an army captain's daughter – for whom he was moved to fire up an entrepreneurial career that would provide her with the comfortable life her beauty deserved.

To that end, he would try anything once. At the age of twenty-two, he and his brother Ebenezer walked through deep snow 150 miles to Vanderheyden (now Troy), New York, where – by rolling up their sleeves in a typically Scottish fashion – they contrived to find themselves in demand as apple-tree sellers, brickmakers and then remarkably successful meat-packers. Betsy must have been a very patient girl, for it was not until Samuel was thirty-one – and she twenty-four – that he felt his financial circumstances could finally do her proud. He returned to Mason, married her, and romantically swept her back to Troy in a jingling sleigh.

While she was busy having four children, Samuel's meat-packing business went from strength to strength – daily slaughtering upwards of 100 cattle and packaging them into barrels also made by the firm, which even had its own ships and jetties lining the Hudson River. But the Big Contract was still to come . . . and with it, the Big Name.

In 1812, although the revolution was over, the British were meddling in American trade and had to be stopped. When the resulting mini-war began, the US Army asked Wilson not only to supply meat for its troops in the northern states but also to act as a beef and pork inspector. As part of the deal, the barrels that made up large shipments of meat to the Army were stamped 'US', and it was during this time – when few people understood the relatively new combination of initials – that some kind of verbal exchange took place, which would lead to Samuel Wilson's name giving birth to the Uncle Sam concept.

As a well-liked boss, Samuel had already become known as 'Uncle Sam' to many of his employees. So when – according to one version of the story – a visitor asked a Troy dock worker the meaning of the stamped letters on the meat barrels, the latter's joking reply, referring affectionately to his employer, was: 'Uncle Sam!'

This tale has the joke travelling well – first to the army's receiving station at East Greenbush, where the soldiers, not knowing Sam Wilson, thought the name was new slang for the US government and quickly adopted it. And the idea spread at the same pace as the barrels crossed the country; so that all the government's property was soon popularly considered to be Uncle Sam's.

Another account says that the legend was born earlier, with some help from Samuel Wilson himself. On seeing people looking curiously at the large letters 'US' on the front of a relative's store in Troy, he is said to have answered their unspoken question by telling them that they meant 'Uncle Sam' – and that he was that very person! And the adoption of his self-nickname spread like wildfire from there . . .

Whichever tale was true (and perhaps the truth was a bit of both), it was always an amusing idea that seemed to appeal to people's sense of humour and belonging.

There is no doubt that it added even more to Samuel Wilson's popularity as he himself – as well as the government – became commonly referred to as 'Uncle Sam'. And soon, the nickname began to appear in print as meaning the country. Legendary status did not begin to take root, however, until after Wilson's death on 31 July 1854. And although the legend was eventually made official when the House of Representatives unanimously approved a resolution establishing his grave as a national shrine; and although President John F. Kennedy signed a resolution in 1961 officially establishing him as the original Uncle Sam, his gravestone at Troy's Oakwood Cemetery reads simply:

SAMUEL WILSON
Died July 31, 1854
Aged 88 Years

# Archibald Binny (1763–1838) and James Ronaldson (1768–1842)

*Makers of the dollar sign*

In the Lawnmarket, a couple of hundred yards down the Royal Mile from Edinburgh's celebrated castle, is a venerable four-storey townhouse called Gladstone's Land – a high, handsome building and the oldest surviving example of the city's Old Town dwellings, dating from the mid-1600s. It is open to the public as a tourist attraction, so Riddle's Court is not hard to find. It is just across the cobbled Lawnmarket street, directly opposite the famous old house.

But why would we want to find Riddle's Court? There should be a clue in the eye-high metal plaque that meets the visitor at the mouth of the tunnel-like close that leads to a dark little square where tall stone walls, wood-canopied stairs, dungeon-type gate and a low weather-worn doorway take you instantly into another, earlier century.

But, no. Like many of the similar 'explanatory' signs placed at such points in the city's most-visited area, the plaque teases more than it tells:

Riddle's Close and Court

In Close lived David Hume before settling in James' Court;
in Court beyond, Baillie MacMorran banquetted in his
house James VI and his Queen and Danish nobles.

There is no mention there, or in the courtyard, of Archibald Binny, who lived there for three years before he emigrated to America in 1795.

But why should there be? Who was Binny and what did he do that he should be honoured with his name on such a wall-plaque? If the minimal records of his achievements are to be believed, it was he – and his partner James Ronaldson, about whom even less is known – who first forged into type the globally recognised American dollar sign.

Although they both came from Edinburgh and one-time baker Ronaldson was already a businessman in Philadelphia when punch-cutter Binny arrived there, it seems they had not known each other in Scotland; but when they met on the far side of the Atlantic they clearly delighted in their shared heritage and hit it off pretty quickly. For within a year of Binny's arrival they were combining their technical and business talents to set up the first American type foundry. Called simply Binny & Ronaldson and based in Philadelphia, it was an immediate success, ending America's dependence on Europe in typographical matters. Today the company is still remembered for having produced, in 1809 and 1812, the first American type specimen books – *A Specimen of Metal Ornaments* and *A Specimen of Printing Types*, respectively.

But it is also credited with nothing less than the first typeset design of the dollar sign, most conspicuously in Updike's *Printing Types: Their History, Forms & Use,* which states that 'in 1797 the Philadelphia foundry of Archibald Binny and James Ronaldson offered for sale the first dollar marks ever made in type'.

It would not have been before time. Up to then, there had been some confusion about the currency of the young country that emerged from the war of independence that began in 1775 and ended in 1783. Before 1775, the nation's monetary system was in disarray, and Congress decided to clarify it by backing all its legal tender with the most commonly circulated coins – Spanish coins minted in the New World. Americans then began trading with the 'Spanish milled dollar' as they shed the British pound . . . though not quite.

For while the word dollar itself comes from the German thaler (the name of a large European silver coin) and the US symbol for it seems to owe more to the Spanish peso, the latter's positioning before, rather than after, the designated amount is a lingering echo of the pound.

Contrary to some popular opinion, the now-accepted dollar sign is not a deliberate placing of a narrow letter 'u' over a letter 's' as an abbreviation for Uncle Sam or the US. Its origins are rather more complex.

The credit for the written – rather than typographical – interpretation of the sign is given by many to one Oliver Pollock, an Irish immigrant who became a wealthy plantation owner in New Orleans, then part of the Spanish Empire, and penned his business in pesos, which he abbreviated by intertwining 'p' and 's' so that the result looked like an 's' with two lines through it.

This habit was adopted by one of his most important contacts, Congressman Robert Morris, financier of the American Revolution, and seemed to catch on more generally, evolving into the dollar symbol that is used today.

But coming soon after the moment that Binny and Ronaldson's design was conceived, the appearance of the dollar sign in print – in a 1797 book by Chauncey Lee – signified the acceptance of the stylised dollar sign as a purely American symbol. And there is little doubt that the two enterprising Scots were responsible for that.

Somebody had to do it, as they say. But what prompted them? Were they inspired by being based in the same city as the US 'Mother Mint', which had come into being in 1792? Were they encouraged by executive nudging? A message from the top? Suffice to say that they were obviously respected enough to enjoy the appreciation of the then-former President Thomas Jefferson, whose help they were not afraid to enlist in sourcing antimony (used in metal type-casting) when an international trade dispute had interrupted supplies. As a champion of homegrown American industry and admirer of the typefaces of Binny & Ronaldson, which had become the most popular in the USA, Jefferson was only too happy to help find them a new source in France.

Such patronage can be rewarding in more ways than one, and both Scots retired as rich men. Ronaldson, who died in 1842, was described as a philanthropist in later life, and Binny, who died in 1838, had retired to a 5,000-acre plantation on St Mary's River – which he called Portobello, after his sandy birthplace on the Forth estuary on which the Scottish capital stands.

He clearly remembered Edinburgh fondly, though the favour was not returned: Edinburgh largely failed to remember either him or his business partner.

# James Gordon Bennett (1795–1872)

*The man who made the news*

To those for whom Gordon Bennett is something more than a name – an expression of astonishment perhaps, or a phrase synonymous with outrageous behaviour – the sight of the peaceful Scottish village of Newmill must be unexpectedly serene. Could this simple little place of a few dozen square-built granite cottages, a population of under 400, and an environment straight out of a dream entitled 'rural peace and quiet', possibly have been the cradle of the man who took New York's blood-and-guts publishing world by storm and spawned a namesake rogue of a son who would make even more of an international impact?

Relieved only by a pub, a post office and a clock tower, the otherwise monochrome Banffshire village hugs the full quarter-mile length of its main street and is embraced in turn by rolling sheep-dotted hills, arable fields and a shaded valley where piled-up regiments of barrels await the lucrative liquid gold of Chivas Regal and other famous whiskies produced in Keith, two miles away.

The handsome, centrally situated clock tower built in 1923 and dedicated to the memory of local men who fell in the First World War is Newmill's most notable landmark. Driving past it going south, you catch a glimpse of Hill Street, pushing up to the hills on your right. Much of it has retained its venerable stone-built character but halfway along on the left are several newish houses, one of which has replaced the modest cottage where the first James Gordon Bennett was born.

Is there any evidence of this today? Nothing. No plaque, no little garden, no acknowledgement of any kind. So perhaps the most remarkable thing about Newmill is that its most famous son has been emphatically, and probably deliberately, forgotten.

No one in the village today seems to want to talk about him (or his son). It is not known what his parents did for a living, though it was 'surely something agricultural', one villager volunteers reluctantly, adding that they must have been relatively well-off to spare a bright son to attend Aberdeen University. Though he had actually intended to train for the Roman Catholic priesthood, in the event his higher education was to serve as a launch pad for a spectacular career abroad. But there is no memory of his ever having come home in a similar way to Scots near-neighbour and fellow US publishing tycoon Bertie Forbes (see page 95). Was it this strange forgetfulness that caused the villagers to conclude that the feeling was mutual – and virtually airbrush him out of their folklore?

If they are remembered at all, the two Bennetts' names tend to fuse in people's memories and, if they don't, the younger one has left such an indelible splash of colour that he is still a preferred subject of controversy. To this day, the son's reputation commands scant respect in the village as – so goes the tale – he was invited by the war memorial committee to contribute to the building of the clock tower and never troubled himself to respond. What more could you expect from such a spoiled brat? This is perhaps an unfair charge, however, as the tower was built five years after James Gordon Bennett Jnr died, in 1918, after a lifetime of high living.

But it was Bennett the elder who put all the hard groundwork into the creation and development of the *New York Herald* as a significant root of the ubiquitous *International New York Times*, the only truly global newspaper, which, in a hugely challenging Paris-based publishing exercise, today has thirty print locations around the world for daily distribution to a quarter of a million buyers in 185 countries.

Bennett senior had acquired a taste for writing at university after his abortive education for the priesthood, and resolved to become a journalist. In pursuit of this, he crossed the Atlantic at twenty-four in the spring of 1819 and while doing a variety of jobs over the next ten years, from teaching (in Nova Scotia) through something menial in book publishing (in Boston) to being a correspondent and associate editor for the *New York Enquirer* and the *Morning Courier,* he began to acquire another taste: for being in command of his own career through ownership. It started with his launch of *The Globe* in 1832, which, despite being short-lived, was a valuable learning process. By 1834 he was beginning to get the idea that perhaps it was not wise to depend on political patronage when launching a paper while doubling as a proprietor and chief editor of the Philadelphia-published *Pennsylvanian*. But it was in 1835 that he really began to spread his wings . . .

That was when he changed the face of American journalism from a cellar in New York. At the age of forty, with just $500 as working capital, he launched *The New York Herald*, the paper that was to make him famous. The first four-page issue of the one-cent publication claimed to eschew 'all politics' and pledged itself to survive on – rather than subsidies from politically interested parties – advertising and circulation, the last of which would demand bizarre stories that might be characterised as 'juicy' today; so that passing people would be curious enough to dig into their pockets. That meant crime and society scandals, lurid illustrations, scurrilous charges, tales of monsters – anything weird and wonderful, indeed, that would capture the public imagination.

But Bennett the journalist was no one-trick pony. The newsman in him demanded that he focus on newsgathering even while developing new editorial techniques that invited wider readership. Therefore, alongside all the offbeat offerings came new ideas and new investment in new ways of covering serious news. During the Civil War the paper had a staff of no fewer than sixty-three war correspondents. On 13 June 1835, it published the first Wall Street financial article to appear in any US newspaper; in December of that year it printed a vivid account of the great fire of New York; and the following year it covered the Helen Jewett love-nest murder, the first such case to be featured in American journalism.

No, he was not cut out for the priesthood.

Bennett the audacious liberal publisher was financially shrewd, interested only in what would sell, and untroubled by moral considerations. This broad-minded approach proved a huge commercial success. So much so that his most desired source of funding thankfully emerged as planned – impressive annual profits for reinvestment. And as these began to blossom and confidence in the product grew, the crassness of his early 'pop' philosophy began to moderate with fresh thinking gradually adding new dimensions. Thus *The Herald* pioneered many innovations in modern journalism, including illustrated news stories, establishment of a team of European correspondents, joint founding of the Associated Press news agency, introduction of a society department, first major use of the telegraph for reporting of a long political speech; the list went on. It all led to a highly successful and profitable news empire, which, by the time it was handed over to Bennett's son in 1867 – five years before the old man's death – was registering annual profits of $400,000.

A rival newspaper greeted news of his death in 1872 with the comment that his character was 'defective' and his career 'a conspicuous example of prosperous infamy'. It went on: 'Visit him, and you would see before you a quiet-mannered, courteous, and good-natured old gentleman on excellent terms with himself and with the world, but . . . that region of the mind where convictions, the sense of truth and honour, public spirit, and patriotism, have their sphere, was in this man mere vacancy.' It considered 'unfortunate' the fact that his newspaper survived him. But it hadn't seen nothin' yet . . .

The younger James Gordon Bennett, born in 1841 with such a silver spoon in his mouth, went out of his way to become an outrageous playboy who conducted the paper from his yacht in Europe; who is said to have spent $30,000,000 of the *Herald*'s earnings; who gave rise to the 'Gordon Bennett!' near-expletive by flying an aeroplane through an open barn; who drove so recklessly he tipped out Winston Churchill's mother; and who appalled the family of his fiancée by urinating in their open fireplace after getting drunk.

The eccentric and capricious Bennett was fond of sports, especially of yachting, and established the James Gordon Bennett cup as a trophy in international yacht races and similar cups for balloon and aeroplane races. Whether or not these are considered good things, he did manage a couple before he expired. In 1869 he sent reporter Henry Stanley on the trail of Dr David Livingstone to register a memorable world exclusive that is still talked about today. He opened *Herald* soup kitchens for the poor during the economic panic of 1873–74, and in 1877 he began the forerunner of what became the *International Herald Tribune* in Paris. But some said this was merely an 'ego' exercise and things were not looking so good at home. In the face of intense competition in the newspaper wars of the 1890s, *The Herald* began to decline and Bennett's absence in Paris did not help. Three years after he died in France in 1918, the ailing *Herald* merged in 1922 with the New York *Tribune*, thereby creating the famous international title (recently taken over by *The New York Times*).

In New York City's Herald Square today, an elaborate monument honours the two Bennetts. But at the time of writing there were still no plans to build one in Newmill, Banffshire.

# Allan Pinkerton (1819–84)

*The first private eye*

On the face of it, the extremely humble beginnings of Allan J. Pinkerton would not seem to have qualified him for the amazingly colourful career and grand roles he enjoyed in later life – as the world's first-ever private eye, dogged pursuer of legendary outlaws, and confidant of America's most admired president, Abraham Lincoln.

The founder of the famous detective agency that still bears his name, Pinkerton was truly a man of many parts; and when all these parts were drawn together, the sum became either a remarkably complex person or a somewhat confused one. On the professional front he was a cooper, a prolific author and a highly accomplished investigator – the expression 'private eye' comes from his agency's logo that depicts a large, open eye above the line 'We Never Sleep'. At various points in his life, he was seen as a drunkard, a defender of truth and liberty, a left-wing troublemaker, an employers' puppet, a patriot, a traitor, a fugitive from the law, an idealist and an adventurer.

Perhaps the last word describes him best, for he managed to turn every stage of his adult life into an adventure of one kind or another. Everywhere he went, in every pond he paddled, he made waves.

And neither was he born into calm waters, when his parents lived in close proximity to the River Clyde that cleaves through Glasgow like a giant sword blade. As Scotland's biggest city, Glasgow is today a vibrant, confident place, which has tackled its historic social problems with a resolve born of a modern awareness that the reputations of its worst neighbourhoods – such as the squalid Gorbals, now comprehensively renewed – were tarring the rest of the city with their dirty brush.

It has been a lot to live down, for when Pinkerton was born in the Gorbals on 25 August 1819, it was a forbidding place indeed: a web of dark, crime-ridden narrow streets where drunkenness, chronic diseases, unplanned children and prostitution were rife, and where murderers (often in the shape of body-snatchers) lurked round every corner. But in a paradoxical way, that formidable scenario probably gave the young Pinkerton a head start in the matter of crime solving, for he must have grown up with an intimate knowledge of human weaknesses. Not only that: his father William was a police sergeant who, until his untimely death, presumably added considerably to Allan's early store of experience.

Having once recalled the excitement at home when his mother brought home 'a precious egg' as a rare treat for her hungry family, no doubt the young Allan also understood the part poverty played in the grim mix of human conditions that surrounded him. And that might also have explained his early motivation to champion the downtrodden.

'Downtrodden' was something he knew about. Born in a crumbling second-floor flat above a corner shop in Muirhead Street, near the spot where the imposing Central Mosque now stands, Allan and his brother Robert were the second brood of William – by his second wife Isabella, a handsome mill girl who also took on his five children from his previous marriage.

Reality and responsibility slammed down on Allan long before adulthood, when his father was killed during a political rally that broke out in a city square – and so the imperative for his heartbroken mother became cash earning by the family for the family. Not that Allan's first job brought in much more than grief. He became a pattern-maker's apprentice and worked night and day in a sweatshop for a pittance. But as his later life would prove, he was nothing if not an enterprising lad, and soon – by the age of twelve – he had acquired another, better, job as a cooper and quickly became pretty good at barrel making.

The carrot-haired rabble-rouser was also good at soap-box oratory, and little did he know it then, but the first skill was to serve him well for the start of a new life in the New World, while the second would provide the spark to launch him away.

That came when his boundary-pushing instinct got him into trouble as a militant member of the Chartist Movement that fought for 'freedom' of the working classes. When he began to advocate physical conflict in speeches to men from the cooperage floor, the authorities took a dim view. Learning that his name was on the King's Warrant list, he was forced to become a fugitive, lie low and weigh up his limited options.

Inevitably, the New World beckoned, promising him a new life and a clean slate; but he wasn't going anywhere without the love of his life, Joan Carfrae, from Edinburgh. She agreed readily to his proposal, but did she know what she was taking on? She certainly got a taste of it the day they were married in March 1842. No sooner had they taken their vows than word came that soldiers were on their way to arrest Allan. And so began – as they were smuggled aboard a Canada-bound ship the next morning – the couple's long life of drama and adventure.

The first alarming scene was the ship's approach to land – in a violent storm – four weeks later. The vessel was blown 200 miles off course and foundered on a reef off Nova Scotia. The newlyweds lost everything they owned in the submerged hold, but luckily not their lives, as they abandoned ship into a lifeboat. It was a close-run thing, though, as on reaching land the rescued passengers were greeted by trinket-hunting Indians, and Mrs Pinkerton was relieved of her wedding ring – after her husband was persuaded by the captain not to risk his life by fighting for it. So the newlyweds began their life together with only the clothes they stood up in, and a few silver coins in Allan's waistcoat pocket.

It would not be so for long, however. Even as the rescue ship that retrieved the stranded passengers passed down the St Lawrence Seaway separating Canada from the USA, new ideas were forming. They heard tempting tales of a fast-growing town called Chicago on the western edge of Lake Michigan. In an age when everything was transported by barrel, Pinkerton reckoned such a booming metropolis would surely welcome his skills as a cooper, and so decided against their original plan of settling in Quebec in favour of the USA instead. In the event, diverted perhaps by the familiar name from home, they settled – after a short stay in Chicago when he made some seed money as a cooper at Lill's Brewery – in a little 'Scottish' town called Dundee north-west of the city. There, they started a much-needed firm, Pinkerton's One and Original Cooperage of Dundee, which soon employed ten men.

Demand for his barrels, which were better and cheaper than those of competitors, was increasing at an impressive pace as customers appreciated their quality and the boss's occasional willingness to exchange his product for theirs. And with the birth of the Pinkertons' first child – William, who was to be followed by twins Robert and Joan – it looked as if they were becoming firmly established domestically and professionally.

Politically, he was feeling pretty satisfied too, as a local leader in the slavery-abolition movement who managed to be both outspoken and covert in his sympathetic activities, working with an underground railroad (by using his cooperage as a 'station') that brought slaves in from the south and up to Canada.

He liked the idea of covert action, but little did he suspect that it was about to seduce him completely. Allan Pinkerton would soon find out that – even more than his barrel-making skills – Chicago would appreciate his as-yet-undiscovered qualities as a detective.

The catalytic moment that revealed his latent talent for detection came in 1846 when, to supplement his dwindling stock of barrel hoops, he made a boat trip to a small, woody island in the Fox River, several miles from Dundee. 'It was commonly supposed that the island was uninhabited,' wrote Sigmund A. Lavine in his book about the Scot, 'but Pinkerton, a most observant individual, noticed that the grass and bushes were bent back, making a path from the shore. Curious, he followed it, and in a thick stand of trees found a campsite that appeared to be used quite frequently.'

Curiosity became suspicion. After he informed the local sheriff and was deputised to help him in this case, both men kept a nightly watch on the spot for five nights, and on the fifth were rewarded with a stunning coup – their arrest, at gunpoint, of a twelve-strong gang carrying spades and sacks full of the kind of counterfeit money that had been spreading uncontrollably around northern Illinois.

Impressed by his success on this case, and by his bravery during the arrests, local businessmen hired Pinkerton to watch for more counterfeiters, and again he registered several successes, not least by putting himself at risk as part of a 'sting' operation.

Seeing that he could also make money at a business he relished, Pinkerton was hooked, and barrel-making quickly lost its appeal. As his reputation grew in Chicago, he literally rolled out the barrels and moved his family back there to accommodate more case-solving offers by the Treasury Department and the Cook County Sheriff's Department, which asked him to find the kidnappers of two Michigan girls. He tracked down and shot one of the abductors, adding a 'biggie' to his record-breaking number of arrests in 1848 and earning himself a full-time position as deputy sheriff. He also became Chicago's first police detective in 1850. He kept on taking freelance commissions, however, and business was so good that by the end of that year he felt the time was right to set up the North-Western Police Agency.

Later to be renamed The Pinkerton National Detective Agency, it was soon also to be known as a highly professional, uncompromising private outfit whose agents would not flinch at the most difficult assignments and would never give up until they got their man (or woman). Its tenacity became legendary among the criminals of Chicago, who, having overwhelmed the regular police, would now quake in their shoes when they heard they were on the Pinkerton target list.

His agency hired no one but the best. His operatives were clean, honest and upstanding with 'vigour of body', but tough-minded and nobody's fool. They were thoroughly vetted and cleverly chosen. Indeed, the agency employed Kate Warne, America's first female private eye, who could get into places male detectives couldn't. The agency's methods were also clever . . . and original. Disguise and infiltration proved effective in case-solving, and although primitive by modern standards, an innovative 'rogues' gallery' – filed photographs to identify criminals – was a breakthrough in the battle against crime; for meticulous research was the essential foundation of Pinkerton's success, along with patient surveillance and often-dangerous undercover work.

In the general atmosphere of lawlessness that prevailed at the time, when the west's expansion was fuelled by gold- and cash-laden trains pushing across often-hostile open country, the post office and the railroads became the agency's biggest clients, and Pinkerton's main work consisted of hunting down railroad thieves such as the notoriously vicious Reno Gang.

But there were also 'security' jobs to be done and one can't help but wonder how the old Chartist firebrand reconciled his past with his agency's investigative work in the area of union activities: he was seen to be responsible for keeping unions out of various trades in the Chicago area for years, and 300 of his agents played an infamous part in the restraint of protesting workers at the Homestead steel plant of fellow-Scot Andrew Carnegie (see page 50). That has proved a lot for both men to live down in the pages of history. And yet, and yet . . .

Perhaps the workaholic Pinkerton was just too busy building his booming business to appreciate the irony of such matters; for another 'security' job, the biggest imaginable, was won at least in part by his abolitionist sympathies (which extended to him and Joan making their fine house in Adams Street busier with fugitives than was his Dundee cooperage). This drew him to the attention of President-elect

Abraham Lincoln who hired his agency for bodyguard services. Just as well; for what then transpired was, without much doubt, Allan Pinkerton's finest hour . . .

As the Civil War boiled up, executives of the Philadelphia, Wilmington and Baltimore Railroad called him in to investigate rumours that secessionists were planning to blow up train ferries on the Susquehanna River. The detective disguised himself, adopted a southern accent and insinuated his way into the company of the suspects – one of whom, in a drunken slip of the tongue, revealed that something much bigger was being planned.

The plot, thus uncovered by Pinkerton, was to assassinate the president as he passed through Baltimore on Saturday, 23 February 1861, on his way from Philadelphia to Washington to take his oath of office and deliver his inaugural speech in front of the unfinished Capitol on 4 March.

Pinkerton requested an urgent meeting between himself and the president in Philadelphia, and there the detective spoke words that made the politician blanch with shock: 'We have come to know, Mr Lincoln, and beyond the shadow of a doubt, that there exists a plot to assassinate you. The attempt will be made on your way through Baltimore, the day after tomorrow.'

The Scot suggested that the president should accompany him directly to Washington that very night; but Lincoln felt too obliged to go through with speeches in his next day's schedule. After that, however, he pledged to follow Pinkerton's advice – and duly did so, by changing his travelling times and passing through Baltimore at night.

Although the move probably saved his life, Lincoln was ridiculed by his enemies for his 'undignified' nocturnal trip to the capital, and was sufficiently stung to express some regret about it later. But with the Civil War breaking out that same year, he was impressed and grateful enough to enlist Pinkerton's help as a spy against the Confederacy. He responded well, with valuable information on rebel supplies, defences and conspirators. And it was an honour indeed when he was appointed Chief of the Secret Service. Though by consensus this turned out to be an example of the Peter Principle in practice – he was clearly rather out of his depth at that level – it was quite a way to rise for the poor boy from the Gorbals.

Indeed, intertwined as his name was with the presidency and all the infamous banditry of the Wild West, the story of Allan Pinkerton's life reads like a Hollywood movie script – or perhaps several. Apart from running to earth four members of the Reno Gang (who were then lynched by vigilantes), he became famed for his dogged pursuit of many legends of the Wild West including the Hole in the Wall Gang, the James Brothers (Jesse and Frank), who returned the compliment by making Pinkerton their number-one murder target, and Butch Cassidy and the Sundance Kid, who always seemed to be one step ahead of Pinkerton agents armed with photos and drawings of the pair.

The elusiveness of Butch and Sundance – vanishing, ultimately, on a South American trail that went cold – was part of their Hollywood-acknowledged sophistication, for Robert Le Roy Parker (Butch) and Harry Longabaugh (Sundance) considered a raid to have been successful not only if it delivered the goods (with the help of inordinate amounts of dynamite) but also came off 'clean', involving no loss of life and no molestation of passengers.

The Molly Maguires were something quite different. An Irish group who claimed to support and defend the interests of their immigrant fellows in the grim coalfields around Pennsylvania, they became a violent secret society who robbed, murdered and spread terror on a massive scale. Into this poisonous stew a brave Pinkerton agent was dropped – a 29-year-old Irishman James McParland, who at great risk to himself, infiltrated the organisation in the time-proven Pinkerton way, befriended its leadership, was instrumental in their arrest, then gave courtroom evidence that sent no fewer than twenty of them to the gallows as a just punishment for all their appalling atrocities. His heroism was hailed by one newspaper as 'one of the greatest works for public good that has been achieved in this country and this generation', but few were surprised by the success, for it came down to the much-acclaimed quality of Pinkerton's people. Even bandits acknowledged it, and in *The Molly Maguires*, one of the books he wrote (about the pursuit of the gang) in yet another career, Pinkerton outlined his expectations of a good private eye: 'The detective should be hardy, tough and capable of laboring, in season and out of season, to accomplish, unknown to those about him, a single absorbing object . . . able to distinguish the real from the ideal moral obligation, and pierce the veil separating a supposed from an actual state of affairs.'

When hiring agents, Allan Pinkerton warned them that he was a hard man who ran his company with an iron hand: 'I am self-willed and obstinate. I must have my own way of doing things.' But it could not be quite as simple as that. The one character strand that ran through all his complexities was surely a deep sense of romance, if not sentimentality.

When he approached retirement and began to pump out a long string of books dramatising his agency's exploits, it was more than an exercise in self-justification. He had a real taste for the adventure-packed frontiers of young America, and he knew he was a significant part of them. He would never forget his beloved Scotland, however, and even as he approached the end of his life, he was building a grand house called The Larches for which larch trees were shipped from Scotland to line the driveways.

When Pinkerton passed away in 1884 his agency, with its branches in Chicago, New York and Philadelphia, was taken over by his sons Robert and William, who continued its movement from detective work to security and protection.

His gravestone in Chicago's Graceland Cemetery reads:

In memory of
ALLAN PINKERTON
Born in Glasgow, Scotland
April 15$^{th}$ 1819
Died in Chicago, Illinois
July 1$^{st}$ 1884
Aged 65 years

A FRIEND TO HONESTY AND A FOE TO CRIME

Devoting himself for a generation to the prevention and detection of crime . . . he was the founder in America of a noble profession in the hour of the nation's peril. He conducted Abraham Lincoln safely through the ranks of treason to the scene of his first inauguration as president. He sympathised with, protected and defended the slaves and labored earnestly for their freedom. Hating wrong and loving good, he was strong, brave, tender and true.

Today the still-thriving company has almost 40,000 employees. In 2000 it celebrated 150 years of service by donating to the Smithsonian Institute in Washington a vast archive of materials, which included once-secret documents on Jesse James, the Hole-in-the-Wall Gang, and Butch Cassidy and the Sundance Kid.

Wherever they and their tenacious old pursuer are now, it would not be surprising to learn that they were still giving each other a hard time.

# Andrew Carnegie (1835–1919)

*Man of steel, heart of gold*

To stand in the tiny, low-ceilinged room where Andrew Carnegie was born in 1835 is to shiver with the realisation that life can deliver some truly unexpected results. It is almost impossible to take in that, from the small wooden box-bed in the darkest corner of the modest weaver's cottage in Moodie Street, Dunfermline – a place that knew real economic alarm, if not sheer poverty – a lad of such simple birth could have grown up to become the richest man in the world. That would be more than adequate achievement for anyone; but Andrew Carnegie, the keen-eyed elder son of handloom weaver William Carnegie and his wife Margaret, also became the world's greatest philanthropist.

That is an easier thing to say than to actually appreciate, of course, and my own means of appreciation came in dramatically physical form when, in the days of telex, I was setting up a feature on the great man for the *Scotsman Magazine* and asked the Carnegie Dunfermline Trust to send a list of the libraries he had funded. There were 2,811 of them in all, and the strip of paper that accommodated the typed list of names stretched from one end of the rather long magazine office to the other. I gasped with amazement – for I realised that, in the days when a million really was a million, the $60,000,000 he had injected into these widely distributed symbols of humankind's instinct for self-improvement represented only a fraction of his spending budget. At his death in 1919 every US state had at least one Carnegie-built library, Britain and Ireland had 660, Canada 156, New Zealand 23, South Africa 13 . . . and so it went until Singapore, with 1. Scotland alone has 147.

But his philanthropy extended well beyond libraries to the establishment of a remarkable range of trusts and foundations in the USA, Britain and Europe. He also set up schools, colleges, teachers' pensions and church organs, and financed – 'to hasten the abolition of international war, the foulest blot upon our civilisation' – the building of the International Court of Justice in The Hague, known as the Peace Palace. Not to mention the museums, institutions and concert halls that still bear his name, from the 600-seat Carnegie Hall in his home town of Dunfermline to the world-famous 2,804-seat Carnegie Hall in New York. Many minor Scottish artists have been known to boast that 'I once filled the Carnegie Hall' – not exactly lying while impressing listeners, but also failing to say that the experience was in Fife, Scotland, and not Manhattan!

Scotland in general benefited, too, from the millionaire's enduring fondness for his native land, as he endowed its universities with large bequests aimed at paying for the fees of the students. Having become a millionaire by thirty-three and worked to about double that age consolidating his fortune, Andrew Carnegie's final years were much concerned with the *purpose* of the accumulation of wealth and self-analysis around that question. By 1900 he was able to outline his thought-out principles when he published *The Gospel of Wealth,* the key points of which he put like this:

> The man of wealth thus becoming the mere trustee and agent for his poorer brethren, bringing to their service his superior wisdom, experience and ability to administer, doing for them better than they would or could do for themselves . . . The man who dies thus rich, dies disgraced.

So – determined not to die disgraced in his own eyes – from the turn of the twentieth century he went about the business of shedding his wealth with the same energy that he had put into acquiring it. The only difference was that he couldn't finish the task – of distributing the allocated $350,000,000 – and had to pass it on to a range of trusts, despite help being offered from all corners. Indeed, even as he arrived on a return visit to Britain in 1901, he found his fellow-countrymen anxious to help him get rid of the money. Newspapers carrying ads from the makers of Mother Siegel's Syrup with a competition inviting readers' ideas on 'how Mr Carnegie should get rid of his wealth'. There were no fewer than 45,000 suggestions.

Devoted as he was to his home town in Scotland and to 'improving the masses', he showered the people of Dunfermline with gifts that still survive and thrive today – not just the Carnegie Hall, but also the town library and two swimming baths. There are other monumental reminders of Carnegie all over the town, such as Lauder College, a well-regarded place of learning founded in 1899 as a tribute to 'the man to whom I owe the most'– his beloved uncle, George Lauder, who played a large part in augmenting the basic education he received at Mr Martin's School in Rolland Street, and taught him to use his memory. There is also a fine statue of Carnegie in the town's green and leafy Pittencrieff Park, not far from his birth cottage, and the story of how he saw that special place given to the people has a delicious element of poetic justice. More of which later . . .

But the town's most poignant reminders of the great man are the well-preserved birth cottage, all that remains of the street of weavers' houses that he knew as a boy, and the now-attached Andrew Carnegie Birthplace Museum which was given in 1928 by his then-widow Louise to display the hundreds of tributes and gifts he received from all over the world.

In stark contrast to this younger companion building and its grand role, the simple cottage recreates the poor atmosphere of the weaving family's home in the 1840s. It is dark and wooden and in one of the two rooms on the ground floor there is a real Jacquard loom, representing the pair that used to clack away making damask linen on that floor. And upstairs, where the family lived, there is only one room, with a table and old grated fireplace – ahead of you as you enter – and two framed box-beds lined along the right-hand wall. It is believed Andrew was born in the bed in the far corner, where there is now a small window (but wasn't in his day). It is a tiny room, perhaps three by four metres, and it is hard to imagine that from here the world was changed so significantly.

Go back downstairs, on the short twist of wooden staircase where the small Carnegie feet once scampered, and in the reception area you may well find visitors from every part of the world, or at least their signatures, in the address book. Walk further into the museum itself and there, under glass, you will find an older visitor book from the cottage, lying open at the entry of one particularly important visitor . . . Andrew Carnegie himself. It reads: 'Andrew Carnegie, Skibo, Sept 27th, 1909. First visit to my birthplace. The humble home of honest poverty, the best heritage of all when one has a heroine for a mother.'

The Skibo address referred to his Scottish home – the magnificent Skibo Castle on the Dornoch Firth in Sutherland, which he and his wife bought, restored and enlarged in 1898. It became their much-loved Scottish retreat, though nowadays, having passed out of the

Carnegie family, is also famous for having hosted the star-studded wedding of pop star Madonna in 2001.

But how did the little weaver's son grow from that simple cottage to such a fabulous home and the worldwide fame and incredible fortune that accompanied it?

Misfortune came first. For his father, William, the cottage served as home and factory, but as Andrew approached his teens, industrial times were changing. The development of power looms meant the days of cottage hand-weavers were numbered, and throughout the 1840s the pressures on Dunfermline's damask linen manufactures became increasingly intense – until the day William had to announce despairingly to his elder son: 'Andra, I can get nae mair work.'

Supporting the family was then down to Andrew's 'heroic' mother Margaret, who earned that subsequent tribute in the cottage visitor-book by sewing shoes at night and running a shop by day. But it was a hard life offering little future, and the grim winter of 1847–48 was the last straw, bringing the Carnegies to the brink. Hope, then, seemed to lie across the ocean.

Margaret's young sisters, Annie and Kitty, had married and moved to Pennsylvania in 1840, and although they had not found the life easy, their letters home had suggested that the USA offered many more opportunities than dreary, depressed Dunfermline. After much agonising, it was decided that the family should try to earn a share in the prosperity of the New World.

In his book *My Own Story*, Andrew recalled that, after the decision was taken, 'my father's sweet voice sang often to mother, brother and me' . . .

> To the West, to the West, to the land of the free
> Where the mighty Missouri rolls down to the sea
> Where a man is a man even though he must toil
> And the poorest may gather the fruits of the soil

Depressed it may have been, but Dunfermline, ancient capital of Scotland sixteen miles north of the current capital Edinburgh, remained a beautiful place to Andrew and one that proved hard to leave. A sale of the Carnegies' house-factory goods and equipment designed to fund their journey proved 'most disappointing', he recalled, and £20 had to be borrowed from a friend before they could set off from the town in the omnibus that ran along the coal railroad to Charlestown. 'I remember that I stood with tearful eyes looking out of the window until Dunfermline vanished from view, the last structure to fade being the grand and sacred old Abbey. And during my first fourteen days of absence my thought was almost daily as it was that morning: "When shall I see you again?" '

They crossed to the west coast and set sail from Glasgow in a converted whaler. And despite his sadness, the young Andrew – he was twelve – kept a firm hand on his five-year-old brother Tom as they breathed in the vivid new experiences of the fifty-day voyage and the 'bewildering' sights and sounds that met them in New York.

Arriving in Pittsburgh in mid-August 1848, after a long, crawling trip from New York via the Erie Canal and Lake Erie, they took a house at Rebecca Street, Allegheny, and William Carnegie returned to work as a handloom weaver making table-cloths 'which he had not only to weave but afterwards, acting as his own merchant, to market himself, selling from door to door' – before again being defeated. Disillusioned by returns that were 'meagre in the extreme', he was forced to take a job in Blackstock's cotton textile mill.

Andrew got a job there too, starting his working life as a bobbin boy at $1.20 a week, before moving to Hay's bobbin factory where, for $2 a week, he tended the steam engine, fired the boiler and, being a conspicuously luckier fellow than his father, managed to be in the right place at the right time when the boss found himself without a clerk. Andrew was asked what his penmanship was like and given a test. 'The result pleased him,' Andrew recalled, and the boss was even more pleased to find the quick-minded young Scot was also good at figures.

He was growing in confidence, and success with another job opportunity – as a telegraph messenger boy for the O'Reilly Telegraph Company – sent him 'wild with delight'. He wrote: 'From the dark cellar running a steam engine, begrimed with coal dirt, I was lifted into paradise, yes, heaven, as it seemed to me, with newspapers, pens, pencils and sunshine about me . . . I felt that my foot was upon the ladder and that I was about to climb.'

He was right there. While also bettering himself in his spare time – by means of the scheme set up by a well-meaning Colonel James Anderson to allow working boys to read books from his private library on Saturday afternoons – Andrew worked hard to become a top telegraph boy, and to this end he became one of the few people in America capable of deciphering Morse telegraph messages by ear. This remarkable skill did not go unnoticed, and in February 1853, he was appointed personal telegraph operator and confidential secretary to Thomas A. Scott, Superintendent of the Pittsburgh Division of the Pennsylvania Railroad Co., at the impressive salary of $35 a month.

Andrew Carnegie was stocky and cherubic of face, with a glint of steel in his eye. While not conventionally handsome, he kept getting himself noticed through his intelligence and initiative. When a rail network failure disrupted systems in his chief's absence he displayed formidable powers of organisation and averted disaster by taking sole charge; a move that did his career no harm at all.

With the sad death of Andrew's father at fifty, Thomas Scott became something of a new father figure to him. It was he who was to lay the foundations of Andrew's formidable fortune when, in 1856, he advised the lad to purchase shares in the Adams Express Company. On later receiving his first dividend cheque (barely eight years after arriving in the USA), Andrew exclaimed: 'Eureka! Here's the goose that lays the golden eggs.'

He wrote: 'I shall remember that cheque as long as I live . . . It gave me the first penny of revenue from capital – something that I had not worked for with the sweat of my brow.'

Under Scott's wing Andrew advanced rapidly in the company and by 1859 he himself had become the Pittsburgh Division superintendent and was able to employ his brother Tom as his personal assistant.

Soon, another fortuitous moment arose that combined Andrew's interest in the railroad with his new-found interest in investment. He was approached by T.T. Woodruff, inventor of the sleeping car, and was so impressed by his inspiration that he put it to Mr Scott – who agreed to test a built vehicle and urged his young protégé to take up the one-eighth interest in the carriage company offered to him by the inventor. Andrew borrowed the $1,250 investment from the bank, and it was quickly repaid from dividends, as the sleeping cars were a big success, bringing him an annual income of $5,000.

This was heady stuff. There was no stopping him now. He threw himself wholeheartedly into moneymaking through many such shrewd investments of small sums, and quickly became wealthy while still working for the Pennsylvania Railroad Company. The Chartist child of Dunfermline was all set to grow into the Capitalist father of America, but not before being seconded to help Washington organise the Union military telegraph service during the Civil War.

When that conflict ended, he quit the rail company to devote all his energy to his expanding business interests, which, by 1865, were giving him an annual income of $50,000. And his cherubic side was not always in evidence as he applied a fast-growing, often aggressive business expertise to oil, railway construction and financing, bridge building, telegraphy, iron and steel.

With the post-war economy expanding and railroads pushing out all over the continent from coast to coast, he invested in companies making related products such as rails, bridges and wheel axles, and quickly saw the potential in a new British system for the mass production of steel. He invested in the process, and so the American iron age became the age of steel, starting with his Edgar Thomson Steel Rail Mill, named in honour of its first customer, president of the Pennsylvania Railroad Company.

The superior qualities of steel, as opposed to iron, proved all-conquering and there was no looking back. But personal tragedy was to spoil Andrew's dreamlike progress, when his mother and brother died within a few days of each other in 1886. At fifty-one, he recovered from that double blow, and from his own bout of typhoid, to marry Louise Whitfield, daughter of a New York merchant, the following year. They soon had a daughter – named Margaret after his mother –and Louise quickly became 'more Scotch' than Andrew, encouraging him to buy a home for them in the Highlands of Scotland, which was when Skibo was welcomed into the family.

It was while they were in Scotland in 1892, when all seemed to be going well personally and professionally – with his web of steel interests now largely consolidated into the Carnegie Steel Company – that the infamous Homestead Affair put an indelible blot on his proud record of good, if paternalistic, relations with the working class. As a child of that class, he had, despite his acquired wealth, felt an affinity with it; but it became apparent that the feeling was not mutual when the workers at Homestead – one of four steel plants that came under the umbrella of the new company – went on strike after management–union talks on wage rates broke down. All hell broke lose, with the executive left in command locking out the workers and getting himself shot twice ('but not dangerously'), 300 Pinkerton agents employed to protect the plant being attacked and beaten by the strikers, and 8,000 state militia being called in to restore order.

Though he did not return to intervene personally, Andrew Carnegie was left with a bitter taste in his mouth from this ugly episode, in which several men were killed, and he later wrote with clear regret:

'Nothing I have ever had to meet in all my life, before or since, wounded me so deeply. No pangs remain of any wound received in my business career save that of Homestead. It was so unnecessary.'

His conscience was much troubled by this affair, and while steel continued to pour from his company's furnaces to the extent of their making almost half of America's requirement by the end of the 1890s, he became increasingly aware of the responsibilities of his ever-growing wealth and developed a compulsion to return it to the people in some way as he came closer to retirement.

The critical moment came in 1901 when the Carnegie Steel Company was sold for $480,000,000 and amalgamated with other steel companies to become the United States Steel Corporation; Andrew Carnegie's personal share was $360,000,000 and, when the deal was done, the organising financier, Junius P. Morgan, shook his hand and said: 'I want to congratulate you on being the richest man in the world.' It was at this point that Carnegie realised the struggle to accumulate riches had come to an end . . . and that the heavier, more responsible task of sharing them had begun.

In all, what he gave away before he died in 1919 – and was buried in New York's Sleepy Hollow cemetery in a grave marked by a Celtic cross of stone quarried near his beloved Skibo – represented almost $3 billion in today's values. And still it goes on: his given-away fortune continues to fund education and research, and the combined incomes of the trusts and foundations he established enables them to spend over $150 every minute 'for the improvement of mankind'.

Despite his despair at the First World War and his own failing health towards the end, he died a well-fulfilled man. For his was the perfect rags-to-riches story. Within it, however, was another story that gave him the greatest gleeful satisfaction of all. Dunfermline never lost its pull on him. 'What Benares is to the Hindoo, Mecca to the Mohammedan, Jerusalem to the Christian, Dunfermline is to me,' he once wrote. And when he was a boy he looked upon the town's Pittencrieff Glen – or Park, as it is now known – as a leafy haven where the chance to play would have been pure paradise. But he was barred from the place because he was related to families who campaigned against the owning laird in favour of the town's rights to the park for the people. Andrew Carnegie regarded it as one of his greatest triumphs that, in 1902, he was able to buy the park for £45,000 and thereby become himself Laird of Pittencrieff – 'the happy possessor of the grandest title on earth in my estimation' – and see it handed over to trustees to bring 'sweetness and light into the monotonous lives of the toiling masses of Dunfermline'.

The intense satisfaction he felt at the 'true romance' of this development – that he should 'arise and become the agent for conveying the Glen to the people of Dunfermline forever' – was more than adequately expressed by the man himself: 'This is the crowning mercy of my career! I set it apart from all other public gifts. Truly the whirligig of time brings in some strange revenges.'

It truly does . . .

# Andrew Smith Hallidie (1836–1900)

*Inventor of the cable car*

It was his witnessing of a heart-stopping incident that inspired Andrew Smith Hallidie to invent the horseless cable car, which, to this day, encapsulates the magic of 'the city by the sea' to virtually the same degree as its acclaimed Golden Gate.

Who can imagine San Francisco, America's fairest city, without its colourful, clanking cable cars crawling up, and clattering down, its picturesque but mountainous streets? And who can forget that so-evocative line – 'Where little cable cars climb halfway to the stars' – in Tony Bennett's classic song 'I Left My Heart in San Francisco'?

But in 1869 the image of the city's horse-drawn streetcars was a deal less magical as the horses struggled bravely to pull the carriages up those challenging gradients. One cold morning in that year, the 33-year-old Hallidie saw several such horses in distress as they lost their footing on the frosty street.

He recalled the moment in a later report to the Mechanics' Institute:

> I was largely induced to think over the matter [of inventing a horseless cable car] from seeing the difficulty and pain the horses experienced in hauling the car up Jackson Street, from Kearny to Stockton Street, on which street four or five horses were needed for the purpose – the driving being accompanied by the free use of the whip and voice, and occasionally by the horses falling and being dragged down the hill on their sides, by the car loaded with passengers sliding on its track.

This enterprising Scot, who had emigrated from London to the United States at the age of sixteen with his Dumfriesshire parents – engineer-inventor Andrew Smith from Fleming and Julia Johnstone from Lockerbie – had good reason to believe that he could come up with something that would put an end to such alarming incidents, while simultaneously improving the city's sluggish transport system.

Taking after his clever father, he was also an engineer-inventor, and one of his many mining experiences in America had inspired him to develop mechanical solutions with wire rope, a field in which Andrew Snr held several patents. Drawing on these, the young Andrew – who had adopted his surname in honour of his uncle, physician to Queen Victoria – solved a problem at a quartz mill, for instance, where cars brought rock down a hillside with the help of gravity and went back up for refilling via rope which lasted just two months. He proposed making a wire rope system to replace it, and the owners were delighted to find that this rope lasted for two years.

Having taken the principle of that system back into the city, where he established a manufacturing plant and saw demand for his product grow in mining and bridge-building contexts, it was as a successful businessman that he was inspired to set about the cable car enterprise 'with the view of obviating these [horse-drawn] difficulties and for the purpose of reducing the expense of operating street railways'.

His plan was to have streetcars propelled by underground cables – or a 'rope railway', as he called it – when he announced his intention in the *Sacramento Record* in 1870.

How would it work? Put simply, the cable car would be hauled by a long, steam-powered cable moving slowly in a loop beneath the street surface and between the rails. But the devil was in the detail, and it was not only a complicated concept to get up and running, it was also a nail-biting one.

Expensive too. Hallidie himself contributed all the spare capital he had – $20,000 – and while design and construction were undertaken, more backing had to be rustled up (mainly from three reluctant friends), a site identified and surveys made for the first test (Clay Street), and a franchise received from the city – which demanded that a test run take place no later than 1 August 1873. 'I devoted all my available time to the careful consideration of the subject,' he later recalled.

But the deadline turned out to be almost impossible to meet. Every day the engineering challenges seemed to be more difficult, and everyone on the construction team was aware that all rights would expire if no cable car were running by the first day of August. On the eve of that day, several exhausted men worked through the night to make the unlikely dream a reality, and they must have felt a deep glow of satisfaction when at last they heard the engine starting to take up the slack of the cable as the grip car was put in place.

Some accounts say that the first actual travelling test did not take place until the following day (though the city did not void the franchise) but a plaque dedicated to Hallidie on the lower terrace of Portsmouth Square, near Clay and Kearney, reads:

> Site of eastern terminus first streetcars in world propelled by cable.
> Commenced operation August 1, 1873. Ceased February 15, 1942.
> Invented and installed by Andrew S. Hallidie . . .

Some accounts also say that, when the car was ready to run down to the foot of the mist-shrouded Clay Street, Hallidie's gripman took one look down the steep hill and, being paralysed by trepidation, refused to operate the car – so that the inventor himself had to spring to the levers. Those watching from the top saw the car disappear into the mist, and learned later to their considerable relief not just that the bottom had been reached safely but that 'the damned thing works'.

It was 5 a.m. As the town was asleep, there were no cheers; but there were strong, silent handshakes and broad smiles among the working team. The horseless cable car had been born.

A month later, a regular service was started with the Clay Street line, and although the system was slow to gain acceptance and ridiculed at first as 'Hallidie's folly', it steadily grew to be a huge popular and financial success, with 600 cars eventually carrying passengers around 120 miles of city streets, and making the doggedly innovative Scot a very rich man in the process.

That in itself might have been reward enough, but Andrew Smith Hallidie could look on in considerable satisfaction as similar cable railroads were adopted by Los Angeles, New York, Chicago, Kansas City, St Louis and Philadelphia.

And you have to wonder if the pioneer – who died in 1900 – is not still wearing a quiet smile. Might he still be watching, from somewhere high above the highest San Francisco hill brow, as – despite setbacks and threats like earthquakes and repeated modernisation proposals – the cars go on and on, protected by the sheer popular affection and enthusiasm that they evoke?

There have been changes, of course. In the early 1980s the present cable car system underwent a two-year-long programme of renovation. But the people of San Francisco have fought many battles to stop their historic streetcars being totally replaced by modern transport, and the result is that forty examples of two types remain, on which natives and delighted tourists can still shake, rattle, bump and grind over ten miles of undulating track.

A favourite position for them is riding precariously on the outer running boards. Which is how they know you have to hang on tight to this unique machine – physically as well as metaphorically.

# John Muir (1838–1914)

*Father of the national parks*

When I was a boy in Scotland I was fond of everything that was wild, and all my life I've been growing fonder and fonder of wild places and wild creatures. Fortunately, around my native town of Dunbar, by the stormy North Sea, there was no lack of wildness . . . with red-blooded playmates, wild as myself, I loved to wander in the fields to hear the birds sing, and along the seashore to gaze and wonder at the shells and seaweeds, eels and crabs in the pools among the rocks when the tide was low; and best of all to watch the waves in awful storms thundering on the black headlands and craggy ruins of the old Dunbar Castle when the sea and the sky, the waves and the clouds, were mingled together as one.

Since the lean, bearded, grown-up John Muir wrote these poetic lines to boyhood memory, nothing much has changed around the rugged coastal shoulder of south-east Scotland on which Dunbar sits. The ancient town may have acquired some new homes and modern shops, but the salty, rocky places of its seashore, where the young John played in the 1840s, still embrace and placate the wild waves that stir where the North Sea joins the Firth of Forth. And though the well-used harbour walls have been repaired here and there, in contrast to the ravaged and lowering remains of the nearby sandstone castle, you can still sense the old fishing community's timeless nearness to nature.

It was here that John Muir's formidable sense of wonder and curiosity about the natural world was awakened; a sense that made him a champion of the environment long before that word acquired its current significance; a sense that powered him around the globe long before aircraft criss-crossed it with ease. Indeed, carried by the wind, the energetic, multi-talented Scot became a truly well-travelled man who could have put any modern peripatetic business executive to shame. Not only did he emigrate from Scotland to Wisconsin while still a boy; as his passion for the study and protection of the God-given environment grew, a fascination with glaciers attracted him to Alaska, a need to know about forests drew him to Australia and Africa, and a driving curiosity about exotic lands in general drove him as far as China and Japan.

He passionately believed that the glory of nature had to be protected from man's avarice and indifference when profitable industry was all that seemed to matter. 'The battle for conservation will go on endlessly,' he wrote. 'It is part of the universal battle between right and wrong.'

Yet wherever he went on his great odyssey through life and geography, John Muir's modest home town in Scotland never lost its place in his heart. Once, after walking 1,000 miles across America, he smelled the sea on the wind. When he was a day's trek from the Gulf of Mexico, he wrote, 'a wind blew upon me from the sea . . . and the Firth of Forth, the Bass Rock, Dunbar Castle and the wind and rocks and hills came upon the wings of that wind, and stood in as clear and sudden light as a landscape flashed upon the view by a blaze of lightning on a dark night'.

And in the fond, proud way that John Muir remembered Dunbar no matter where he wandered, the town now remembers him. For another significant thing that has remained unchanged in that venerable place thirty miles south of Edinburgh is the facade of the three-storey house at 126 High Street where he was born on 21 April 1838. It is still a square unremarkable building, sitting shoulder-to-shoulder with its neighbours in a street that has held its historical integrity; but it has been painted white and its deteriorated interior fabric stripped to create a light, airy and superbly designed visitor attraction in the form of 'a stunning interpretative centre highlighting the work and achievements of this remarkable man'. Established in response to a new awareness that relatively few Scots had ever heard of Muir (while in America his writings are as celebrated as those of his fellow Scots Robert Burns and Robert Louis Stevenson), the centre graphically presents records of his global travels in written and drawn sketches of places, flora and fauna, while generally paying tribute to the farmer, inventor, botanist, explorer, naturalist, writer and conservationist who became 'the father of the US National Park system'.

Of course, there is no shortage of tributes to the man in America, where over 340 historic sites – parks, woods, mountains – comprising over 80 million acres of wild land cared for by the National Park

Service, have been named in his honour. They include the John Muir Memorial Park near the Muir homestead at Fountain Lake, Wisconsin; the John Muir Wilderness and John Muir Trail in the High Sierra; the Muir Woods and Muir Beach near San Francisco; the Muir Glacier and Mount Muir in Alaska . . . the list goes on and on. His later home at Martinez, California, is designated The John Muir National Historic Site 'in recognition of his campaigns and books that celebrated America's natural heritage'.

Until lately, it had been quite different in what was a relatively indifferent Scotland. But now the very existence of various Muir-inspired bodies and initiatives which helped East Lothian Council bring about the Dunbar visitor centre – the John Muir Birthplace Trust, John Muir Trust and local John Muir Association – represents a fair indication of today's changing perception of a now-more-famous son at home. And just across the High Street, there is a relatively new, handsome statue of John as a boy setting a bird to flight. To the west of Dunbar, there is also the John Muir Country Park, eight miles and 1,760 acres of 'unspoiled nature'. Not to mention the John Muir Way, a pathway developed to provide a continuous coast-hugging path linking East Lothian with Edinburgh.

The significance of the Dunbar spark that ignited the famous man's future fire should not be understated, but the catalytic moment came when John, the eleven-year-old first son and third child of the seven-strong brood of grain merchant Daniel Muir and Anne Gilrye, was hard at homework with his nine-year-old brother David one evening in 1849. Their well-to-do father had been unable, it seemed, to find a compatible context for his intense religious beliefs in Scotland, and so had decided to join the Disciples of Christ sect in America. It was for very different reasons that John was pleased about that decision, and later he recalled the thrill of the moment when it was put to him: 'One night, when David and I were at Grandfather's fireside solemnly learning our lessons as usual, my father came in with news, the most wonderful, the most glorious, that wild boys ever heard. "Bairns," he said, "you needna learn your lessons the nicht, for we're gan to America the morn." '

Why was the news so 'wonderful and glorious' when John loved Dunbar so much? If a note sent from a Scottish visit back to daughters in America some forty-four years later was anything to go by, he was no doubt feeling relief that he would no longer have to suffer the singularly brutal regime of a Scottish schooling:

July 12, 1893

Hello Midge, My Sweet Helen

Are you all right? I'm in Scotland now, where I used to live when I was
a little boy, and I saw the places where I used to play and the house
I used to live in. I remember it pretty well, and the school where the
teacher used to whip me so much, though I tried to be good all the
time and learn my lessons.

It was not anticipation of America being a 'schoolless and bookless
wilderness' that so enthused John as he, David and their thirteen-
year-old sister Sarah set sail from Glasgow with their father, leaving
the eldest sister Margaret and the three youngest of the family to
follow on with their mother after a farm and comfortable house
had been found. Reading was an important impulse, but he hated
being obliged to perform on pain of stern punishment and hoped
that his new life across the Atlantic would at least see the end of
the double pressure of his despotic father and harshly strict school.
And indeed, that proved the case, according to his first impressions
(recorded later in life) of the Fountain Lake Farm virgin land bought
by his father:

> This sudden splash into pure wildness – baptism in Nature's warm
> heart – how utterly happy it made us! Nature streaming into us,
> wooingly teaching her wonderful glowing lessons, so unlike the dismal
> grammar ashes and cinders so long thrashed in to us. Here, without
> knowing it, we were still at school; every wild lesson a love lesson,
> not whipped but charmed in to us. Oh, that glorious Wisconsin
> wilderness!

True to plan, then, the homestead was found in 'glorious' Wisconsin,
and the rest of the family sent for; but the establishment of home and
farm required much hard labour, and father Daniel then seemed to
transfer his harshness in education to his sons' physical work. He
pushed and beat the boys hard, even denying them a doctor when they
buckled with illness, but John at least had other diversions – whenever
he could, he would wander into the country to study the flora and
fauna, and his enthusiasm for book-learning remained strong.

He was also something of a carpenter and, to satisfy his father's
diktat that he should not stay up reading late at night, he came up
with an ingenious invention that tipped him out of bed at an early
hour to maximise the day and allow for more reading. Installed in

his bedroom in the family's log cabin, it consisted of a home-made wooden clock that, on reaching the requested time, set off an alarm mechanism that, in turn, activated a cross-bar to push his bed (and his body) into a vertical position.

As he showed such an imaginative talent, it looked to family and friends as if he might become an inventor; but he himself was not sure about a career direction. He had done enough reading to enter the University of Wisconsin, where he dipped into chemistry, geology and botany, emerging in 1863 still without a clear idea of how to employ his hard-won education and ingenious, if butterfly-like, mind.

The answer came to him by accident – literally. In 1867, while working at a carriage parts shop in Indianapolis at the age of twenty-nine, he suffered a blinding eye injury that was to change his life. When he regained his sight a month later to his great relief, he resolved – by seeing the world through even more appreciative eyes than before – to devote himself to observing, recording and protecting the beauty of nature. And so began his years of travelling that would take him from North and South America (including Panama and Cuba) to Australia, Africa, Europe, China and Japan; but it was closer to his adopted American home that he registered his greatest triumphs.

He walked 1,000 miles, for instance, from Indianapolis to the Gulf of Mexico, observing 'fields, mountains and forests' and keeping a day-by-day journal, in which he discussed animals and plants, geological formations and forests, people and his deeper thoughts. Other arduous walks and climbs, initiated to understand the geography of unmapped areas, took him to Nevada and Utah, to the north-west and to Alaska, and as he went he filled some seventy books with sketches and observations. In California, where he eventually settled, he was captivated by the Yosemite Valley and the Sierra Nevada, where he found living glaciers in the High Sierra, and proposed their role in sculpting entire mountain ranges over vast stretches of time. His theory that the Yosemite Valley had been so formed was laughed at by the famous Californian geologist Josiah Whitney ('What does a sheep herder know about geology?') but proved correct by Louis Agassiz, the father of glaciology.

Muir never lost his sense of awe at nature's power and complexity, just as he never lost his Scottish accent or the influence of his strict Scottish upbringing. When he wrote, the language of the King James Version of the Bible – which he was compelled by his father to learn virtually by heart – rang through his sentences with a certain drama. He was not conventionally religious, but his father gave him a sense of his own destiny and conviction in his message, and his word power was compelling. His fine turn of phrase could inspire and influence. Example: 'When we contemplate the whole globe as one great dewdrop, striped and dotted with continents and islands, flying through space with other stars all singing and shining together as one, the whole universe appears as an infinite storm of beauty.'

Realising that his pen was probably mightier than anything else he could think of to bring about responsible care for the natural world, Muir started his writing career seriously in 1874, and by the end of it he had had 10 major books and over 300 articles published.

Encouraged by the respected editor Robert Underwood Johnson, he fought through magazine columns to bring to public attention the devastation of mountain meadows and forests by cattle and sheep – 'the hoofed locusts', as he colourfully called them – and by 1890 an act of Congress created Yosemite National Park, which would further protect the area from the devastating effects of farming. He was also involved in the creation of Sequoia, Mount Rainier and Grand Canyon national parks and he laid the foundations for the creation of the National Park Service.

There were essential pauses in his driven life, of course. He married the daughter of a Polish immigrant, Dr John Strentzel, and bought from his father-in-law part of a fruit farm. From 1881 to 1891 he worked hard to establish this as a viable business, eventually earning enough to look after himself, his wife and two daughters – before resuming his travels and the non-stop campaigning that was to win over public opinion and a succession of presidents and defeat the lobbying of the timber barons.

Muir fought hard to save the giant redwoods of California, and in 1892 he and some supporters founded the Sierra Club environmental organisation 'to do something' – in his words – 'for wildness and make the mountains glad'; and as its first president, he led the battle to enlarge the protected boundaries of Yosemite Valley. Today the club continues to do important conservation work, and is now the premier conservation body in the US with more than 600,000 members.

Muir's advocacy of national parks culminated in the highest power in the land being converted to his cause. In 1901 he published a book, *Our National Parks*, which brought him to the attention of Theodore

Roosevelt, and in 1903 the president – persuaded by Muir to come camping – visited the conservationist in Yosemite where, over four days that were catalytic to the president's mindset, they discussed plans and ideas for the many conservation programmes which he subsequently undertook

Could the lad from Dunbar ever have imagined pulling such influential strings of power? Not then, perhaps. But the level of his success in the fullness of life can be gauged from the fact that, under his influence, Roosevelt's first years of office were marked by the establishment of no fewer than sixteen new national parks, taking in 148 million acres. But that was only the beginning. During his lifetime John Muir also influenced presidents Wilson and Taft as they designated more than 50 national parks, 200 national monuments and 140 million acres of National Forest.

But the depth of his energy and commitment was staggering, even – and especially – as he approached the end of his life. As we are told in the introduction to his book *John Muir's Last Journey*, for over forty years he kept alive the dream that he might yet journey to the 'two hot continents' to study their richly biodiverse flora and fauna. And so, just three years before his death, he set off in 1911 on an epic trip that would have daunted many a man half his age (he was seventy-three). Leaving from New York and travelling alone, he embarked with enthusiasm on his eight-month, 40,000-mile voyage to South America and Africa. He first went 1,000 miles up the Amazon, then down the Atlantic coast and across the continent to the Chilean Andes before re-crossing the pampas to Buenos Aires, Argentina. From there, he sailed east and travelled through south and central Africa and to the headwaters of the Nile, before returning to New York via the Red Sea, Mediterranean and North Atlantic. It was a gigantic, life-maximising journey inspired by a gigantic curiosity that the world must still be grateful for.

When he died at the age of seventy-six in a Los Angeles hospital, the lad from the seashore of Dunbar had left an immeasurable legacy to mankind.

After his death, Roosevelt wrote of him in 1915:

> His was a dauntless soul. Not only are his books delightful, not only is he the author to whom all men turn when they think of the Sierras and northern glaciers, and the giant trees of the Californian slope, but he was also – what few nature-lovers are – a man able to influence

contemporary thought and action on the subjects to which he had devoted his life. He was a great factor in influencing the thought of California and the thought of the entire country so as to secure the preservation of those great natural phenomena – wonderful canyons, giant trees, slopes of flower-spangled hillsides . . . our generation owes much to John Muir.

Muir has been voted 'Most Famous Californian of All Time' and appeared on two US postage stamps. Truly a man of many parts, in all senses of the expression, he lived a life filled to the very brim, with so much left over for the edification of succeeding generations in perpetuity. To the roles of farmer, carpenter, inventor, philosopher, botanist, climber, geologist, explorer, naturalist, writer and especially pioneer of conservation, we could fairly add the phrase 'all-round visionary genius'.

He more than deserves the last word . . .

They will see what I mean in time. There must be places for human beings to satisfy their souls. Food and drink is not all.

# Robert Dollar (1844–1932)

*Grand Old Man of the Pacific*

What more apt surname could a self-made Scots-American millionaire have? It is almost as if Someone Up There had decided Robert Dollar's fate at birth, though it is conceivably more likely that the name's provenance was the picture-postcard town of Dollar about twenty miles across the Forth River from the bigger central-belt town of Falkirk, where he was born in 1844. And like Andrew Carnegie, his fellow Scots-born millionaire, Dollar came to consider that the mountains of dollars he acquired during his long lifetime – largely and ultimately through his ocean-going fleet of steamships – were somehow rather vulgar if kept to himself; and so, in an echo of Carnegie's end-of-life generosity, he gave at least $1 million away (when a million was a million) and among the gifts he scattered on both sides of the Atlantic were several impressive ones for his home town: swimming baths, a park, a set of church chimes, a fountain and the book-stock for the town library.

Today, that library – the building of which was funded by Carnegie – remembers both men's benevolence with a large brass plaque on an interior wall, while Dollar's many letters of negotiation about his books donation ('it will all be paid in a few days') are treasured by its staff. But few people in Scotland now seem to even know the name that ranged so conspicuously over the world's oceans, emblazoned as it was across the hulls of Dollar Steamship Company ships – whose smokestacks carried the not-so-subtle logo of a large dollar sign. An obvious device, yet one that 'Captain' Dollar had doubts about . . .

His love–hate relationship with money was clearly evident in a letter he wrote to a friend:

> In this world all we leave behind us that is worth anything is that we can be well regarded and spoken of after we are gone and that we can say that we left the world just a little bit better than we found it. If we can't accomplish these two things then life, according to my view,

has been a failure. Many people erroneously speak of a man when he is gone as having left so much money. That, according to my view, amounts to very little.

Which of his Falkirk contemporaries could have guessed, however, that the humbly born lad who once confessed to having 'practically no education' would have grown into the elegant, confident shipping magnate who strode across the world stage and mixed with presidents and kings as he became known as 'the Grand Old Man of the Pacific'? He even had the enviable honour of being portrayed on *Time* magazine's cover in March 1928.

But, perhaps a touch ironically, the way he grew in stature owed more than a little to the simple trade that defined his upbringing in Falkirk, where his father William ran a sawmill. Robert and the rest of the family – his mother Mary and two brothers – were accommodated in a house above the building, which was later demolished to make way for new housing, though that sadness seems to have been compensated for by the birth of Dollar Avenue.

Wood-processing being the business he knew, it sustained Robert when at fourteen – after the death of his mother – he emigrated to Canada with his father in 1858 and started work as a cook's boy in a lumber camp. By 1866 he was camp foreman and, in 1871, he bought his first piece of timberland. Broadening his scope, he then moved to Michigan, and, in 1888, to California where he opened an office in San Francisco and set up home with his wife Margaret in San Rafael. By 1893 Dollar had a mill and lumbering business at Usal in Mendocino County, and shortly after, at the age of fifty, embarked on his second career – in shipping.

But how did that come about? Frustrated at finding his lumber deliveries to be at the mercy of unpredictable schedules operated by unreliable shipping companies, he acquired in 1895 a vessel of his own to transport his products from the Sonoma coast to San Francisco.

The steam schooner *Newsboy*, which had been owned by the recently bankrupted Navarro Mill, proved a shrewd investment and, as it began to effect improvements in his operation's efficiency, it simultaneously awakened the beginnings of his steamship line. He continued buying vessels to ship lumber, and by 1901 had bought his first large steamer and established the Dollar Steamship Company.

It was the start of something big. Being internationally minded,

Dollar had an instinctive feeling about Eastern promise – the potential market across the sea – and decided to make a test-run with one of his ships, which was memorably successful. He thus became the first to transport American lumber across the Pacific to the Orient, and his frequent subsequent trips to the Far East convinced him of the need for development of foreign trade across the Pacific. Each year he increased the number of ships carrying lumber and freight to Japan, China and Singapore. But that bold, successful strategy was not just a matter of international prestige. There were two winning commercial angles to it. One was the signal it sent to encourage leaders of various other American industries to explore Asia as an exciting new market; the other was the incalculable boost to his own Dollar Steamship Company, which was to boast, by 1930, the largest fleet of cargo and passenger liners that ever operated under the US flag.

Dollar became such a respected name in Asia that, by the First World War, his word alone was enough 'collateral' to allow the US government to commission the construction of ships in China to the value of $30 million.

But he not only became a pioneer and leader of American trade with the Orient, he also developed a round-the-world cargo service in 1920, which was followed in the mid-1920s by the purchase of seven 'President' ships owned by the US government; the acquisition of the Pacific Mail Steamship Company and its trans-Pacific routes; and the inauguration of a round-the-world luxury passenger service that was the first to publish scheduled departure and arrival times.

And what luxury! With a history of travelling extensively on his own ships on business – he made eight circumnavigations of the world and over forty trips to the Orient – Dollar was supremely qualified to commission the construction of two of the largest ocean liners ever built in the United States – the *President Hoover* and *President Coolidge* – with which he impressed even himself. When he boarded the former on 6 August 1931, he gasped: 'The ship is a wonder!'

He was not wrong there. Each ship carried 988 passengers in super-plush accommodation, and how they were pampered, not least by the attentions of a crew of 324. There were phones in every room, stunning art deco furnishings, outdoor pools and even gymnasiums.

The luxury and elegance of these two vessels were in stark contrast to the hard time of the Great Depression, which lasted until the Second World War. And although the Dollar Line lasted through it, when it came to an end it was plain that the effect had taken its toll. Fortunately, Robert Dollar did not live to see the collapse of his dream: the scrapping of the *President Hoover* in 1937 after she ran aground near Hoishoto Island; the arrest of the *President Coolidge* in San Francisco the following year for an unpaid debt of $35,000; his family's passing of the line's ownership to the government in return for a cancellation of its debts; and the renaming of the company to American President Lines – whereby a white eagle replaced the famous dollar signs on its funnels.

A true workaholic, Dollar had remained active in the business until several weeks before his death at the age of eighty-eight on May 16, 1932. Control of the company went to his sons, but A. Melville Dollar died several weeks after his father, and J. Harold Dollar in 1936. R. Stanley Dollar then headed the company until his death in 1958. Today, what remains of the family business consists primarily of lumber operations.

But it was a blaze of global glory while it lasted. During it, Dollar amassed a fortune of $40,000,000 and was rated number 88 in a survey of the wealthiest 100 men in the US – not a bad conclusion for a poor immigrant from Scotland who became an astute American businessman with remarkable vision. Throughout it all, he made several trips back to his home town of Falkirk – where he enjoyed being noticed and followed by admiring groups of children who reminded him of his own childhood – and back in America a particular source of pride for him was his grand house in San Rafael, which he bought in 1906 and named Falkirk (and which today houses the Falkirk Museum).

It is from here that we get a picture of his character, as described by his granddaughter, Grace Dollar Dickson Kleiser, who went to live there with her sister after their mother died in 1920. 'Grandfather sat at the end of the table and said grace before each meal,' she recalled. 'At festive occasions he would tell us a story about his life in the Canadian north woods and have us all spellbound and laughing. He had dark brown, very sparkling eyes and a white beard and you couldn't keep your eyes off him when he was talking. Although we heard the same stories over and over, we always asked him to tell them again.'

More than 3,000 people attended his funeral at the First Presbyterian Church just down the road from the house, and among friends and family were many foreign dignitaries, business associates and government officials. The US government even sent the giant airship *Akron* over the scene to drop flowers from the sky. Honorary pall bearers included the mayor of San Francisco and Governor James Rolph Jr of California, who said: 'Robert Dollar has done more in his lifetime to spread the American flag on the high seas than any man in this country.'

But Dollar did not make his exit without leaving a message to those who wished to do as well as he had. It came in the form of four simple instructions:

Do not cheat; do not be lazy; do not abuse; do not drink.

# Alexander Graham Bell (1847–1922)

*The man who rang the changes*

In any competition to name one person who has changed the world more than any other, Alexander Graham Bell would have to be well worth putting your shirt on as a potential winner. That may be a big statement, but just think for a moment of the sweeping alterations in our way of life that this Scot's invention of the telephone has wrought. It was big enough back then, in 1876, when he made the momentous breakthrough; but even after conquering the challenge of worldwide communication – where before were only horses and sailing ships and an inadequate telegraph service – the telephone's development continues thunderously today, as new ideas are added to it virtually by the day, to feed an endlessly demanding and seemingly ever-young market.

Surprising, then, that the man's birth home in a handsome Georgian building just off Edinburgh's celebrated Princes Street is acknowledged by little more than a few words engraved into the one of the building's 32-inch-wide fluted fascia blocks:

Alexander Graham Bell

Inventor of the Telephone

Born here on 3rd March, 1847

Set to the left of its high, dark-green main door, the words draw little attention to the wood-panelled apartment in South Charlotte Street, on the corner of the classical Charlotte Square, where Alexander's parents – Eliza and Melville Bell – lived and worked; where they were more than a little interested in communication with and for the deaf, as his mother had seriously impaired hearing and his father and grandfather were elocution teachers specialising in that area.

To their surprise and delight, no doubt, the young Alexander chose not to rebel against family tradition in the predictable way of each new generation, but to embrace it with a lifelong fascination for deaf education and acoustics. And he brought to the exercise an invaluable something extra – an inventive mind capable of conceiving ingenious devices to facilitate laudable objectives.

The bearded man with his rich, rounded vocal tones may have been modest himself, saying some years after the world hailed his invention: 'I am sure that I should never have invented the telephone if I had been an electrician. What electrician would have hit upon so mad an idea? I must confess that, to this day, I don't understand how it is possible that someone can speak in Washington and someone else hear him at the foot of the Eiffel Tower.'

But only a few words on the wall? Where better, after all, than the Bell birth-house to create an Alexander Graham Bell Museum (of the history of telecommunications) to add to the Scottish capital's rich mix of money-spinning tourist attractions?

Its absence becomes even more bizarre when you consider that, but a few years ago, the house was actually owned by the very people who live by his invention as an industry – British Telecom.

Today, the company protests that during its year-long ownership it was seriously considering developing the property into a heritage centre. But several insurmountable problems got in the way – it was too small, it didn't lend itself to a large turnover of visitors (disabled access being difficult) and, most serious of all, BT found itself in deep financial trouble after the dot.com bubble burst and had to urgently divest itself of much valuable property.

Now, at time of writing, the recently refurbished building – acquired by property developers – is a series of 'small office suites' housing software firms and such like. No further mention of its world-famous earlier incumbent; no exciting exhortation to use the head and crank up something special.

To give BT its due, it has been instrumental in providing a large variety of fascinating artefacts for an impressive £1 million telecommunications permanent exhibition entitled 'Communicate!' and opened in October 2003 at the National Museum of Scotland in Edinburgh.

Bell's great-grandson, Hugh Müller, seventy-one, who made the journey from Nova Scotia for its official opening, said at the time: 'I think my great-grandfather would be very pleased. He always prided himself in being a Scot. When he went to Scotland for the last time he was given the freedom of Edinburgh and he told people that, of all the awards and honours he had, that was the one he prized the most.'

Showing the many different ways in which people have communicated over the centuries – from bongo drums, carrier pigeons and telegraph wires to the internet and the mobile phone – 'Communicate!' pays implicit tribute to the pioneering work of Scotland's telephone inventor, and is the only formal celebration of his achievements in Scotland. One of its champions argues: 'Some people might find this museum exhibition the most appropriate home for a Scottish tribute to Bell.'

But this writer is not convinced. Surely, the birth-house would have been more apt. Where a great, custom-made museum should naturally be, there is nothing.

Likewise in Elgin, in the northern county of Moray, where the teenage Alexander enrolled as a student teacher of music and elocution at Weston House. There is today no sign of his having been there. And it was an important, formative time in his life when, after teaching during the day, he learned in the evenings about electricity, became fascinated by telegraphy, and conducted experiments on the pitch of vowel sounds, even building a machine to produce them electronically.

Fine old Weston House was demolished in 1955, to be replaced by a car-sales garage, which has since become a branch store of a well-known electrical chain. And at no time has there ever been a public note on the site of the illustrious Scotsman's presence.

It is a different story in North America, of course, where he went at the age of twenty-three – first to Ontario – with his surviving family to recover from the tuberculosis that killed two of his brothers in 1870. Though it was not a big step from Canada to the USA, where he then took a job teaching deaf children in Boston, it would stay close to his heart, and vice versa.

On Cape Breton island, Nova Scotia, there is an Alexander Graham Bell National Historic Site on ten hectares of land. Overlooking Baddeck Bay and Beinn Breagh, Bell's second home, where much of his scientific work was pursued and where he and his wife Mabel are now buried, the centre commemorates and interprets his scientific and humanitarian work, illustrated by fascinating artefacts such as books, photographs, material from his archives, personal furniture and awards received during his lifetime.

A more-than-fitting tribute to a well-remembered man. But Bell's early professional sojourn north of the border lasted only a year. It was 'down south' in Boston, where he taught at a special day school for deaf children and became a renowned educator by opening classes to train teachers of speech to the deaf, that he began to lay the groundwork that would lead to the invention of the telephone.

Encouraged by a number of local scientists interested in acoustics, in his spare time he sought to combine his work for the hearing-impaired with his interest in invention, and began to believe with growing conviction that it might be possible for an electrified wire to carry the human voice over great distances. To this end, his keen ear helped him experiment with musical notes in trying to develop a device that would record the rising and falling of voice tones in speech. As he saw there was little difference in the harmonics, he realised speech transmission must be within reach.

It was during this time, when he was also professor of vocal physiology and the mechanics of speech at Boston University, that he determined to move on through inventions of the phonautograph (a device for converting sound into visible traces) and the multiple telegraph (increased capability for the dot-and-dash system) to the 'speaking telegraph' itself.

He was encouraged in this by the entry into his endeavours of Tom Watson, a skilled electrician who seemed to understand his ideas and was capable of developing devices to support them. The two men were to become one of history's most legendary partnerships – reminiscent almost of Sherlock Holmes and his 'elementary' Watson – and, as their goal came tantalisingly close, Bell gave up teaching to focus all his considerable brainpower and energy on reaching to grasp for his holy grail. By 1874, he had worked out the principles for electronic transmission of speech; by mid-1875, Bell and Watson proved that a fluctuating current could carry sounds as a whole variety of them were transmitted through their wires; and by 7 March 1876, Bell had got his patent for the invention he called the 'telephone'.

How does it work? Simply described, it is a system that converts sound, specifically the human voice, to electrical impulses of various frequencies and then back to a tone that sounds like the original voice. To some degree Bell's work on it reflected that of the German Johann Philip Reis who, in 1864, nearly solved the problem of long-distance talk by constructing an apparatus capable of transmitting music – but not the spoken word; and it cut across the bows of American Elisha Gray who had been doing similar work to Bell's. Indeed, both Bell and Gray filed for a patent on their designs at the New York patent office on February 14 1876, with Bell beating

Gray by only two hours! Although Gray had built the first steel diaphragm/electromagnet receiver in 1874, he did not master a workable transmitter design until after the tireless Bell – who had slaved over various types of mechanism year after year. But there were many legal challenges.

To the highly principled Bell, every lawsuit was an assault on his integrity. 'He took it very personally,' Hugh Müller, his great-grandson, told the *Scotsman* newspaper on his 2003 visit to Scotland:

> His lawyers would tell him not to worry about it, not to react, but he found that very difficult. He was a man of very high integrity. What really bothered him was when people thought he was stealing ideas, that he had been fraudulent. He was a product of the Victorian age, not necessarily religious, but of very tight morals. After the lawsuits about the telephone he didn't write on a scrap of paper without first dating it.

Court battles over his patent went on for almost two decades, and although all were eventually resolved in his favour, Bell must have wondered to himself if it had not been granted a touch prematurely. For it was not until 10 March 1876, three days after his Gray-beating green light, that the famous verbal request that was to become possibly the most recorded one in human history, was sent out over the wire from one room to another, and was clearly understood by the recipient, Tom Watson.

The many reports of that moment have produced, like Chinese whispers, various versions of the immortal words spoken, and there have been dramatised accounts of the reaction such as 'Watson dropped the receiver and rushed with wild joy across the hall to tell Bell the glad tidings' – so here, just for this record, is the event as told through the horse's mouth, from the pages of Bell's experimental notebook for that fateful day. It began with a drawing of his latest, most refined instrument:

> The improved instrument shown in Fig 1 was constructed this morning and tried this evening. P is a brass pipe and W the platinum wire, M the mouth piece and S the armature of the receiving instrument.
>
> Mr Watson was stationed in one room with the receiving instrument. He pressed one ear closely against S and closed the other ear with his hand. The transmitting instrument was placed in another room and the doors of both rooms were closed.

I then shouted in to M the following sentence: 'Mr Watson – come here – I want to see you.' To my delight, he came and declared that he had heard and understood what I had said.

I asked him to repeat the words. He answered, 'You said, "Mr Watson – come here – I want to see you."'

We then changed places and I listened at S while Mr Watson read a few passages from a book into the mouth piece M. It was certainly the case that articulate sounds proceeded from S. The effect was loud but indistinct and muffled. If I had read beforehand the passage given by Mr Watson I should have recognised every word. As it was I could not make out the sense – but an occasional word here and there was quite distinct. I made out 'to' and 'out' and 'further', and finally the sentence 'Mr Bell, do you understand what I say? DO-YOU-UN-DER-STAND-WHAT-I-SAY' came quite clearly and intelligibly. No sound was audible when the armature S was removed.

And so the telephone, that boon and blessing to mankind, was born. Among the many huge consequences of that historic moment was the burgeoning of telephone exchanges, the first of which was installed in Hartford, Connecticut, in 1877, and the founding of the Bell Telephone Company (later AT&T), which grew to be the world's largest phone company.

It is difficult now to appreciate the sense of wonder the invention engendered at the time; but at the back of one of my bookshelves I have found a musty volume of the *New Harmsworth Self-Educator*, published in the 1920s, that seems – in its introduction to the chapter entitled 'Transmission of Speech: Invention of the Telephone' – to capture the true impact and magnitude of the development. It reads:

Of the many inventions which distinguished the latter half of the 19th century, it is safe to say that none excited greater wonder and interest than that of the Telephone.

It was looked upon as the first step in the direction of realising the 'Arabian Nights' dream of a magic carpet – the brilliance of the conception cannot easily be realised.

For thousands of years men had been content to transmit their speech sounds over at most but a few hundred feet. In 1876 Graham Bell astonished the world by showing how the energy of sound vibrations could be transformed into electrical energy, transmitted along a wire at a speed approximating to that of light, and re-transformed into sound waves under conditions which seemed to annihilate all the pre-existing limits of time and space.

When we remember that sound in air travels at about 1,100 feet per second – a speed which would require over half an hour to traverse the distance between London and Glasgow [400 miles] and at the same time know that every day men converse between these towns as easily as if in the same room, we appreciate more fully the modern miracle of the telephone.

As has occurred with many other epoch-making inventions, so in this case all the necessary component parts were in existence, and only the touch of genius was required for a great forward step.

It must have been an indescribably exciting time in the life of the young Scot. Thanks to the stunning achievement of his 'touch of genius' at the tender age of twenty-nine, his professional and domestic future – on the brink of marriage, as he was, to one of his students, Mabel Hubbard – looked not just secure but remarkably bright in 1876. Indeed, Mabel's well-off father became a funding champion of Bell's system, and it is amusing from this remove to read the response he and his son-in-law got when they offered his patent to the Telegraph Company (which became Western Union) for $100,000 in 1876. Chauncey M. DePew, president of the company, had a committee investigate the offer and here is part of its report . . .

The Telephone purports to transmit the speaking voice over telegraph wires. We found that the voice is very weak and indistinct, and grows even weaker when long wires are used between the transmitter and receiver. Technically, we do not see that this device will ever be capable of sending recognisable speech over a distance of several miles.

Messer Hubbard and Bell want to install one of their 'telephone devices' in every city. The idea is idiotic on the face of it. Furthermore, why would any person want to use this ungainly and impractical device when he can send a messenger to the telegraph office and have a clear written message sent to any large city in the United States?

The electricians of our company have developed all the significant improvements in the telegraph art to date, and we see no reason why a group of outsiders, with extravagant and impractical ideas, should be entertained, when they have not the slightest idea of the true problems involved. Mr. G.G. Hubbard's fanciful predictions, while they sound rosy, are based on wild-eyed imagination and lack of understanding of the technical and economic facts of the situation, and a posture of ignoring the obvious limitations of his device, which is hardly more than a toy . . .

In view of these facts, we feel that Mr. G.G. Hubbard's request for $100,000 of the sale of this patent is utterly unreasonable, since this device is inherently of no use to us. We do not recommend its purchase.

For this astonishing lack of prescience, Bell got his poetic justice in the end – when in 1882 he acquired a controlling interest in Western Union!

But, back in 1876, the timing of his breakthrough couldn't have been better, with the Centennial Exposition in Philadelphia – to celebrate 100 years of US independence – coming up in June of that year.

Surprisingly, the stand displaying his groundbreaking invention was largely ignored – until a VIP recognised Bell himself, as the distinguished expert in speech training who had helped him in a training session at Boston University. This was the Brazilian Emperor Dom Pedro II, who came over to say hello then accepted an invitation to hear the inventor reciting Shakespeare over the telephone. 'Great heavens! The thing talks!' exclaimed the emperor, as heads all over the hall turned. From that point on, the telephone was the star attraction.

Bell could have been forgiven for being content with the success of his world-changing invention and being ready to take life rather more easily. But such a thought never crossed his mind. The following month, two days after forming the Bell Telephone Company, he married Mabel and they set out on a year-long working honeymoon in Britain to introduce the telephone there.

While he was to make a great deal of money on selling his interests to big business, Alexander Graham Bell was also a man driven to the end by his inventive impulses. The Bells had two daughters, Elsie and Marian, and eventually settled in Washington and Nova Scotia. But he never stopped experimenting and inventing. In 1881, he invented a probe to locate bullets in a body; in 1886 he sold his patents for making wax phonograph discs to open a place to carry out his work for the deaf; in the 1890s he conducted experiments with flying machines, earning his portrait a place on a US postage stamp between the Wright Brothers' heads; and so on it went.

Late in life, he told a reporter, who was clearly awed by his mental energy: 'There cannot be mental atrophy in any person who continues to observe, to remember what he observes, and to seek answers for his unceasing hows and whys about things.'

Interested in aeronautics and physics, he worked on a variety of projects as diverse as flying machines, metal detectors, automatic switchboards, hydrofoil designs and – after his new-born son Edward tragically died from respiratory problems – an early version of the iron lung. And all the while he remained a prominent advocate for new methods of teaching the deaf to speak and lip-read; for he saw himself, above all, as a dedicated teacher of the deaf.

For the rest of the world, of course, he would be principally remembered for his momentous invention of the device with which his name has now become almost synonymous. In 1915, in New York, he spoke to Watson in San Francisco, in celebration of the first transcontinental telephone link. And in a tribute that seemed to match the size of his achievement, when he died seven years later, the entire telephone service of the United States – something that simply didn't exist before the kindly Scot crossed the Atlantic – stopped operating for one minute in his honour.

# David Dunbar Buick (1854–1929)

*Who gave the car its name*

You can't find No. 26 these days, and you can barely discern the vestigial shape of Green Street itself in Arbroath, the east-coast fishing port famed for its piquant smoked haddock and now-ruined abbey, where the Declaration of Arbroath (a model for the American Declaration of Independence) was signed in 1320. The one-time position of the little house in question can be vaguely perceived between the cluster of newish homes that have ambushed it and the wider outer circle of older houses built in the town's distinctive red sandstone – the same stuff, hewn by monks from the nearby shore's dramatic cliffs, that made that celebrated abbey. Indeed, in the absence of the house and its one-time neighbours, the only building that still holds the street's virtually vanished line is the little Victorian Milne masonic hall, on one of whose walls, just above head height, is the brass plaque I have been advised to seek out.

This intrigues me for two reasons: the first being that I grew up through babyhood only a few metres from this spot – with my back-bedroom in Lochlands Street well within dummy-throwing distance; the second being that, until recently, and in common I assume with most townspeople, I knew little of my famous fellow-toddler from this street. For many decades he had been something of a forgotten hero at home as well as in his adopted country of America.

In people terms, Arbroath had been known for being the home town of James Chalmers, who famously developed the adhesive postage stamp; for lawnmower inventor Alexander Shanks, and for the kilted entertainer Andy Stewart. But here was evidence that the little town just north of Dundee could boast yet another important son. The plaque, which was placed on the hall by a group of US car industry executives more than a decade ago to mark the hundred and fortieth birthday of the man who gave his name to the Buick automobile, reads:

David Dunbar Buick Sept 17, 1854–March 5, 1929. American motoring pioneer and founder of the Buick Motor Company of America, David Dunbar Buick was born at No. 26 Green Street, Arbroath, which lay approximately 90 metres north of this, the only remaining building to show the line of the original street.

Sponsored by the Buick Motor Division of the General Motors Corporation of America.

To accompany its unveiling, the Buick bosses brought along a brace of their most handsome cars – one from 1937 and one hot off the 1994 presses. They were put on display lined outside the hall for locals to gasp at in a cathartic moment of great local rediscovery – for although his story did not have a traditional happy ending as the person himself almost vanished out of the history books, paradoxically David Buick's name is one of the most enduring in automotive history.

It was only two years after he was born that his parents decided to up sticks from Arbroath and take the family to America. They settled in Detroit, where his carpenter father died three years later and his mother then worked in a candy store to support the family.

At the age of fifteen, David was hired by the Alexander Manufacturing Company, a Detroit fabricator of plumbing fixtures – where Henry Ford had also worked as an apprentice – and there he acquired and developed the inventive and tactile skills that were both to serve him well and lead him astray. He became a prolific engineer and inventor of many new applications – thirteen patents for valves, water closets, bathtubs and a lawn sprinkler, not to mention his ground-breaking process for heat-binding porcelain and wrought iron to make white bathtubs – and by 1882 he and an old school friend, William Sherwood, had taken over the plumbing business.

Buick & Sherwood, of which Buick was president, was successful and would undoubtedly have made them considerable fortunes, but . . . When he saw his first automobile, bathroom fittings were immediately a thing of the past for David Buick. Always an innovative thinker, and always more interested in making things than making money, he turned his attention to petrol engines and became so obsessed with developing them that tension began to play on the delicate business partnership with Sherwood, until it cracked under the latter's change-or-else ultimatum.

'Or else' it was. The company was sold in 1899 for $100,000 and Buick, then forty-five, used his share to form a new firm to build petrol engines for farm and marine use. The Buick Auto-Vim and Power Company, as he called it, was the cradle of a smart Buick prototype, which the cash-strapped David sold for $225 to its chief engineer, Walter Marr, in 1901.

That was a signal of how things were about to go. Buick's ambitions to build a great car were driving him on, but he did not have deep enough pockets to match them, as his company's name was constantly changed to reveal his burning intent.

In 1902 it was transformed into the Buick Manufacturing Company – where the famous Buick valve-in-head engine was designed. Indeed, so advanced did his designs become that the Buick Motor Car Company – formed the following year – was overspent before it began, and did not have an easy birth. It completed fifty experimental cars at $1,200 each before selling any, and often had to be saved from financial failure by optimistic believers such as Walter Marr and Buick's businessman friend Ben Briscoe, who believed in Buick's hands-on talents but was wary of his business abilities. His patience with the Scot often grew thin, and he once said the Buick story 'is so fraught with romance that it makes the Arabian Nights tales look commonplace'.

And the terms of the new firm's organisation would haunt Buick all his life. It was capitalised with $100,000 in stock – $300 for Buick and $99,700 for Briscoe. As president, Buick could gain control of all the stock if he repaid Briscoe $3,500 he owed him within four months. If he couldn't, he would forfeit all interest in the company. In what he probably reckoned was a smart move, Buick sold the company before the deadline – to Flint Wagon Works, which was looking for a way into auto manufacturing and was impressed by his car, settled his corporate debts, and embraced both the Buick set-up and its name.

But while Buick became entangled in what was actually a bad bargain with the new owners, the Buick Motor Company was moved from Detroit to Flint. He became secretary of the new car works and was allotted 1,500 shares but would not receive the stock until his dividends paid off his personal debts.

Meanwhile, the show had to go on, and a catalytic moment for the fledgling car giant came in the summer of 1904, when the first Flint-built pre-production Buick was taken on a test run to Detroit and back by Walter Marr and Buick's son Thomas. Here is a contemporary account of that historic drive in the Model B . . .

They started out on Saturday, July 5, 1904, at 1:15pm from Flint's Sherman House Hotel on a 90-mile route to Detroit via Lapeer. A rear-bearing failure caused them to spend a night in Lapeer. They arrived in Detroit on the Sunday, the *Flint Journal* reporting that 'the distance from Pontiac to Birmingham was covered in ten minutes'. They bought car license No. 1024 Monday and headed back to Flint Tuesday. Driving in a steady rain through the small towns of Pontiac, Oxford and Lapeer, Marr averaged more than 30mph. 'The roads were deep in mud every mile of the way,' Marr said. 'I did the driving and [Tom] Buick was kept busy wiping the mud off my goggles'.

In one town they were challenged to a race by an electric car, but the Buick 'showed them the way', Marr said. 'We went so fast at another time that we could not see the village's 6mph sign. At one place, going down a hill, I saw a bump at a bridge too late to slow up. When I hit it I threw in all the power and landed over it safely in the road. Buick was just taking a chew of tobacco when a lump of mud as large as a baseball hit him square in the face, filling his mouth completely. We were plastered with mud from head to foot when we reached Flint.

Marr drove his first Flint Buick directly to the office of the *Flint Journal* on his return. 'The machine made the run without a skip,' he boasted. 'It reached here in the best of condition. We took the hills handily with our high-speed gear and the machine sounded like a locomotive.' Back at the plant, Marr told the directors: 'Well, we are here.'

The test was so successful that the order was given to start production immediately, and by the end of the year, thirty-seven Model B Buicks had been built. But the company ran into financial trouble again – and turned to prominent local entrepreneur William C. Durant, a horse-drawn carriage builder who didn't particularly like automobiles . . . until he saw how the Buick could climb hills and run through mud like no other car he had ever seen.

Once Durant made the decision to switch (from) horses, there was no going back. The Buick's success was assured. Few people could raise money and interest in a product like 'Billy' Durant, and when he went to the 1905 New York Auto Show he took orders for 1,000 Buicks before the company had built 40.

None of which was particularly good news for David Buick, personally or professionally. As a non-commercial animal with little interest in company politics, he began to lose out dramatically.

Like Henry Ford, Durant knew the motor industry's future lay in speeding up production and cutting assembly costs. But Buick was a craftsman who saw each new car as a unique piece of work. His role in the business declined rapidly until he finally lost the manager's title to Durant in early 1906. The company was clearly not big enough for both of them, and one would have to go. Buick sold his stock to Durant for $100,000 – stock that would soon be worth $115,000,000.

So in 1906, at the age of fifty-two, David Dunbar Buick severed all his links with the company he had started, and returned to Detroit with his wife and son. He had been involved in the making of only 120 Buicks and, after a while, the only vestige of his input was his name, which continued to suit the car as its technology advanced with the company's growing strength. In 1908, Durant acquired Cadillac and Oldsmobile to form General Motors – which, as it grew towards today's global conglomerate, then took in Chevrolet (1918), Britain's Vauxhall (1926) and Germany's Opel (1929).

By 1923 Buick production had reached 100,000 units a year, a figure that has risen steadily until now – when there is a 300-acre complex employing 20,000 people producing 350,000 cars a year.

It is a remarkable and romantic story, but it ended less than sweetly for David Dunbar Buick. Forgotten and impoverished, in the last years of his life the automobile pioneer held a series of low-paid jobs. When he was found in 1928 by the young reporter Bruce Catton – who later became a Pulitzer-Prize-winning historian of the American Civil War – the once dapper bespectacled executive had become 'a thin, bent little man' working behind the information desk as an inspector at the Detroit School of Trades. He was described as having, at seventy-four, grey hair, a slight frame and a deeply lined face, but bright and cheerful eyes.

In his talk with the reporter, he was candid about the way his life had worked out and seemed nevertheless to be looking forward. He was not to know that less than a year later, on 5 March 1929, he would die of colon cancer complications in Detroit's Harper Hospital.

In that same year, while he couldn't afford to keep a telephone in his home, let alone buy one of the automobiles that bore his name, General Motors produced 196,104 Buicks, making it the sixth most popular car line in the United States. Eight years later, GM adopted the Buick family crest as the logo for the car line. To date, the Buick name has been stamped on over 25 million cars.

But in his talk with Catton, Buick was neither bitter nor regretful. In response to a question comparing what had gone before with his current situation, he said: 'I'm not worrying. The failure is the man who stays down when he falls – the man who sits and worries about what happened yesterday, instead of jumping up and figuring what he's going to do today and tomorrow. That's what success is – looking ahead to tomorrow.'

David Buick was not alone in ending in a destitute state. Perhaps he allowed himself an ironic smile when he learned, wherever he was, that Billy Durant eventually lost control of GM and ended up running a bowling alley in Flint.

The Buick name has lived on, however, in the handsome badges of sophisticated state-of-the-art models that cruise across America today, and it has come to mean guaranteed quality and luxury.

Come to think of it, the car-crazy boy from Arbroath might just have been happy with that.

There is still a Buick living in Arbroath who has a strong relationship with the car company. Eric Buick, an industrial cleaning contractor, was keen to find out if he was related to the Buick founder – and, after some research in the early 1990s, was saddened to find that he wasn't.

That didn't stop him making friends with the company's executives, however, and it was at his suggestion that they came over to fix and unveil plaque the DDB plaque in 1994.

'I told them I thought it was a shame that David Buick was not commemorated at his birthplace and their PR man Larry Guston responded quickly with a bit of a challenge,' he recalls. 'If I could come up with a good idea, they would come up with the funding.'

Eric did . . . and they did.

So strong is his relationship with Buick that he was invited by his company contacts to attend the record-breaking 'Buicktown centenary gathering of the cars' at Flint, Michigan, in July 2003.

Eric still feels he might one day find some living relatives of the auto pioneer. 'His grandson, David Buick II, died in the late '80s and, on the face of it, that seems to have marked the dying out of the family name. But I'm still researching and I live in hope . . .'

He feels David Buick had 'a pretty rough deal', being pushed out of the firm early.

# Bertie C. Forbes (1880–1954)

*Founder of* Forbes Magazine

If you care to look for them, there are many pearls of wisdom attributed to Bertie C. Forbes, some of them pertinent to living in general ('Jealousy is a mental cancer' or 'The truth doesn't hurt unless it ought to') and some with particular reference to the decent conduct of business ('A shady business never yields a sunny life' or 'Real riches are the riches possessed inside'). But the one aphorism that seems to have particular relevance to the unfolding of his own thoroughly fulfilled life is: 'To make headway, improve your head.'

He might easily have added 'and use it', because using his head was what the remarkably enterprising Scot seemed to do from the moment he was born in 1880 – the sixth of the ten children of Agnes and Robbie Forbes, a modest tailor and ale purveyor in the small farming community of Whitehill in the parish of New Deer, Aberdeenshire.

It is tempting, while telling such rags-to-riches tales, to overuse the word 'poor' in characterising the parents or offspring; but I suspect even the little Bertie Forbes knew the word could not apply to him – his early life may have been hard, with little on the table and an often-chilly mile walk to school and back every day from his cottage home known as the Cunnyknowe, but his earthy agricultural environment was rich indeed, characterised by rolling fields of oats, glossy cattle and good fresh air.

He was a well-loved lad, too. But if you could ask him now what he considered his greatest blessing, he would doubtless answer with the name of one man. It would not be that of a US president or any of the famously rich people he met in later life; it would be that of Gavin Greig, a man who was the very embodiment of the legendary idea (now sadly faded) of a 'guid Scots education'.

This enlightened, erudite man was not only a respected playwright, poet, composer and collector of the region's folk songs but also the headmaster of the little school at Whitehill where he taught the three Rs – reading, writing and 'rithmetic – and the classics with equal dedication and passion to the simple country children in his charge.

Some, of course, were less simple than others. And as a man of letters himself, Greig sensed and encouraged an aptitude for words and hungry curiosity that he saw in the keen young Bertie Forbes. So when an exciting opportunity presented itself in class one day, the teacher was not surprised to see Bertie stick up his hand in instant response. Dauvit Scott, publisher of *The Peterhead Sentinel* local newspaper, was on the look-out for a printer's devil, and had asked Gavin Greig to announce his requirement in class to the older children.

There was no doubt in Bertie Forbes' mind that this chance, which he immediately related to his interest in writing, was a golden one. And so, with his eager response taken positively, he set off at the age of fourteen on the long journey to be a publisher himself – and one of America's most important ones. It is intriguing to wonder now, with hindsight, at the catalytic significance of that small moment, when the first seed of America's most prestigious business and financial magazine was sown.

Headquartered on New York's Fifth Avenue, a few blocks from the Empire State Building, *Forbes Magazine* quickly grew into something of an institution, the American business person's long-established 'bible' – full of intelligent, conscience-searching and respected features but perhaps best-known for its many periodic 'wealth' lists. Today, these include the Forbes 400, a list of the richest people in the United States; a list of the richest people in the world; and the Forbes 500, a list of largest companies taking into account market capitalisation, revenue, income and assets.

The magazine's own income and assets have been mightily impressive too over the years, making many of its prime family movers multi-millionaires. Not the least of them, of course, Bertie Forbes.

And it all surely began in the fishing port of Peterhead, not far from his family home. There, his first job might not have been the world's greatest, at a wage of a few shillings a week, but its importance in the great scheme of his life could not be underestimated. He spent three years typesetting there and acquired not just a vital grounding in technical understanding but a valued introduction to editorial work. Any veteran journalist will tell you how important these things used to be, and in the same breath will surely mention the *Dundee Courier* – long acknowledged as Britain's best in-at-the-deep-end training ground for journalists in the days before computers and formal training schemes.

And that was where Bertie went next, to be a fast-learning *Courier* cub reporter – who, while still in his teens, was transferred to Montrose, an important harbour town on the east coast between Aberdeen and Dundee, as boss of the branch office there.

So before he was twenty-one and on his way to new horizons at the turn of the century, Bertie had a formidable secret weapon under his belt – he was already a relatively tried and trusted journalist. Did he look it? Probably not. And that misperception, as we will see later, was something he relished having to counter with the surprising revelation of his skills when the right moment presented itself.

For many of the facts and memories in this chapter I am indebted to another man of letters from the Greig family, my old journalistic colleague Jack Webster, great-grandson of the great teacher. In his tender trade-choosing years Jack actually met Bertie on several occasions and was even encouraged into journalism by him – with satisfying results, it has to be said. For Jack, now in his seventies, has a distinguished career in national newspapers behind him and is quietly famous himself thanks to his finely written books, features and star-spangled interviews, which have included names like Charlie Chaplin and Bing Crosby. It is to him, then, that we turn for some unique memories of, and insights into, Buchan's formidable son:

'Bertie was in my granny's class at school and he always felt very much indebted to our family because of my great-grandfather,' recalls Jack.

> He just idolised Gavin Greig. In later life he said he thought Greig was a greater man than any of his great American pals like Henry Ford and John D. Rockefeller. This was because of the superb education he gave his pupils, turning them out not just with top-class English but also Latin and Greek and a real appetite for the world. They were incredibly well educated by the age of 14.

That included Bertie, of course. And when the Boer War stirred his appetite for worldly adventure, he left the *Courier* to set sail for far southern horizons. In Johannesburg the (later) great mystery writer Edgar Wallace, who had been a war correspondent and decided to stay on, was looking for help to revamp the post-war *Rand Daily Mail*. When he met Bertie Forbes he knew this was 'just the kind of guy he was looking for, a hard-working Scot prepared to get his jacket off'.

Eventually, Bertie became so trusted by Wallace he would be allowed to take over his columns as if he were the master himself.

'But he had another important string to his bow,' says Jack. 'Having developed an interest in golf, he would often be on the golf courses caddying for the big diamond merchants, and as he did so he would keep his ears open to learn about high finance from their conversation.' Though he was doing well on the new paper, Bertie decided that if he was going to be so interested in stocks and shares, the best city to be in was New York. And so, by 1904, he was waving Wallace goodbye and steaming off to another new life in the Big Apple.

> He had no contacts there. Nobody knew a thing about him. He tried to get a job but nobody would take him on. Who was this Scottish country bumpkin anyway? At twenty-four he was too old to be an office boy, and he probably wasn't experienced enough for a real editorial job. Seeing this problem of perception, Bertie offered to work for nothing, but the *New York Journal of Commerce* yielded and grudgingly admitted him to its humblest post for a few dollars a week.

With his feet thus under the table, Bertie began to push in articles, which were received – and published – with great approval and surprise. Which must have been very gratifying for the unknown country boy, who suddenly found himself rising quickly up the ladder so that, in next to no time, he was the paper's respected financial editor.

'Soon he was doing syndicated columns under different names, and at one of our meetings,' recalls Jack,

> I listened open-mouthed as he told me how William Randolph Hearst, the biggest newspaper tycoon in the world, was so keen to hire him he gave him a blank cheque to sign his own salary. He asked for a massive $20,000 and Hearst told him later that, although he had been prepared to pay much more, he had calculated that a Scot would under-estimate his own value.

By 1917 Bertie Forbes had become so famous as the most widely read financial writer in America that he decided to capitalise on his name by starting *Forbes Magazine*. To acquire much of the needed (borrowed) capital, he knocked on the Fifth Avenue door of the industrialist Charles Frick and won him over in a charm offensive. And once the magazine was up and running, he pulled no punches.

The very first issue reminded readers that 'business was originated to produce happiness, not pile up millions' and carried a column with the biblical exhortation 'With all thy getting, get understanding'. Indeed, he became known as 'the great humaniser of business' and, despite becoming a friend – and fellow-millionaire – of people like Henry Ford, Andrew Carnegie, John D. Rockefeller and Frank Woolworth, he practised an unusual morality in the magazine and would not pull back from criticising, say, Ford for slave-driving in his factories.

In time, however, as the magazine steadily grew in stature and financial stability between the two wars and between the great sprouting skyscrapers of Manhattan, Bertie Forbes found himself thinking more and more of his simple Scottish roots, and how he would like to honour the people from whom he came. And so, after he got himself established around the early 1920s, he started going back to Scotland every two years, and his picnics at Whitehill became something of an institution.

'The idea of Bertie coming always caused tremendous excitement in the parish,' recalls Jack.

> We weren't used to mixing with millionaires, and he always paid special attention to my family when he came back – my granny was still there, of course, and as I was the great grandson of his great hero, I got a bit more attention than most.
>
> I first remember him when I was a little lad, about 1935 or '37. He was quite Americanised by that time – a small, rotund, fairly typical cigar-smoking American, with gold-rimmed specs. But he wasn't long back before he was speaking with something of a Buchan accent again, with local words . . . the American nasal bit would gradually give way to the voice of the real Buchan boy.
>
> Then of course the war came so we didn't see him again until 1946, and by then I was 15 and keen to be a journalist. So he devoted a lot of time to encouraging me, thinking I suppose that he was paying back a debt to Gavin Greig. He told me stories about his friends like John D. Rockefeller and Frank Woolworth . . . and he aroused great excitement in me to be a journalist, though I was keen anyway by that time. All the stuff about his life in New York was fascinating . . . playing Saturday night poker games with Mrs Gershwin, mother of George, and me being a great Gershwin fan!'

In all, Jack Webster met Bertie Forbes five times after the war.

He would come over to our house in nearby Maud, two miles from Whitehill, and play poker with my father . . . and I'd just sit and listen. He would sit in our best room and just chat away over a cuppa – for which the best china was brought out – or a dram. He exuded tremendous personality. You could still see the wee butter ball of a Buchan boy in him, but you had to look through all these layers of American sophistication. He had just grown hugely in stature.

The millionaire's picnic two-yearly visits after the war started in 1946, and so then took place in 1948, 1950, 1952 and . . .

For the next one we shouldn't have been expecting him until '54. But word got around that he was coming for Christmas '53, and my mother – who was a bit intuitive – said 'That's very odd. I wonder why he's coming then, he's never been here at Christmas'. So he came and played Santa Claus for the kids, and visited our house as usual. But when he left in his big limousine with his chauffeur to drive back to Glasgow to catch his ship (he often came on the *Queen Mary*) I remember my mother saying: 'We're never going to see Bertie again.'

Indeed, the following May the millionaire publisher was found dead – lying on the floor of his office – by a night security man who wondered why his light was still burning. He had had a heart attack and died there and then, with a pen in his hand. So he would not have made it to Scotland for the summer of 1954.

Bertie had been editor-in-chief of *Forbes* until his death, though he was assisted in his later years by Bruce and Malcolm, the two oldest of the surviving four of his five sons (Duncan had been killed as a teenager in a car crash). Bruce took over the business, but within a few years, in 1964, he too had died – of cancer, in his forties. So Malcolm, the colourful third son, who had not been thinking about taking the helm, was called into service, and proved a godsend, as he developed Bertie's worthy company into a billion-dollar business.

In fact, Malcolm not only sorted out the company; he sorted out his father's position for eternity. The old man was buried in a New Jersey cemetery, but thirty-four years later Malcolm brought his body home to Scotland be re-interred in the old churchyard at New Deer. Jack Webster has a story to tell about that too . . .

Malcolm had asked me to help him bring back the old picnic tradition, and after the first revived one in 1987 I was driving him back to the airport when we passed New Deer cemetery. I said: 'Your ancestors are buried in there' and I could see his mind working . . .

When he got back to America, he summoned a family conference which then decided that Bertie would probably be happier back among his ain folk in New Deer. That was when he got on the phone and said: 'We've decided to dig up Dad and bring him back'. So in 1988 about 18 members of the family came flying in and we reburied Bertie in the old churchyard in New Deer just across the road from the village church, St Kane's, that he used to attend with his whole family, all ten of them.

I had a cord to lower him into his new grave. The coffin had been sent in advance. I can't remember if it came by sea, but it sat for some time in the potting shed of the village joiner, who was also the local undertaker.

Malcolm was a flamboyant man whose colourful lifestyle included lavish star-studded parties, motorcycling interludes with Liz Taylor, flying hot-air balloons, and an unsuccessful stab at New Jersey's 1957 gubernatorial election; and when he died in 1990, he left a fortune estimated at over $1 billion.

Times soon began to get relatively harder for the Forbes family, however, as much of that sum went on taxes, and the eldest of his four sons who took over, Malcolm Stevenson Forbes Jr (known as 'Steve'), spent an estimated $76 million on two unsuccessful bids for the Republican presidential nomination in 1996 and 2000.

It is no secret, of course, that such expenditures – combined with the advertising downturn that followed the Twin Towers catastrophe – prompted the organisation to pull in its belt a little and, at time of writing, Steve's brother Kip was mounting a big effort to shore up the family finances and was initiating a number of commercial ventures, including a wine label, jewellery and designer furniture.

Other measures designed to keep the family fortune intact included the selling of their father's collection of Fabergé eggs to a Russian collector, and the licensing of the company's business name for products ranging from calendars to furniture. But setbacks and challenges are what the Forbes dynasty has been always about, and it seems unlikely that its foundations can be seriously shaken now. Indeed, one can almost hear the ghostly voice of Bertie Forbes booming out across the Atlantic with another of his memorable advisory observations:

History has demonstrated that the most notable winners usually encountered heartbreaking obstacles before they triumphed. They won because they refused to become discouraged by their defeats.

# Tommy Armour (1895–1968)

*The one-eyed golf champ*

> It is not solely the capacity to make great shots that makes champions,
> but the essential quality of making very few bad shots.

Many a frustrated amateur – and even professional – golfer will recognise the wisdom in that memorable quote by Tommy Armour, one of the few club-swinging Scots to really capitalise on the fact that he was born in the land that claims (although the Dutch might dispute it) to have invented the game.

This baker's son was, in fact, born in full view of a cemetery in Edinburgh's Balcarres Street, which skirts the vibrant shop-rich Morningside area, in a foursquare Victorian block, which must have appeared quite pristine when he entered the world on 24 September 1895. It looks a little worn at the edges today, with eight flats spread over four floors, but it could well be good for another 100 years.

And although he died in 1968, it looks as if Tommy Armour's reputation could also live on for a century or more. Already more than a half-century since the height of his fame, his name remains one of the more recognisable among golf aficionados largely because of the respected and sought-after range of golf equipment still marketed under its branding.

The resonance of the name also has much to do with the man's achievements, of course – as golfers always like to be associated with success – and the Silver Scot, as he was fondly known, registered a jaw-dropping list of these. He chalked up no fewer than twenty-five tour victories and three major championships: the 1927 US Open, the 1930 Professional Golfers' Association (PGA) Championship and the 1931 British Open (the first to be staged at Carnoustie, about seventy miles north of his birthplace – for which he returned from a new life in America). He was also made a member of the World Golf Hall of Fame, posthumously, in 1976.

But the most remarkable thing about his achievements was that he accomplished them with only one eye. How did that come about?

There was nothing too precious about golf in Scotland when he was growing up. In many places, especially near the undulating dunes and links immediately inland of the shores, it was still a game most people could participate in. There were public courses galore where youngsters could pay and play, and Tommy honed many of his skills while growing up with his full sight.

The First World War put a rude stop to his progress, however, when he was called up. After enlisting with the Black Watch, with which regiment he gained quite a reputation as a keen-eyed machine gunner, the Fettes College alumnus transferred to the Tank Corps in 1918, where he rose to staff major. In the heat of battle, however, he was blinded and badly injured in a mustard gas explosion, and surgeons had to add a metal plate to his head and left arm. During his convalescence, he regained the sight of his right eye and was understandably deeply relieved that he could – to some degree – take up his beloved game again.

But neither he nor his friends expected he could ever measure up, thereafter, to the performances of fully sighted players. Such an obvious disadvantage as having no sight in his left eye was almost certain to inhibit the development of his golfing career. But they were all surprised. While he certainly had to give himself a good deal more time to line up his shots, his game remained stunningly effective at home in Scotland after the war, and he was soon making his mark in amateur competitions, reaching the final of the Highland Open and taking second place in the Irish Open in 1919.

After winning the French Amateur the following year – the same year he married Consuelo Carrera, with whom he later had two children – Tommy decided to head for America, hoping to make his mark in the professional big-time there. It took him no time at all. On the transatlantic voyage he met the golfing legend Walter Hagen, who was returning from the British Open. By the time the two men disembarked in New York they were good friends, and Hagen soon helped the young Scotsman land a job as secretary of the Westchester-Biltmore Club in that city.

The Silver Scot went increasingly native in his adopted land. Though he represented Britain in 1921 in an informal match against an American team at Hoylake and played for Scotland against England in 1922, some four years later he was playing on the American team in a US-v.-Great Britain competition at Wentworth that some now consider to have been the 'unofficial' precursor of the Ryder Cup.

By 1926, he had become a US citizen after quickly establishing a reputation as an excellent player. But his playing career really took off in 1927, his fourth year as a professional, when he achieved seven tournament victories, including the Canadian Open and the highly prestigious US Open, in which he defeated 'Lighthorse' Harry Cooper in an eighteen-hole play-off, taking the title by three shots.

While still riding high, he went on to win the 1930 PGA and the 1931 British Open, becoming just the third golfer – after Jim Barnes and Walter Hagen – to take all three titles.

Other big wins included the 1929 Western Open (then considered a major) and two more Canadian Open titles. But things were not going so smoothly in his personal life: around this time he was going through a traumatic divorce from Consuelo Carrera to enable his marriage to Estelle Andrews, with whom he later had one son.

And painfully soon after he had registered his greatest triumphs, another trauma lay just around the corner. His putting began to let him down in the early 1930s, as he was increasingly afflicted with what he called 'the yips' – a jerky, nervous stroke – and he had a tough decision to make. Regretfully, he retired from major competitions in 1935 and decided to take up teaching full-time. This he did with considerable success, however, in Washington and New York in summer and Saratoga or Boca Raton, Florida, in the winter months.

His putting might have been his eventual downfall in competition but, having very strong hands, the Silver Scot was considered one of the finest iron players of his generation, though he himself considered his driving – to set up things nicely for the irons – was his strongest point.

When teaching, he worked not just with great golfers but with ordinary amateurs, charging some of the highest rates of the time: upwards of $50 a lesson. But many of his students appreciated his blunt Scottish style as he told them – among other things – to 'just knock hell out of it with your right hand'.

As he watched each pupil hit twenty balls, which he sharply analysed before asking for another twenty, he became almost as famous for his quotable sayings as for his golfing prowess. Example: 'Golf is an awkward set of bodily contortions designed to produce a graceful result.'

Indeed, the author Ross Goodner once recalled of him: 'At one time or another, he was known as the greatest iron player, the greatest raconteur, the greatest drinker and the greatest and most expensive teacher in golf.'

He may have been an expensive tutor, but he was a colourful, larger-than-life character who believed in giving value for money on all fronts. With his endless store of reminiscences and anecdotes told in a sharp, waspish style, he would keep students and co-players constantly entertained on the practice ground – or in the clubhouse – over the inevitable gin and tonic

He augmented his healthy income with a bit of betting, often on himself. He would challenge visiting golfers to matches for stakes of $50 or $100, and he would seldom lose.

Another lucrative sideline was the writing of best-selling how-to books. In 1953, he co-wrote *How to Play Your Best Golf All the Time* with Herb Graffis. It became a best-seller and was for many years the biggest-selling book on golf ever written. Six years later he brought out another must-read for serious golfers: *A Round of Golf with Tommy Armour.*

Both books are still widely available, and so the Silver Scot who lives on in memory has achieved another, more tangible form of immortality. His body may have gone – he died in New York on 11 September 1968 and was buried there – but his body of work lives on.

# Harry Benson (1930–    )

*Photographer of ten presidents*

When Robert Kennedy fell to an assassin's bullet on 5 June 1968, one of the many newspaper photographers who found themselves almost literally on the spot was Harry Benson of the London *Daily Express*. Most of them seemed to seize up – 'out of respect for Bobby or something,' he recalls – but, as they were paralysed, he was galvanised. 'I thought to myself: "This is it, kid. This is what all your training and experience have been about . . . this is what you're in the business for. You can mess up tomorrow but not today, not now . . ."'

Benson's sensational monochrome pictures of the prone, dying Kennedy sprawled in his own blood swept around a shocked world, elevating the photographer in the process to global status. It mattered not that the hastily shot images were badly focused, claims Benson, suggesting that this even added to their drama, freezing the shock and confusion of the moment for posterity.

Kennedy had been on his way to the White House. He had won major primaries in Indiana, Nebraska and California. And on leaving a celebration in Los Angeles after his victory in the California primary was assured, he was shot in the back of the head at close range by the Jerusalem-born Jordanian Sirhan Sirhan, and died the following day. His gravesite in Arlington National Cemetery is near that of his brother, President John F. Kennedy.

JFK had also been photographed by Harry Benson – in rather happier circumstances – as one the many famous people to have filled the Scotsman's lens in studio conditions; and had his brother reached the Oval Office, he too would doubtless have had the pleasure of being benignly photographed by the talented man who was eventually adopted by *Life* magazine to capture memorable images of the great and the good for its readers and then, no doubt, the history books.

Happily ensconced in his favourite seaside hotel on Scotland's west coast, the cheekily handsome and smartly dressed Benson is the first to admit that representing such a highly regarded magazine, albeit well-earned by his previous work, was his unique and enviable entrée to the world of the rich, important and famous. And neither would he deny that such a prestigious sponsor had given him an enviable lifestyle, in which his first home is a luxurious apartment shared with his Texan wife Gigi in New York's 73rd Street.

'Of course, with a name like *Life* behind you, all doors open like magic,' he says; and indeed a roll-call of his photographic subjects over the years sounds like a *Who's Who* of the last century . . . no fewer than ten American presidents since Eisenhower, and many more legendary names to conjure with such as Churchill, Beaverbrook, Solzhenitsyn, Bobby Fischer, Norman Mailer, Dolly Parton, Liz Taylor, Jack Nicholson, Roman Polanski and Michael Jackson. The A-list goes on.

Regardless of how famous his subjects are, Harry Benson finds it easy to strike up personal relationships with them. 'I'm not overawed by anybody,' he says. 'You can't get Willie Nelson into a bathtub for an absurd picture if you don't have a nice rapport with him.'

Perhaps it is a veteran's understanding of who makes the newsmakers (that is, people like him) that keeps Benson singularly unimpressed by such names, or by the things he has done. He has just had a 'big show' in a Palm Beach museum, for instance; but big names and big shows are his work. For pleasure, he prefers the company of old home town buddies and returns to Scotland 'about once a week these days to keep up old ties, eat fish and chips, and walk along the beach at Troon, contemplating things'.

In fact, he visits about three times a year because he doesn't want to forget the land of his birth, nor does he want it to forget him, and often there's an exhibition in Edinburgh or a book being published in Glasgow. Being at time of writing well into his seventies, with fifty-five years of brilliant picture-taking behind him, perhaps he is anxious to appreciate the basic values of human relationships after a lifetime of looking for depth in the glittery world of celebrities. He found some too, and with matter-of-fact acceptance that his is a trade like any other, he now describes himself as 'a people photographer'.

The son of a curator of Glasgow Zoo ('I've always hated the caging of animals'), he was born in the Knightswood area of the city before being moved to Troon on the west coast 'within five days of my birth'. His career got off to a racy start as a holiday camp photographer at Butlin's in nearby Ayr, and the steps from there were logical if not as rapid as the impatient and ambitious young man would have liked.

Weddings and fires are the staple stuff of local papers and it was in recording these that he learned his trade on the *Hamilton Advertiser*, Scotland's biggest weekly and once the local paper of the famous explorer of Africa, Dr David Livingstone: 'our darkroom used to be the chapel where he prayed on his way to his home at Blantyre'. About a dozen bleary-eyed night train trips to London with his portfolio finally landed him a job in the national *Daily Sketch*'s Scottish office, and that in turn provided the stepping stone to London when he was seconded for a while to its Fleet Street office.

The *Sketch* was ailing at the time, and the *Daily Express* booming. So how did he manage to change horses?

> I gatecrashed a top people's party which happened to be attended by Max Aitken [son of *Express* proprietor Lord Beaverbrook] and as I was snapping away, I heard he wanted to speak to me. I went over and introduced myself. He said he liked the way I was working, and if I gave him my number someone would call me. I did, but nothing happened. Then, about six months later, I saw him coming out of Caprice restaurant and said: 'Remember me?' He nodded and recalled my name as I added: 'I haven't heard from you'. He smiled, walked on, and said: 'You'll hear tomorrow.'

And he did. At the *Daily Express,* Benson was quickly seen to be a great photographer – and charmer – of people. So when The Beatles began their amazing transatlantic rise in the 1960s, the *Express* sent the Scot to accompany them and cover their every move. Inevitably, he became a good friend of the Fab Four and, as such, had access to many of their private moments – like their famous feathery pillow fight at the George V Hotel in Paris, of which he took some memorably happy snaps.

Benson recalls that John Lennon once even wrote a poem about him. 'Can you believe it? I just lost it. It didn't seem important at the time. I remember how it finished up – "and Harry, I want you always to have a happy Beatlebrook" – playing with the words Beatle and Beaverbrook.

> Ironically, many years down the line I found myself photographing the guy who shot and killed Lennon, Mark David Chapman, and he seemed to feel the need to apologise to me. When we met in prison he took me aside and said: 'I know he was your friend and I'd like to apologise to you for killing him.' What could I say? He seemed

genuinely sorry, but they'll never let him out. Celebrity killers are
not well treated.

Like Lennon, Benson could not get America out of his blood. Like
Lennon, he had chosen to stay in New York. Indeed, Benson was
hooked on the place by the time the touring Beatles left him in
America in 1964. 'After I'd had a few more stimulating years there,
the *Express* editor told me I ought to come home and give someone
else a chance, but I couldn't leave. America had been so good to
me. In many ways, I'd have liked to have chosen Britain – especially
Scotland – but the pull of America and its big, prestigious magazines
was too strong.'

It was when he and the *Express* parted company that he started
developing his contacts on such magazines, and the fact that he could
eventually command thousands of dollars for a *Life* cover suggests he
did so with no small degree of success.

Having now photographed every president in living memory, who
is his favourite? He warns that his answer might surprise . . .

'Nixon,' he says.

Why?

Because the most interesting things happened to and around him,
and they weren't all bad. They were often very good. He was strong on
civil rights and opening up to China, for instance. And it's very hard in
our business to dislike somebody who just allows you to do your job. I
mean, if he had stepped out of line I'd have zapped him – and I did;
some of my shots of him were not so flattering; but he was kind to me
and helped my career a lot.

I was the only journalist allowed on the plane with him to San
Clemente after his resignation and I spent a couple of days there with
him. This was not the best time of his life. He was deeply humiliated. I
was photographing him for *Life* and thanked him very much for giving
me his time and patience under such trying circumstances. He just
smiled wryly and said: 'Well, Harry, you've got to allow professional
people the chance to do their job' – which was a very nice thing to
say.

And his other favourites?

I found George W. Bush a good guy too. I was photographing him
swinging a golf club outside the governor's mansion when he was
running for president. I told him I'd become an American citizen

and he just shrugged. But then it seemed to dawn on him. He pointed his club at me and said: 'That means you can vote, Harry . . . and I'm asking for your vote.'

It's very personal, as you'd imagine, when a presidential candidate asks you for your vote. But I said: 'Well, Governor, I'll see how it goes today.' And he laughed. We got along like a house on fire. But in general I don't really get too close to my subjects. I wouldn't say I was a friend, as such, because they might step out of line, and where would you be then as an objective journalist?

Often I don't pick up a phone after I've done a job because I don't want some big star saying to me, 'Hey, Harry, that picture of me in the bath, please don't use it . . .' I don't want to have to choose between my best shot and my new best friend.

Has he ever had a political influence on any of his famous sitters? He laughs:

I would hate to think so . . . I would hate to think that a little pipsqueak from Glasgow would have any say in world events. But I did discuss the war on drugs with Nixon – he was the strongest advocate of that – and also with Nancy Reagan. I told her I'd been to a few parties with famous movie stars and that they'd all been sniffing cocaine. She wasn't surprised. Disappointed maybe, but she wasn't naïve. She knew what went on.

Not surprisingly, Benson found the Reagans, as two former film stars, easy and professional in front of the camera:

I took them kissing each other for *Vanity Fair*. They were terrific – polite, and knew exactly what to do; and Nancy was quite the opposite of the painted doll everybody thought she was. She combed her own hair and came on the set with no make-up at all.

And Ronald Reagan used to tell funny stories. There's nothing worse than some big shot telling you a story that isn't funny and you have to laugh. But his were genuinely funny stories, not patronising jokes.

You get amusing moments too. Take John Kerry, who was the Democrats' presidential candidate at the time I photographed him. This guy with the war-hero image wanted to be captured for posterity looking macho on his sparkling new Harley-Davidson. But I'd taken only about five shots when it started to rain and he started complaining: 'Oh, I'm getting wet . . . I'm getting wet . . . we can't go on anymore'.

His aides said I should follow him to his next stop, where he was meeting senior citizens indoors, but I said no, I wasn't interested in senior citizens, and in any case the few shots I'd taken turned out fine.

Next thing I know I'm going though airport security and my cellphone rings. It's Kerry himself – phoning to apologise for looking such a wimp, afraid of a little rain. He could laugh at himself at least, and I thought that was OK, and it was nice that he called personally.

We journalists do rub shoulders with famous – and infamous – folk. Almost literally. I mean, take Sirhan Sirhan, who killed Bobby Kennedy. I was standing right next to him when he did it. Sometimes when you tell these things it sounds like you're really bullshitting, but they are all truths . . . just part of the job.

Though he has lately used the 'people photographer' label for convenience, Harry Benson doesn't like to be pigeon-holed. He points out that he has also done 'starvation in the Ogaden, the IRA on manoeuvres, Russian prisoners-of-war in Afghanistan, the Iraq war, and lots of stuff like that, because I'm also a photo-journalist'.

It is vital, he says, for a good photographer to be multi-dimensional.

I'll do high fashion for French *Vogue* as soon as anything else. Some photographers are caught off-base if they have to work outside their strengths. You shouldn't stay just in your most comfortable area. You've got to come out and work on your weak sides, too . . . keep challenging yourself. But in the end, all I want is a good picture.

The last comment sums up Harry Benson precisely. Despite his place in American photographic history and his obviously ambivalent feelings about home – is it Scotland or New York? – he is essentially an uncomplicated, hard-working picture-taker. From his wallet he produces a print of his latest famous subject and shows it with almost boyish pride. Yes, it's a good picture, you concede; and he's happy, if a little puzzled, about how he can get along so well without the artist's mystique.

But his Scottish west-coast humour defines his sense of perspective. 'My last book was rather unpretentious,' he says with a small laugh. 'I think I'll try to make the next one pretentious.'

And his final laugh is explosive: 'As I've said hundreds of times, I don't know what I'd have done if I'd had to work for a living.'

# Hugh Grant (1958– )

*Controversial GM crops boss*

Love them or loathe them, there is no doubt that genetically modified (GM) crops can induce strong feelings in people. But however much he might be demonised by those who dislike his company's raison d'être, Hugh Grant – not the film star – is anything but satanic and often reveals to those who meet him a surprisingly sincere interest in agriculture and its possibilities.

Perhaps that should not be so surprising, given his background and education. The gentlemanly president, chairman and chief executive of the controversial Monsanto company was born in 1958, in Larkhall, fifteen miles south-east of Glasgow, right on the edge of the picturesque Clyde Valley where – in his words – 'coal and steel stopped and dairy farms began'. He earned a bachelor of science degree in agricultural zoology with honours at Glasgow University before going on to take a postgraduate degree in agriculture at Edinburgh University and a master's in business administration in England.

He now lives in St Louis, Missouri, which is also home to the headquarters of his company, which employs 15,000 people and records revenues of $5 billion. But as he travels the world from there – explaining the benefits of GM crops, as he sees them, to farmers from South Africa to China – Scotland remains his anchor. He comes 'home' regularly to visit friends and relatives; he is an international advisory board member of Scottish Enterprise; and he still speaks with a soft Scottish accent of which he is clearly quite proud. 'He is very measured and very careful,' says an acquaintance, 'but he is still very much a Scot.'

It is ironic, however, that the land of his birth – Britain, if not Scotland – has given one of the world's most hostile receptions to Monsanto's cause.

Those on his side believe that, as the earth's 6 billion population will double in fifty years, GM foods will help increase food production in the same given cultivation area. And genetic engineering can create plants that are resistant or tolerant to 'danger' factors such as disease, cold, insects, drought and even weed-killer. It can also change a crop's properties, reducing growing time, adding nutrients, making better taste.

But opponents have many concerns – the first being environmental. They argue that GM foods can cause harm to other organisms unintentionally and that in reality they will largely be used to feed the power and profits of agri-food corporations rather than alleviate Third World hunger.

Not that the lurid 'Frankenstein Food' headlines faze Hugh Grant. He is a patient man who is in it for the long game and said, in a *Financial Times* interview with Stefan Stern:

> You have to keep going. I don't like it much, but what I've learned is that you can't get too discouraged by some of the rogue headlines.
>
> There's the headline, and then you go to the letters page. It's changing. Seven years ago it was 'absolutely not'. Today, if you go to the letters page, there's a discussion . . .
>
> Companies like mine are in the process of learning to speak a language that people understand. I think that's more than high theory – I think that's how this is evolving.

Hugh Grant joined the company in 1981 as a product development representative in Scotland, and spent the first ten years there in a variety of European sales, product development and management roles. Being keen to see the world, he needed little persuasion to relocate in 1991 to St Louis as global strategy director of the agriculture division. In 1995, he was named Monsanto's managing director for the Asia-Pacific region, with responsibility for the company's agriculture, nutrition and pharmaceutical businesses in South-east Asia.

A succession of bigger executive jobs followed and each seemed increasingly to suit his instincts and education: in 1998 he was named co-president of the company's agriculture division, in which role he jointly oversaw global business operations and led the business and product strategy. As co-president, he reported to the president of Monsanto and was responsible for the operational and commercial performance of all agriculture division business units and brands worldwide.

In 2000, he became an executive vice president, and not long after that he was entrusted with the very top job. But he is not one to ensconce himself behind a gigantic desk and issue orders from there. As a lad he grew up on the edge of rural Scotland and learned to appreciate the joys of fresh air. So he likes to be on the road – the world's highways and airways anyway – spreading his message to all who will listen.

He may or may not win the argument, but he will have enjoyed himself trying.

'There were two passions for me,' he told the *FT*, with reference to his early life. 'I was really intrigued by the idea of getting the chance to work outside, rather than being chained to a desk – a bit naïve, maybe – and the other was the chance to travel, to see the other parts of the world. I've been very lucky. Agriculture is a global industry and it happens outside.'

# The Scottish Influence

*Some Scots have impacted on America and its culture without actually living there. Here are a few of them . . .*

# Alexander Selkirk (1676–1723)

*The original Robinson Crusoe*

Just how indelibly the romantic tale of Robinson Crusoe has imprinted itself on the American imagination was illustrated by the modern movie version – *Castaway* – which updated Daniel Defoe's much-loved 1719 classic through the acting talent of Tom Hanks, playing a Fed-Ex engineer marooned after a plane crash en route to Malaysia.

We all dream of such a telling experience – of being left alone on a desert island with only our initiative to keep us alive – and wonder how we would fare if stripped of our layers of civilisation. Hanks' Chuck Noland almost loses his mind but survives for four years by spearing fish, extracting his own teeth, treasuring a picture of his girlfriend, creating a buddy called Wilson from a volleyball and lashing together a rough getaway raft.

It was not so different in the early eighteenth century when such an experience really happened, not to a fictional Robinson Crusoe, but to a real person: Alexander Selkirk, a sailor from the little Fife coastal town of Lower Largo on the north bank of the Forth estuary.

His story was every bit as exciting as the Crusoe one – which was probably based on his experiences after an assumed (but unrecorded) meeting between him and author Defoe – but there were some essential differences. Whereas Crusoe's story had the hero being shipwrecked, adopting a native servant as Man Friday and living for twenty-eight years on his tropical island, Selkirk's experience was shorter and sharper. He actually asked to be let off his ailing ship when she came upon the island of Juan Fernandez 400 miles west of Chile; and he lived there without human company for four and a half years before being rescued.

Perhaps the most convincing parallels between the two versions, which fuse in the mind's cinema screen, are the identical visual impressions of the fictional and real heroes at their moments of salvation. As described by his shocked rescuers, Selkirk's coat and cap of many goatskins, which had replaced his worn-out conventional clothes, surely provided the model for Crusoe's famous ragged image. And indeed, any uninformed visitor studying the handsome bronze statue of Selkirk above the door of the house in Lower Largo, Fife, that replaced his original family home, would immediately say: 'Crusoe!' It's an impression the town does nothing to discourage, keen as it is to attract tourists; so its biggest hostelry is called The Crusoe Hotel and local shops sell booklets with titles like *Crusoe's Village*.

The plate under the heroic Selkirk statue, created by Stuart Burnett of Edinburgh, reads:

> In memory of Alexander Selkirk, mariner, the original of Robinson Crusoe, who lived on the island of Juan Fernandez in complete solitude for four years and four months. He died 1723, leiutenant [sic] of HMS *Weymouth*, aged 47 years. This statue is erected by David Gillies, net manufacturer, on the site of the cottage in which Selkirk was born.

Holding a musket in his left hand, the bronze Selkirk has raised his right to shade his eyes while apparently searching for a ship on the far horizon. It is an impressive piece of work and a fine posthumous honour. Indeed, there was another that faded away with the demise of the famous sailor's last relatives to be resident in the town in the 1990s. The Jardine family gathered as many Selkirk-related artefacts as they could to create a little museum in the town – for which this writer was once asked to trace the sailor's gun. After a month on the telephone, a battered-looking claimant for the title – with the words 'Alexander Selkirk' burned into its butt – turned up in the attic of a private home in Ely, Cambridgeshire, and was duly bought and proudly returned to Scotland.

But the town was not always so proud of its famous son . . .

Born in 1676 the seventh son of local shoemaker John Selkirk, Alexander was often in trouble with the girls and the Church and, after a particularly unruly episode, was summoned to give an account of his behaviour to the Kirk Session in 1695 – but made his getaway to sea before the case came up.

He was to have a very different impact on the Kirk when he returned some seventeen years later after making his fortune.

But first, he had to endure a few episodes of less good fortune. Having taken to mathematics at school, he became an accomplished navigator and made several relatively uneventful journeys before joining the sixteen-gun *Cinque Ports* galley in 1703 as sailing master on a privateering venture to attack Spanish shipping and possessions in the New World. Commanded by William Dampier, the famous buccaneer, navigator and man of science sailing in the *St George*, the expedition had more than its share of bad luck as opportunities for taking plunder were missed or bungled and crew members fell out.

When the *Cinque Ports* parted company from the *St George* off Panama in 1704, Selkirk, now second-in-command of the former, was not seeing eye-to-eye with her new captain, Thomas Stradling, particularly about the condition of the worm-eaten ship with its ragged sails. Frustrated by the captain's lack of action on these points, the Scot opted to be abandoned on Juan Fernandez rather than stay on a ship he considered too rotten to float much longer.

Despite that, watching her depart he had severe second thoughts as he sat on the beach among his few possessions – a sea chest with clothing and bedding, a gun, a pound of gunpowder, ammunition, a flint and steel, a few pounds of tobacco, a hatchet, a knife, a kettle, a Bible, navigation books and mathematical instruments. Suddenly, he ran into the sea, calling after her, but she sailed on, ignoring him. And just as well, for the *Cinque Ports* did sink, just off Peru, with loss of most of her crew, although Stradling and seven others survived to be jailed in Lima for seven years – so no word got out that Selkirk was on the island.

He had been left there with enough food for two meals, and while that was initially alarming, he was relieved to find that the seventeen-mile-long, seven-mile-wide island was inhabited by goats and cats left by some previous (probably Spanish) visitors. He befriended both – and even danced with the easily tamed goat kids – though he sometimes had trouble catching the larger goats, which would supply him with the occasional stew.

There were also hundreds of rats to contend with, which added to his sense of challenge as he kept a fire burning on a high hill in the hope of being spotted by a passing ship. For the first eight months he had to bear up against a gnawing melancholy, and fear of being alone in such a desolate place. He built two huts with pimento trees, covered them with long grass, lined them with goatskins, and gradually began to feel at home. Juan Fernandez certainly had its compensations. The climate was fine, there was plenty of fresh water, fruit, cabbages, herbs, crayfish, goat meat and milk; and as he began to accept that he was not going to be rescued quickly, he resigned himself to appreciating the quality of his life and surroundings.

He acquired another piece of real estate – a cave in a nearby hillside – and his constant traversing of the island maintaining his 'properties' and searching for sustenance and sails on the horizon certainly kept him fit. And just as he began to enjoy his good health and his solitude, he saw sails – Spanish ones – twice. But he found himself running away from them, on one occasion even hiding up a tree. He did not want to reveal himself as he had heard of the inquisition methods of the Spanish. And he was not even sure if he could speak English now, far less Spanish. Indeed, when he was eventually rescued in February 1709, his lack of speaking ability was only one of the impressions that shocked his saviours.

Selkirk was taken on board by two Bristol privateers, the *Duke* and *Duchess,* under the command of Captain Woodes Rogers, who later wrote about the rescue in *A Cruising Voyage Round the World* (1712):

> Immediately our Pinnace return'd from the shore, and brought abundance of Craw-fish, with a Man cloth'd in Goat-Skins, who look'd wilder than the first Owners of them. He had been on the Island four Years and four Months, being left there by Capt. Stradling in the *Cinque-Ports*; his Name was Alexander Selkirk a Scotch Man, who had been Master of the *Cinque-Ports*, a Ship that came here last with Capt. Dampier, who told me that this was the best Man in her; so I immediately agreed with him to be a Mate on board our Ship.

Being taken on as a mate – and later put in command of one of Woodes Rogers' captured vessels – was a fortunate turn of events for Selkirk, who had to thank his lucky stars for the coincidence that Captain Dampier had recognised him through his weird and wonderful outfit – about which Woodes Rogers wrote:

> When his clothes were worn out he made himself a coat and a cap of goat skins, which he stitched together with little thongs of the same, that he cut with his knife. He had no other needle but a nail; and when his knife was worn to the back he made others, as well as he could, of some iron hoops that were left ashore, which he beat thin and ground upon stones. Having some linen cloth by him, he sewed him some shirts with a nail, and stitched them with the worsted of his old stockings, which he pulled out on purpose. He had his last shirt on when we found him on the island.

Such clothes were in stark contrast to the finery that he wore on a visit to Lower Largo after he returned to Britain a rich man in 1711. The Woodes Rogers expedition had been a great success and his share of the booty was £800 (about $100,000 today). It is said that he arrived in the town while the kirk service was in progress on a Sunday morning. He threw open its doors and heads turned and gasped to see the richly dressed prodigal standing in the aisle. As his parents and the rest of the congregation rushed up to greet him, the minister had to abandon the service.

It would be nice to end the story there, but its real conclusion is less happy. The truth was, Selkirk missed Juan Fernandez (now renamed Robinson Crusoe Island) and in Largo, he took to finding spots above the town where, overlooking the River Forth, he could sit and remind himself of life on his island. His love life became messy, too, as he ran off to London – and the Navy – with local girl Sofia Bruce in tow. Whether or not he married her was unknown and became a moot point after he definitely married another, English woman, Frances Candish, and made out a will in her favour.

For his first voyage as mate on HMS *Weymouth* was his last. Along with many other crew members, he died of yellow fever while sailing off the Gold Coast in December, 1721.

Sofia, the modest girl from his home town, lost the bitter battle over his considerable estate.

# William Cullen (1710–90)

*Creator of cold comfort*

Scots are not normally shy about trumpeting their inventive achievements – 'Wha's like us?' is their not-so-tongue-in-cheek war cry – and while this might not always be an attractive trait, they can often reclaim a listener's affection by being self-deprecating about their lack of aptitude in other fields. This is historically evident in the way they can make significant breakthroughs then see the amusing side of not knowing quite what to do with them. Which is why they have often had to bow to America's conspicuous flair for taking an idea and running with it – developing a product so that it becomes not just marketable but an object of desire for consumers all over the world.

One such case in point is the refrigerator. Necessity being the mother of invention (most of the time), it would always have been hard to imagine that, in a small northern country as cold as Scotland, there would be much demand for the cooling of food and drink.

In hot countries, before the invention of refrigeration, the idea of artificial intervention to keep perishable food relatively fresh – and drinkable liquid more refreshing – had been around for millennia, despite absence of the ideal technology required to achieve best results. Various methods of drying, smoking, salting, pickling, heating, and icing were employed to preserve edibility, and the chill factor first found its place in caves before gradually moving, along with human ingenuity, from the cold depths of rivers, lakes, streams, or wells to cellars, snow holes, specially dug pits, outdoor window boxes, underground store-rooms lined with wood or straw and packed with snow and ice.

As far back as 1000 BC, the value of coldness in preserving food was recognised by the Chinese, who knew how to cut and store ice, while ancient Egyptians stayed cool by putting earthen jars full of boiled water out in the cold open air overnight. The more privileged people of Cairo also used their camel postal system to transport snow all the way from the Lebanese Mountains.

By similarly gathering ice or snow from their own mountains, first-century Romans cooled their drinks much as we do today; and in more recent times, the empire-building British would send tons of Norwegian ice 8,000 miles around the Cape of Good Hope to India and other UK charges, while the shipping of ice from America to tropical climes was undertaken by America's 'ice king', New Englander Frederick Tudor.

The obvious disadvantage with all these exercises was the fact that, due to melting or evaporation, the receivers always ended up with a good deal less than the dispatchers started with. While Tudor managed, through experiments with insulating materials, to build ice-houses that reduced in-storage melting from 66 per cent to less than 8 per cent, it might have been reasonable to expect a cool solution from a hot country.

It has to be something of an irony, therefore, that the first artificial refrigeration (cooling air by the evaporation of liquids in a vacuum) was invented by a shivering Scot as long ago as 1748. William Cullen got successful results at the University of Glasgow by letting ethyl ether boil into a partial vacuum, but – given the geographic factor – it was almost forgivable that in this case he did not develop the result into any practical purpose.

Indeed, while today's internet references (generally sourced from other countries) invariably credit him with the invention of refrigeration, Glasgow's own Mitchell Library can find little or nothing in terms of book references that place their man emphatically in that context.

Be that as it may, after Cullen's invention, it was left to a succession of clever people from various nations to apply the principle to commercial and domestic use. While the English physicist Michael Faraday liquefied ammonia to cause cooling in 1823 – leading to the development of compressors, changing gas to liquid – and the American inventor Oliver Evans designed the first refrigeration machine that used vapour instead of liquid in 1805, it was another Scot who, more than a century after Cullen's breakthrough, introduced vapour-compression refrigeration to the brewing and meat-packing industries.

Soon after moving from Glasgow to Australia in 1837, an overheated journalist called James Harrison felt compelled to set about designing his own refrigeration machine, and by 1855 he had succeeded in creating and patenting an ether liquid-vapour compression fridge.

To be fair, he was not being particularly indulgent or prescient about the current Oz enthusiasm for cold beer (and food) but he did have that country's long-term interests at heart: he realised that the export-marketing of her abundant livestock to, say, Europe would be practically impossible without large-scale shipboard refrigeration to survive the boiling equator. Unfortunately, he bankrupted himself trying to prove it, after setting up a shipment to London that was ruined because of a leak from the cooling chemical tanks. His bold move was not in vain, however. As other successful exporting voyages followed, it could be said that Harrison won the consolation prize of credit for opening the door to Australia's economic salvation.

In the meantime, icy developments had been going on apace elsewhere. In 1834, the first cumbersome refrigerating machine, using ether in a vapour compression cycle, was built by American inventor Jacob Perkins. In 1844, American physician John Gorrie built a refrigerator based on Oliver Evans' design to make ice to cool the air for his yellow fever patients. In 1876, German engineer Carl von Linden patented not a refrigerator but the process of liquefying gas that is part of basic refrigeration technology. And in 1879 and 1891 improved refrigeration designs were patented by the African-American inventors Thomas Elkins and John Standard.

It was about this time that nature stepped in with a timely push. Shortages of natural ice – which would normally be used in people's basic iceboxes that depended on simple insulation – were created by super-warm American winters in 1889 and 1890. And it wasn't just a domestic problem. Food shops and industries that were not equipped with large, albeit primitive, refrigerators to freeze and store fish, dairy products and meat just had to stand and watch their produce go bad. The imperative to develop and market the domestic refrigerator was now as clear as day, and by the early 1900s they had started to appear: basic wooden cabinets with water-cooled compressors.

Two American corporate giants took the lead. General Electric and General Motors were the early innovators, the first releasing a home refrigerator designed by a French monk in 1911, the second introducing in 1915 the first Guardian refrigerator, which was a predecessor of the famous Frigidaire.

In 1923, Frigidaire introduced the first self-contained units. Britain got its first batch of these in 1924, and the march of the fridge was halted only briefly by the consequences of their having used the toxic gases ammonia, methyl chloride and sulphur dioxide, the leaks of which caused several accidental deaths up to 1929. Thereafter, compressor fridges generally used Freon – a trade name describing a whole class of chemicals known as chlorofluorocarbons – with relatively minimal health risks. Soon, the production line was rolling again, and Frigidaire, GM's brand, went on to sell 50 million units by 1965. Nowadays the fridge is one of the world's most common domestic appliances – to be found in 99 per cent of North American and European homes.

If by some miracle William Cullen were to make his way back to today's world for an iced tea, would he be happy to take the credit for this? Probably not. He was a charming man by all accounts, and not a seeker of fame.

Yet even he would have to admit that, while he had never come closer to America than a couple of trips to the West Indies as a ship's surgeon, he had some influence on it, and not only through refrigeration.

William Cullen was essentially a medical man, though he developed a keen interest in chemistry. Born in Hamilton, Lanarkshire, in 1710, he went from the local grammar school to the University of Glasgow – where he was later to make his name in the world of science. His early medical training and experience included apprenticeship in Glasgow, service as a ship's surgeon, a period as assistant to an apothecary in London, and general medical practice in Scotland.

In 1744, after marrying minister's daughter Anna Johnstone, with whom he was to have seven sons and four daughters, he moved to Edinburgh University. Everywhere he went, his verbal skills were admired. His contributions to medicine and his widely used textbooks earned him an international reputation. He was elected a Fellow of the Royal Society of London in 1777.

His single published paper relating to chemistry was 'Of the Cold produced by Evaporating Fluids, and of Some Other Means of Producing Cold', which prompted Alexander Fleck, a former director of ICI, to say: 'His contributions do not seem to have been effective in causing improvements in practice.'

But Cullen's lively personality, rich imagination and compelling delivery as a teacher were legendary, attracting great attention and attendances from the student body. Advertised enthusiastically by word of mouth, his classes in Edinburgh grew rapidly from 17 students to 145. And the word even crossed the Atlantic. During his eleven years as professor of chemistry, the charismatic and articulate

William Cullen had forty American students, many of whom in turn sent their own promising students to Edinburgh in later years. Warm and welcoming to them all, he became something of an idol among two generations.

Could that be why, despite Scotland being unusually shy to make claims for a son of some achievement, he is generously given credit for inventing the cooling system that makes a Coca Cola taste so good on a hot summer's day?

In any case, he died on 5 February 1790 at his country home at Kirknewton in Midlothian, probably quite unsuspecting of the fact that his casual little experiment in 1748 would one day help to change the world and the operation of its food and drink supply lines.

# Adam Smith (1723–90)

*Free thinker for a free-trade world*

The covered pend still looks quite grand in a neglected kind of way, defined as it is by a pair of cracked and stained ionic columns next to Greggs the baker on Kirkcaldy's bustling, chain-stored and pedestrianised High Street. Many passers-by don't notice the rusting 1950s plaque suspended at eye level on the separating wall, which reads:

> *ADAM SMITH*
> *1723–1790*
> *Born in Kirkcaldy*
> *On this site stood the house of his mother in which he lived*
> *from 1767 to 1776 and completed 'The Wealth of Nations'*

Every shopper is too busy spending and putting into direct practice the human acquisitiveness of which the plaque's subject wrote so eloquently. But even if you're interested, you can abandon hope of seeing Adam Smith's one-time home. Walk through the columns where the great moral philosopher and pioneer of political economy once walked, and at the alley's end you find only a few parked cars and a shaky wooden fence. For, as the plaque suggests, the pantiled, crowstepped house where Smith worked on his great book, a remarkable treatise on economics that's been translated and celebrated by the free market all over the world – not least in America – since it was first published in 1776, is no more.

But before we curse the brutal removers of that impressive house with its even more impressive claim to fame, we should note that the replacement of it by a not-so-charming building now straddling the alley happened in the less appreciative 1830s; a dire deed presumably regretted by 1899, when Andrew Carnegie opened the Adam Smith Halls, a big and elegant foursquare Victorian edifice on the leafier outskirts of town. Dedicated to 'Kirkcaldy's Greatest Citizen', it is now known as Adam Smith Theatre, where new movies are screened and children's shows are unapologetically performed.

Indeed, if you look around more closely, it's clear the memory of Smith remains almost tangible, if rather taken for granted in this busy seaside town – with not just the eponymous theatre itself but ubiquitous signs pointing to it, a new-build development down by the Forth shore recently dubbed Adam Smith Court, and of course a special display devoted to his life and work in the Kirkcaldy Museum and Art Gallery, just across the road from the theatre.

It would be easy to argue that such a man deserves a home-town museum of his very own. But this surprisingly modest showing informs us that – in the spirit of his instruction to his executors to destroy any of his unpublished works – he made sure there was little left of him for future generations to view.

So what *is* there physically here to remember him by? Specifically, there is his pewter inkstand, which held his busy quills and sand-shaker while he wrestled to articulate his ideas for posterity; his ivory snuff mill, with its mounted silver lid bearing his initials; an example of the Kirkcaldy Penny, a copper trade token of the time which bore his image; another glass-plate portrait of him by Glasgow sculptor James Tassie; three of his well-thumbed books (by Rousseau, Locke and Necker) and one of his two major self-written ones.

And no, it's not the lesser known but still prodigious work entitled *The Theory of Moral Sentiments* in which one particular sentiment ('If we saw ourselves in the light in which others see us . . . a reformation would generally be unavoidable') is said to have inspired Robert Burns to write 'To a Louse', with its similar theme.

The star item is at first invisible under one of the two display cases. You have to pull out a drawer to find an original near-tabloid-size example of *Inquiry into the Nature and Causes of the Wealth of Nations* – to give his famous tome its full title – lurking there under glass and opened at a spread touching on the subject of employee/master relationships. The book is globally renowned – still – for its explanation of how rational self-interest and competition between enterprises can lead to general well-being and prosperity.

Oh, and then there is Mum on the wall. Apparently guarding all this with a stern look of downright disapproval of the world at large is the dark-clad lady who brought him into it, with the help of her late husband, a senior solicitor and local customs officer, also called Adam Smith. The sizeable, ornately framed oil painting of Margaret Douglas of Strathendry by Conrad Metz is captioned: 'This formidable-looking woman is Adam Smith's mother. He was close to her throughout her life and lived with her in Kirkcaldy and later Panmure House, Edinburgh'. (Of which more later.)

That closeness suggests, of course, that she was not so formidable in real life. But while he lived with her, just a (lengthy) stone's throw from the shoreline, he often needed to lift his head from his work and clear it by walking down by the waves. The one-time British Premier and Chancellor Gordon Brown, long Kirkcaldy's MP and an ardent Smith student, once recalled how Smith 'took long solitary walks on the foreshore as he thought through his great plan'. And Smith himself, writing from the town to his friend and fellow Enlightenment philosopher David Hume, said, 'My business here is study. Amusements are long solitary walks by the seaside.'

But his early adult life was not spent in Kirkcaldy. He studied social philosophy at Glasgow and Oxford universities before returning to Fife in 1746 – from where he established his reputation with a series of public lectures in Edinburgh. In 1751, Glasgow called again. He was appointed professor of logic at the university and, a year later, professor of moral philosophy. Meanwhile, he became a leading light in the latter half of the century's Enlightenment, befriending not just Hume but other big names such as the playwright John Home, the historian William Robertson, the poet Allan Ramsay, the distinguished judge Lord Hailes and Kirkcaldy-born architect Robert Adam.

There were to be even more high reputations to mingle and conjure with abroad when a decade or so later he left Scotland to travel on the Continent as a tutor to Henry, the future Duke of Buccleuch. It was during this time that he met many leading European intellectuals, including Rousseau, Quesnay and Voltaire.

Between 1767 and 1776, as that High Street plaque confirms, Smith was back living with his mother in Kirkcaldy, before moving yet again – this time to London, where he published the fruits of his seaside studies: the volume he intended to be the first part of a complete theory of society, covering ethics, theology, politics and law. *The Wealth of Nations* was the first major work of political economy, in which he argued against the regulation of commerce and trade, and wrote that if people were set free to better themselves, it would produce economic prosperity for all.

'The invisible hand' is one of his phrases made much of by followers. It refers to the unseen mechanism that maintains equilibrium between supply and demand, eliminating the need for government intervention in the market and so setting the foundation for laissez-faire economic philosophy.

But rather in the way religious texts can be selectively interpreted by different parties, there have long been co-ownership claims from left and right – and even centre – for the ideas of a man often called the father of capitalism. He himself contended that capitalism requires a moral centre if it is to function effectively and to the benefit of all. But in the 1980s his nuanced free-trade view seemed to open a gateway to the greed-is-good theme of the Thatcher/Reagan meeting of minds.

Indeed, at a memorial service in 2004 for the then-late president, his one-time senior aide Bruce Chapman wrote: 'Ever since Ronald Reagan studied economics at Eureka College, Adam Smith was his hero. So everybody in the administration quoted Adam Smith. Neckties with Adam Smith busts on them festooned every male conservative chest in Washington when I was there. You had a wide range of choices: there were green, maroon, red, white and blue Adam Smith neckties . . . There were even Adam Smith scarves for women. If Ronald Reagan had been allowed to run for a third term, I imagine there would have been Adam Smith hats and Adam Smith raincoats.'

Thatcher was an early convert. In 1975, as leader of the Tory party four years before becoming the British Prime Minister, she gave a speech in Chicago that linked *The Wealth of Nations* with the Declaration of Independence. She asserted that Adam Smith 'heralded the end of the straitjacket of feudalism and released the innate energy of private initiative and enterprise which enables wealth to be created on a scale never before contemplated'. In other words, Smith gave her debatable philosophy credence and justification. In an apparent reference to him, she once said, 'The Scots invented Thatcherism long before I was thought of.'

A relatively solitary man with no political allegiance, Smith himself was hardly a rampant enemy of simple folk. Indeed, he was once accused – by economist Thomas Malthus – of confounding 'the wealth of the state' with 'the happiness of the lower classes of the people'.

Gordon Brown has often questioned the right's presumed absolute right to Smith, of course; and another event that underlined that proprietorial conflict was an Edinburgh University symposium in 2002 entitled 'Can both Left and Right Claim Adam Smith?'

Introducing it, Brown, then Labour's UK Chancellor, further asked, 'Would the Adam Smith who has been the inspiration behind the right-of-centre [London-based think-tank] Adam Smith Institute be more likely to feel at home with the left-of-centre [late Labour leader] John Smith Institute?'

With Brown by his side, the US Federal Reserve chairman Alan Greenspan chose his words carefully when delivering the Adam Smith Memorial lecture in Kirkcaldy in 2005: 'With Smith, the emerging elite found their voice and sanction. Smith's sanction, however, was directed to the freedom of markets and trade, not to the new business elite, many of whose business practices he severely deprecated. He concluded that the competitive force unleashed by individuals in pursuit of their rational self-interest induces each person to do better. Such competitive interaction, by encouraging specialisation and division of labour, increases economic growth.'

But however he is seen by whoever, it can't be denied that Adam Smith has had a profound and long-lasting impact on the world, with his works having been produced in dozens of languages from Japanese and German to French, Russian and Korean. There are plaques and colleges and institutes everywhere bearing his name. Streets, too. The Adam Smith Institute, with its mission to be 'an influential centre for the promulgation of free-market doctrines', is based in London's Great Smith Street.

And then of course, there is Edinburgh, where a relatively new but traditional-style statue of the man has been erected in the High Street near St Giles Cathedral; and where another superb stone tribute to him was, at time of writing, yet to be inaugurated. To explain . . .

When in 1778 Smith inexplicably accepted the role of Commissioner of Customs and the Salt Duties at an annual salary of £600, he settled into the last phase of his life with his mother in Panmure House, a seventeenth-century mansion built by and for the 4th Earl of Panmure. Key figures of the Scottish Enlightenment were regular visitors there until Smith died in 1790, leaving instructions for his unpublished manuscripts to be destroyed.

Now the house, to be found through a close opposite the Royal Mile Primary School, is being restored both inside and out as his last surviving home. Scheduled to open in the autumn of 2017 as a prestigious business centre, with state-of-the-art facilities for lectures, seminars and webinars, it is the Adam Smith-inspired vision and inspiration of its future administrator, the Edinburgh Business School.

Smith did not travel far on his last journey.

Three hundred or so paces back up the Royal Mile is the Canongate Church, where his is the first name you find – at your feet – on a 10 by 24 cm brass cobble among the many setts that wrap around the front entrance. 'One American lady thought this wasn't much of a marker for such an important man's grave,' the kirk's property convenor Stuart McFarlane told this writer. 'So I had to explain that it's just one of several guiding signs to his tomb.'

And his elevated tomb, rising above several hundred in this famous graveyard, is anything but small. With its elaborate headstone against the wall of the street-side Canongate Tollbooth building, it stands behind a padlocked cage of iron rails with an inscription that reads:

*Here*
*are deposited the remains of*
*ADAM SMITH*
*Author of the*
*Theory of Moral Sentiments*
*and*
*Wealth of Nations*

On the stone lying flat below that, and above the great man's buried bones, are inscribed his words: *The property which every man has in his own labour, as it is the original foundation of all other property, so it is the most sacred and inviolable.*

'This is by far the kirk's most visited grave of them all,' says Mr McFarlane. 'In the summer months we have a regular stream of visitors from all over the world – and especially America – asking to be directed to it.'

As if to prove his point, two young foreigners immediately appear in search of it . . . this in the middle of January.

They will have heard all about the great man in their respective countries, then?

'Oh yes, the value of labour!' says the bearded Argentinian.

'*Mais oui,*' says his French companion. 'We are both here as students of the economy.'

And so he lives on. Wherever his spirit is now, Adam Smith cannot complain that he has been ignored or forgotten.

# James Small (1740–93)

*Inventor of the swing plough*

In today's world, so diverted as it is with personal advantage and profit, it is hard to imagine such a truly altruistic man as James Small, carpenter and ploughwright of the Scottish Borders, who seems to have been limitlessly ingenious as an inventor yet happy to remain relatively unsung and largely unrewarded for the huge advance he brought to the world through his inspired development of the swing plough in 1765.

His unique design revolutionised the face of agriculture for ever, and not just within his own environment and community. Often feeling that he was too shy for the good of his own reputation, no member of the latter has ever been, to this day, similarly reticent about making one specific and gigantic claim for Small's invention on his behalf – that it enabled the great prairies of America and Canada to become 'the breadbaskets of the world'.

But we don't even know what the man looked like. Seeking out his image today, his most ardent admirer would fail to find one; for even in his own land there is no painting, statue or commemorative plaque – though there are illustrations aplenty of his brainchild, which was the result of much thought, application and perseverance.

How did he go about realising it? From his birthplace in Dalkeith, a small town just south of Edinburgh, Small went to England to study various plough designs that were finding favour – or not – and took careful note of his observations before returning to Scotland, to Blackadder Mount in Berwickshire, in readiness to make the first-ever attempt at the development of a plough on a scientific basis. After many days and nights of candle-burning at both ends, he was satisfied with his design for the iron swing (or wheelless) plough – intended to replace the old Scotch plough of James Anderson of Hermiston, which itself had been a huge improvement on Scotland's previous labour-intensive, cumbersome and mainly wooden model that required up to twelve oxen. That unlamented affair often broke down, and while needing several people to operate it – one guide, one to keep it from getting choked with roots and stones, and another to 'whip' on the team – failed even to turn neat furrows.

As bad as that machine was, Small felt he had developed something good to the same degree. When he was ready, in a moment of high excitement, he took his concept to the recently opened Carron Iron Works in Falkirk to be cast and transformed into reality. It was an anxious time for him. Would the resulting metal contraption perform its intended purpose or would its theory prove to have been more promising than its practical application? He need not have worried. After exhaustive testing in the field – literally – his two-horse plough was hailed an immediate success, a dramatic improvement on its predecessor. And soon the neighbourhood – and the entire country – got to know of its effectiveness, not least its ability to carve clean, clear furrows of turned earth with a fraction of the energy that had once been required.

By 1780 James Small found himself turning out 500 of his ploughs per year for his customers – and turning a blind eye to the increasing number of blacksmiths and foundries that had quickly started mass-producing and adapting with impunity his basic design to suit *their* customers' particular requirements.

Soon, emigrating farmers were taking the Small-style machines with them to America, or having them built on arrival, and all the while the inventor took – rather than monetary profit – a quiet, private satisfaction from seeing how his invention swept the prairies to the general benefit of the world.

Not only had it made life easier for the farmer, it had thereby helped to combat humankind's most ancient enemy, hunger. Consequently, he rejected any entreaties to patent his design. And thus overworked and underpaid, James Small died a poor man, at sixty-three, in 1793. It may be hard to understand today, but it is also said that he died a happy man.

# John McAdam (1756–1836)

*Roadbuilder extraordinary*

He was neither a dirty-fingernailed builder nor a grand engineer in the accepted sense, but John Louden McAdam was certainly a frequent coach passenger whose shoulders had been well and truly shaken. Such rough riding had presumably irritated him to the point of distraction before he got out his quill, his candles and his resolve to do something about it. The result was a significant contribution to making the world move more rapidly and smoothly than it had before he addressed the annoying impact of mud-puddled holes, stone bumps, wheel-breaking cracks, collapsing edges, unpredictable cambers and all the other drawbacks of tracks and carriageways that had grown organically over the years.

Borrowing some ideas from the ancient Romans, he came up with a new process for road-building, with three graded layers of broken and crushed rock and gravel which would, with the passage of time and traffic, firm into a smooth, hard surface considerably more durable and less hazardous than the usual composite of stones with compressed dirt and mud. Slightly convex surfaces saw that rainwater would effectively drain away, making his roads dryer and less rutted than those they replaced. It was a commonsense solution that proved to be a welcome and remarkably enduring one.

Indeed, McAdam's principles of road-making are still used on many of the world's highways today, and the system's success has elevated the Scot's name to the point that the highly adventurous word 'macadamization' has entered the (American) English language without apology.

John McAdam was born in Ayr, south-west Scotland, in 1756 and emigrated to America as a young man in 1770 after his father died, immediately entering the financial world of New York in the counting house of a merchant uncle. The plan was that he would stay and prosper as a merchant too but, while he initially managed to do the latter to an impressive degree, his failure to support the Revolution put the seal on the eager Tory's budding American career. After the war he was no longer welcome in the now-United States and he returned to Scotland in 1783, with his American wife Gloriana and their two children.

Having been metaphorically shown the road from that side of the Atlantic, John McAdam was not to know then that there would be a rich irony in the manner of his making his presence felt for the second time in the United States – the showing of his road-making system before its adoption by the people who had happily seen the back of him.

Despite much of his property and assets having been confiscated by the new American government, the still-young McAdam had sailed back to Ayrshire with a considerable fortune after little more than a dozen lucrative years away, and he soon purchased a fine estate near Maybole. It was there and then that his interest in road-making was truly sparked, for the estate's roads were rather less fine, as were its adjoining and nearby public roads.

Though wealthy enough to feel unobliged to bother with such apparently mundane matters, he determined to do something about them. He became a local road trustee, then – not content simply to register that the district's road network was in poor condition – applied his own agile brainpower to them. Then he put his hand in his purse to set up a series of road-making experiments at his own expense; not least among these being the first 'macadamized' road – on his Sauchie estate – which is still in use today.

Having thus learned a few things about effective road-surfacing techniques – and feeling his experiments were promising success – he became more ambitious and began looking to spread his ideas to improve the notoriously bad roads of the entire British Isles. His first step was a move to Falmouth in the southernmost county of Cornwall, where he continued his experiments as a government appointee. Then in 1806, with his subsequent appointment as paving commissioner in the western port of Bristol, he had a chance to really put his theories into practice, appalled as he was by the condition of the roads he oversaw.

He developed an inexpensive technique for implementing the new surfacing system and wrote two treatises documenting his work, *Remarks on the Present System of Road-Making* (1816) and *Practical Essay on the Scientific Repair and Preservation of Roads* (1819). Also responsible for reforms in road administration and adviser to many turnpike trusts, he ensured that public roads became the government's responsibility, financed out of taxes. His impressive efforts did not go unappreciated. In 1820 parliament awarded him £2,000, and in further recognition of his work, he was put in charge of all British highways as Surveyor-General of Metropolitan Roads in 1827. The consequent 'macadamization' of the country's roads did a great deal to improve travel and communication, and soon his road-paving methods were not only ubiquitous throughout his own land, they were adopted by almost all the major European countries – where coverage was almost 90 per cent – and by the USA,

America's first McAdam surface appeared on the Boonsborough Turnpike Road between Hagerstown and Boonsboro, Maryland, in the early 1820s; the second was laid in 1830 on the seventy-three-mile National Pike (or Cumberland Road); and soon 'tarmacadam roads' became standard, used on a massive mileage of highways and lesser roads all across the land.

So his system had well and truly taken root in America by the time John McAdam was struck down by a heart attack in 1836 on a visit to his Scottish boyhood haunts at Moffat in Dumfriesshire. He was eighty years old and, having put so much into his mission, he had worn out his health and his wealth. Though he died a poor man – but 'at least an honest one', he said shortly before his death – he was unquestionably rich in achievements acknowledged the world over.

And although 'macadamization' was replaced by more modern techniques in the early 1900s, his name lives on – mainly in the affectionate form of 'tarmacadam', shortened to 'tarmac'.

# Robert Burns (1759–96)

*The immortal poetic memory*

When you consider how his name and work have travelled and grown in global celebration over the centuries, it fairly makes a Scot's fingers tingle to touch the tiny recessed bed in which Robert Burns was born in a modest thatched cottage – to a 'blast o' Janwar win'' – on the twenty-fifth of that first month of the year 1759.

How could his humble parents, William and Agnes Burnes, ever have expected that, nearly two and a half centuries after it, the birth of their first son in the rural hamlet of Alloway in Ayrshire would be annually hailed all over the world; that in a creative span of twenty-two years he would have composed 28,000 lines of verse and restored a huge body of Scotland's dying folk-song heritage; and that, by his death thirty-seven years later, he would have become Scotland's best-loved, most respected poet ever – apparently to remain so in perpetuity?

For some, it can be puzzling that Burns' poetry, which works best euphonically in the rhythmic roughage of an archaic country dialect that even Scots can strive to grasp today, has been such a successful export. So much so that countries like Russia and Romania have produced postage stamps in his honour; that the new year is greeted in scores of lands by the singing of his 'Auld Lang Syne' lyrics; that his 'immortal memory' is toasted not just at annual Burns suppers wherever Scots blood flows, but also by non-Scots in hugely important arenas – such as the United Nations. There, in 2003, 300 international guests heard Secretary-General Kofi Annan deliver the inaugural Robert Burns Memorial Lecture on the theme of the brotherhood of man. Speaking movingly of anti-Semitism, Islamophobia and racism in general, he quoted the key lines from the poet's 'A Man's a Man for a' That' as the touchstone of his address: 'That man to man the world o'er, shall brothers be for a' that.'

Such fame! And so deserved – for such soaring thoughts so well expressed despite their vehicle being the poet's local tongue; or perhaps because of. Is it this very closeness to his humble roots that seems to speak to people so eloquently? In any event, and perhaps in any tongue, his craftsman's lyrical skill would surely make his work an emotional delight.

His spontaneous surrender to a picture, a thought or a moment was also uniquely appealing. An inspired Burns would write wherever he found himself – at candle-lit desks, of course, but also on horseback, on country walks, or in inns where he was known to scratch his tumbling words on walls or windows. One such etched glass pane, from the Cross Keys Inn in the central town of Falkirk, is now preserved in the Victorian museum that sits beside his birth cottage. It begins: 'Sound be his sleep and blythe his morn / That never did a lassie wrang.'

Also among the museum's many fascinating exhibits relevant to the poet's work and life (including some original manuscripts) is a tiny leather 'travelling companion', holding a set of quill nibs, a knife and an ink bottle, which he presumably carried at all times. So why he did he have to scratch on glass? Was it writing surfaces he lacked when his inspirations came?

And of inspirations he was never short. He could be as angry as he could be sensuously gentle. When not puncturing lordly pomposity, he would be responding to the joys and tribulations of life and nature, from animal and human foibles through the 'fresh and fair' blooming of a riverbank, to the 'fond kiss' of a lover.

And neither was he short of lovers among the ranks of what he called 'rapture-giving Woman'. The handsome Burns could see the funny side of sex, as expressed in this mock epitaph to a wild friend in the town of Mauchline . . .

> Lament him, Mauchline husbands a'
> He often did assist ye;
> For had ye staid awa',
> Your wives they ne'er had missed ye!
>
> Ye Mauchline bairns, as on ye pass
> To school in bands thegither,
> O, tread ye lightly on his grass
> Perhaps he was your father!

But pursuit of females was a most serious enthusiasm for him – the father of eight illegitimate children – and love found him in a wide variety of ways, according to whims of his objects of desire. Apart from his loyal wife Jean Armour, the 'jewel' of 'The Belles of Mauchline' with whom he had four offspring, his many amorous adventures included, to list only the most notable: Nelly Kilpatrick, his harvest-field co-worker who first moved him to verse; the mystery of 'E'; Peggy Chalmers, who cast him aside; Clarinda, who never succumbed to him despite their intense love-letter romance; Maria Riddell, whose charms included intellectual challenge; and . . .

Perhaps the most piquant of his extramarital loves was Mary Campbell, with whom he fell in love in 1786, just before his career as a poet took off. With her, his life could have taken a completely different course and the world might have been deprived of his fabulous contribution. That year, pursued by creditors and the angry family of the pregnant Jean, he had accepted a position as a bookkeeper in Jamaica and 'Highland Mary', having agreed to go with him, went to the port of Greenock to await him while he set about raising the nine-guinea fare.

But she was to wait in vain, for his desperate attempt to do that – through publishing some of his stocked-up young man's poetry – was stunningly successful. The Kilmarnock Edition of his *Poems, chiefly in the Scottish Dialect* was an instant success, receiving reviews like this from the *New London Magazine*: 'We do not recollect to have ever met with a more signal instance of true and uncultivated genius.'

No one was more surprised than Burns himself. The praise echoed throughout the country and especially in Scotland's refined capital, where the name of the 'ploughman poet' was soon spoken with awe. Never had there been such a dramatic transformation of a penniless, reviled womaniser into a celebrated son of a diminished, post-Union Scotland that had been longing for an unapologetic champion of its identity and language. The young farmer with little formal education but a poetic gift of passion, wit and power was fêted and called by popular request to Edinburgh.

On arrival, he was greatly in demand to be the focus of fashionable parties and – though he sometimes feigned resentment of this, comparing himself to the 'intelligent pig' in a popular sideshow – he generally enjoyed the attention. And at one such party, another young man destined to be a companion of his in the Scottish hall of literary fame was there to see him relish it. Walter Scott, who was sixteen when he saw Burns at Dr Adam Ferguson's house, later recalled the buckskinned hero's impact thus:

I think his countenance was more massive than it looks in any of the portraits. I would have taken the poet, had I not known what he was, for a very sagacious country farmer of the old Scotch school; that is, none of your modern agriculturalists who keep labourers for their drudgery, but the *douce guidman* who held his own plough. There was a strong expression of sense and shrewdness in all his lineaments: the eye alone, I think, indicated the poetical character and temperament. It was large, and of a cast which glowed (I say literally *glowed*). I never saw such another eye in a human being, though I have seen the most distinguished men of my time. His conversation expressed perfect self-confidence, but without the least intrusive forwardness; and when he differed in opinion, he did not hesitate to express it firmly, yet at the same time with modesty.

To Highland Mary's misfortune, Burns was quite overwhelmed not just by the acclaim and celebrity prompted by his book but also by the fact that Jean Armour had now given birth to twins, with whom he was delighted. His head spinning with such distractions, he repeatedly postponed his departure for Jamaica and in October of the same eventful year in which he had met her, Mary died of a fever (or, some say, of pregnancy complications) while still waiting at Greenock. It would be several years before the poet could bring himself to express the pain he felt at her loss.

Yet another diversion was an intense and surprisingly enduring love-letter relationship begun in Edinburgh with the married Nancy Maclehose – whose pen name was Clarinda, while she called him Sylvander – which was never to be physically fulfilled, despite its on-paper passion.

In the meantime, Burns published new editions of his poetry, toured Scotland and began working on one of his most important projects, collecting and restoring traditional Scots songs for *The Scots Musical Museum*. Through his rewriting, repairing and completing scores of old, half-remembered folk songs, he did Scotland an immeasurable (and unpaid) service, generating interest in the country's culture across Europe and the world.

Generally speaking, though he felt he had finally found his calling after trying his hand unsuccessfully at flax dressing and farming in his now-late father's footsteps, he was aware of the fickle nature of his new-found 'friends' and fame and felt the need to secure an 'honest' living. Also being honest to her, he finally married Jean Armour and moved with her to a farm at Ellisland near Dumfries; but when the town seemed to hold more attractions than the too-familiar strain of farming, the family moved on to Dumfries itself, taking a house in Bank Street in 1791. While also working actively as an exciseman, in which job his uncanny ability to get fines from wealthier defaulters secured him promotion, Burns' pen became increasingly prolific. Here, he wrote some of his best-known works such as 'Scots Wha Hae', 'Is There for Honest Poverty', 'Ae Fond Kiss' and the acclaimed classic comic poem 'Tam o' Shanter'.

But hard work would be his downfall. As the new century approached, his health began to decline and he was plagued by recurring bouts of rheumatic fever. The tragedy came as his family expected. Far too young and with so much yet to offer, he died on 21 July 1796, probably from endocarditis contracted while toiling in the fields as a boy.

Thousands attended his funeral. But he was never to be forgotten. In 1801, on the fifth anniversary of his death, the first-ever Burns Supper was held by a small group of friends in his simple little birth cottage in Alloway, which is now open to the public – unlike its replica in Atlanta, Georgia – and within a few years Burns clubs were springing up all over Scotland and eventually (as we know) well beyond.

But from where had this great talent sprung up? William Burnes was a gardener from the north-east of Scotland, who moved south for self-improvement and built the Alloway cottage to support not only his market garden, but the family he and his local wife Agnes began in 1759 with Robert (who would remove the 'e' from his surname). By bringing together other parents to pay for a school-teacher for their children, William put a big effort into making sure Robert and his younger brother, Gilbert, got a good schooling – and the teacher, John Murdoch, would later report how well they could memorise whole passages of text.

It was in Alloway, too, that Robert's creative imagination was stimulated – by his mother's frequent singing of traditional songs and distant cousin Betty Davidson's telling tales of ghosts and witches. He was also inspired by animals and plants in the countryside around the farms the family later tried in vain to work successfully as tenants – Mount Oliphant, Lochlea and Mossgiel. It was seeing his father struggle that made Robert turn his hand assiduously to the plough; but it also embittered him about landowners' exploitation.

And sadly, William never lived to see his elder son's success that owed much to the parental gift of a thorough education and its basic acknowledgment of received standard English. And just to show he could use it if he felt inclined, Robert would occasionally write in that mode, as in his 'Ode For General Washington's Birthday' . . .

> See gathering thousands, while I sing,
> A broken chain exulting bring,
> And dash it in a tyrant's face,
> And dare him to his very beard,
> And tell him he no more is feared –
> No more the despot of Columbia's race!
> A tyrant's proudest insults brav'd,
> They shout – a People freed!
> They hail an Empire saved.

But fine as it was for the occasional stanza, he must have known there was some magic missing. Nothing could compare with his poetic command of the vernacular, as shown in his gloriously simple, Scottish and evocative 'Ye Banks and Braes o' Bonnie Doon':

> Aft hae I rov'd by bonnie Doon
> To see the rose and woodbine twine
> And ilk bird sang o' its luve
> And fondly sae did I o' mine

# Charles Macintosh (1765–1843)

*The long reign of his raincoat*

There is something indefinably dramatic about a raincoat. Sometimes it's sinister, worn by shadowy, cigarette-smoking movie spies lurking behind its high-winged collars; sometimes it adds a certain dark glamour to the good guys – detectives, say, like Marlowe or Columbo or even Inspector Clouseau. But mostly that romantic Third Man image, combined with its sheer practicality, has made it an enduringly loved garment for ordinary Americans, especially when they visit the cold and wet far northern shores of Europe. For ordinary Scots, however, there is something ironic about how they recognise their transatlantic cousins principally by that dress code. For while refusing to share American appreciation of it and choosing to shun such a reliable protector themselves as something rather 'wet', they can't escape the widely acknowledged fact that, whether you call it a trench coat or a mac, the wonderfully waterproof creation that has survived a thousand lesser fashion trends was invented in Scotland.

It might seem odd to say that a coat is 'invented', but the word seemed apt when this species emerged, as it hinged on the development of the material with which it was created. Had he been alive today, the Scottish chemist who made the breakthrough, Glasgow-born Charles Macintosh, would have been gratified to see his brainchild's remarkable longevity 'across the pond' – where it is affectionately known by a misspelled version of his own name – but bemused by his own countrymen's less-than-enthusiastic feeling for what should have long been regarded as a godsend in the damp Caledonian climate.

It was no doubt such weather conditions that inspired him in the first place, when in 1823, at the age of fifty-eight, while working in the family fabric plant, he set about the challenge of creating the waterproof material that promised to minimise the discomfort of a hard Scottish winter.

In the context of a long quest to find uses for waste gasworks products, he began experimenting with India rubber – an exciting new substance – to see how its qualities might provide a waterproof element when applied, somehow, to a normal woollen cloth. Noting that coal-tar naphtha dissolved the rubber, he applied the resulting preparation to one side of the cloth then placed another layer of wool cloth on top. It worked! With important input and help from James Syme, an Edinburgh University medical student (and later eminent surgeon), his system was refined enough to produce a truly waterproof material that he was able to patent that same year – though, by adding a 'k' to make his name 'Mackintosh', the patent office made a historic error which has stuck to the resulting product to this day, when belted raincoats made from refined versions of the Scot's material are still known affectionately as mackintoshes, or macs, mainly in America though also to a lesser degree in Britain.

Introduction of the early products to the market was not so easy, however. While Macintosh did not attempt – initially – to get into tailoring himself, he supplied the waterproof material to tailors to make up. And while there were some notable successes (such as the outfitting of Sir John Franklin's Arctic expedition in 1824) it began to seem almost impossible to successfully tailor such an inflexible fabric. For soon after the manufacture of coats and other garments with his new material began – advertised as 'life preservers' for anyone who had to go out in the rain – some major problems became apparent, not least the frequent puncturing of the garments' fabric by tailors engaged in seaming them. The resulting penetration of rain into the cloth's natural oil caused the rubber cement to deteriorate too quickly. Another significant problem to beset early Macs was the fact that they reacted oddly to weather extremes – becoming stiff in winter, while in hot weather, they had a tendency to melt, sometimes causing two people wearing them to become literally inseparable.

Nonetheless, in 1830 Macintosh finally took on a partner – the Manchester firm of Thomas Hancock – to move into the ready-to-wear business . . . and on to more challenges. Their 'macs' were voluminous, neck-to-ankle garments, designed to keep the wearer completely dry in the era of the stagecoach; but soon, the enclosed comforts of the railway carriage were to render that style almost redundant. The aforementioned problems persisted too, and there was also the small matter of smell: wearers and their companions complained about the peculiar rubbery odour that was given out by the garments.

Yet it looked as if rubber and its various applications were here to stay. In a few years, the Amazon would be booming as the stuff began to feature in much more than rainwear. And in America, the cavalry was getting ready to ride to Macintosh's rescue . . .

Working in his garage to get away from his nagging wife, the innovative Charles Goodyear discovered in 1839 how to vulcanise rubber to produce resistance to temperature fluctuations, making it much more elastic and non-sticky in heat and less brittle in cold. And about ten years later, Joseph Mandleburg of Lancashire, England, successfully got to grips with the rubber smell in woollen waterproof garments, and then launched the first odour-free waterproof coat.

The invaluable input of these two men – plus the fact that the still-prominent waterproof-wear company Hodgman in Framingham, Massachusetts, had begun to import and sell Macs to set down the roots of their remarkable popularity in the United States – meant that Charles Macintosh's original dream was to prevail and indeed triumph after all. And that in the process the Scotsman's name was to be immortalised among all those for whom his waterproof material still reigns supreme.

The son of a well-established Glasgow dyer, Macintosh recorded several other scientific achievements for which he is not particularly remembered – notably a conversion process which used carbon gases to convert iron to steel much more quickly than any other method of the time – and was elected a Fellow of the Royal Society in 1823. He died twenty years later.

# Walter Scott (1770–1832)

*Scotland's romantic literary hero*

Unlike his ploughman companion in Scotland's hall of literary fame, Walter Scott did not have to make any kind of class-crossing journey to be the toast of Edinburgh's polite society (and eventually far beyond). He was born into it as the son of a lawyer and a professor of medicine's daughter, and was quite at ease in it. Indeed, after a good Scots education, he followed his father's footsteps to also become a distinguished lawyer, counting among his professional achievements his posting as Sheriff-Depute of Selkirkshire. But other conspicuous talents tugged at his heart and at a certain moment he knew he was fated to live a life of two strands, exercising his brain, like a nineteenth-century John Grisham, not just on dusty old law books but on the creation of romantic adventure books, for which he became famous as 'the father of the regional and historical novel'.

But what was that certain moment? Scott was only sixteen when he met Robert Burns on *his* epic class-crossing journey in 1786, as the poet stepped on to the fine Edinburgh carpets of the Scotts' family friend, Dr Adam Ferguson. The boy never forgot the impact of their meeting, later recording it breathlessly in a keenly observed, and now precious, description of 'Caledonia's bard' (see pages 136–7).

As he was never shy of attention himself and indeed veered a touch towards flamboyancy, there can be little doubt that young Walter Scott was well impressed by old Edina's celebration of Ayrshire's champion versifier – and suitably inspired by it to find a similar kind of celebrity for himself. He did not fail.

Childhood polio had left him lame in the right leg, but Scott grew to be handsome and tall – over six foot – and managed to minimise his disability with the confidence and encouragement he found on frequent visits to his paternal grandparents' home in the Scottish Borders. And it was there, listening to his grandmother talk, that his fascination with the old tales and ballads of the area was awakened.

He had already started to collect such ballads as a teenager but –

after graduating from Edinburgh University in 1783 and qualifying as an advocate in 1792 – he did not begin to find his publishing feet until an avenue opened in the context of his interest in German works; so his first efforts to see the light were translations of ballads by Gottfried Augustus Burger (1796) and of Goethe's *Götz von Berlichingen* (1799). Overly academic for some, perhaps; but they gave Walter Scott a taste for publishing that he would thoroughly indulge and never lose in his lifetime, and his quill soon became a very prolific scratcher indeed.

His first major work, an impressive collection of old ballads with introductions and notes entitled *Minstrelsy of the Scottish Border,* appeared in 1802. He went on to write poetry for several years with the hugely successful *The Lay of the Last Minstrel* (1805), about an old Borders legend. That was followed in 1808 by *Marmion,* a historical romance concerning the attempts of a lord to marry a rich lady; then came *The Lady of the Lake* (1810) and *Rokeby* (1813) before his last poem, *The Lord of the Isles* (1815).

Some say Scott gave up poetry to sidestep comparison with Lord Byron, but he turned to fiction with astounding success, whatever his motives. One was surely to raise money to pay for the building of his own personal Gothic castle – Abbotsford, near Galashiels – which his flamboyance had driven him to begin in 1811. Another was a crisis in the business affairs of his printer-publisher associate James Ballantyne, to which he had contributed not just money but hack editorial work. When the final crash came, he accepted all Ballantyne's £130,000 debts and decided to literally 'write' them off. 'I am become a sort of writing automaton,' he wrote in his diary, 'and truly the joints of my knees, especially the left, are so stiff and painful in rising and sitting down, that I can hardly help screaming – I that was so robust and active.'

And he told Lord Henry Thomas Cockburn, with whom he had founded the Edinburgh Academy boys' school, that 'my right hand shall work it all off'. So in his later years there could be no respite in the prodigious output he had maintained while also practising as an advocate.

So busy was he that, to keep several projects going at the same time, he used two massive desktops. He began to write his way out of financial trouble with his first novel, *Waverley* (1814), which was essentially a historical fiction vehicle designed to retell swashbuckling tales of the '45 Jacobite rebellion while ostensibly following young

Edward Waverley's coming of age. It defined a new literary genre and was followed by a stream of similar successes, such as *The Tale of Old Mortality* (1816), *Rob Roy* (1817) and the widely loved *Ivanhoe* (1819) – depicting the rivalry between King Richard I and his evil brother John – which was made into a memorable film starring Robert Taylor and Elizabeth Taylor in 1952.

In all, Scott's passion for the printed word was expressed in no fewer than twenty-seven historical novels, and his last few years' work included *Woodstock* (1826), *A Life of Napoleon* (1827), *Chronicles of the Canongate* (1827), *The Fair Maid of Perth* (1828), *Anne of Geierstein* (1829) and *Count Robert of Paris* and *Castle Dangerous* (1831). His novels made him one of Europe's most famous literary figures, and he was created a baronet in 1818, making him a 'sir' and prompting George IV to remark: 'I shall always reflect with pleasure on Sir Walter Scott's having been the first creation of my reign.'

Scott's talent was also acknowledged in the respect and admiration of fellow scribes such as Hogg, Goethe and Wordsworth; of portrait painters like William Allan and Henry Raeburn; and of admiring 'Edinburghers' who saw to it that the city's soaring Scott Monument (built in 1844) and the nearby Waverley Station represented enduring tributes to the author's elevated status in the Victorian world.

While some critics have accused him of going too far in over-colourfully portraying wild Jacobite clansmen, credit is largely due to Scott for rehabilitating Scotland's image in the 1800s, reviving an interest in tartan, and even persuading King George IV to wear a kilt during his visit to Edinburgh in 1822.

And still the writer, poet and born storyteller had time to bring up the five children he had with Margaret Charlotte Charpentier, whom he married in 1797. And still he had time to become clerk to the Court of Session in Edinburgh.

But all his efforts would inevitably take their toll, and after a trip to Italy and a short illness, he died at his beloved Abbotsford in 1832, at the relatively young age of sixty-one. He was buried beside his ancestors in Dryburgh Abbey and all his debts were ultimately paid off from the profits from his books.

*American Note.* The march traditionally played to honour the US President, which includes the line 'Hail to the Chief who in triumph advances!', is based on verses from Sir Walter's *The Lady of the Lake*, put to music by James Sanderson (1769–1841).

# Johnnie Walker (1800–59)

*The man behind the drink*

In this age of clever marketing ploys, when a new ice cream is given an old-sounding foreign name to imbue it with a sense of long establishment, you would not be surprised to learn that the famous red-coated figure of Johnnie Walker – whose ageless dynamic image so helps the world-beating sales of his eponymous whisky – was just an invention. But how surprised would you be to learn that he was real?

Of course, the original Johnnie Walker did not stride briskly around Kilmarnock in monocle, top hat and breeches like the figure on the whisky bottle; he was just an average Ayrshire lad who, after his farmer father's death, left his family's home at the age of fifteen to set up a grocery business in that town in 1820.

Well, not quite average. He turned out to be something more than a regular shopkeeper. Gradually, his shop began to find favour not so much for its groceries and dry goods as for its wines and spirits, particularly its own brand of whisky. It seemed John had a keen nose for blending tea, and as he began to apply the same principles to the qualities of Scotland's water of life, his talent found expression in Walker's Kilmarnock Whisky, which he sold to many a grateful customer.

Up to that point in the west of Scotland, malt whiskies and grain whiskies had been bottled singly, and there was little appetite – and even less of a market – for the oily stuff outside its native land. How that emphatically changed in the latter half of the nineteenth century owed much to the art of whisky blending refined by several pioneers, among whom the dedicated John Walker was an important player. With the invaluable help of a selection of his favourite Islay malts, he created a consistent taste and quality and, in so doing, managed to capture a certain depth of flavour that the 'single' could not match.

And appreciation of it did not just happen locally. When John's son Alexander joined him in 1856, the younger man spread its fame further and wider as he continued this tradition of creating harmonious blends 'to make our whisky' – in his own words – 'of such quality that nothing in the market shall come before it'.

By the time John died, in 1859, the single-minded Alexander had brought his own talents to bear on the business, not just revealing an inherited flair for blending, but also an aptitude for product promotion. This he did initially by getting over his message (with the aid of a few complementary drams, no doubt) to the many travelling salesmen who visited Kilmarnock as a centre for carpets and textiles. But he was soon pushing the Walker brand of whisky all over the world. His big helpers in that respect were ships' captains who, under the merchant venturers' system, would, wherever they landed, sell bottles on commission at the best price they could.

And as the British Empire expanded, Alexander made sure his product, now called Old Highland Whisky, went with it. Offices and representation were found in England (1880), Australia (1890) and South Africa (1897); and as he enhanced his whisky's reputation by winning the first special award for blended whisky at the Sydney International Exhibition and introducing the square bottle design with black-and-gold slanting label, he planned the conversion of John Walker & Sons to a limited liability business. That happened in 1886.

But it was not until 1906, nearly twenty years after Alexander's death, that the family's famed whisky took on the memorable brand name 'Johnnie Walker', which has since become known all over the globe. Alexander left the burgeoning business in the hands of two of his sons, Alexander Walker II and George Paterson Walker. And it was George who, having inherited his father's flair for marketing, masterminded the image of the much-loved 'Striding Man' in 1908 to give life and identity to the Johnnie Walker name and support the recent launch of Red Label and Black Label (which have since become respectively the world's largest-selling Scotch and its best-selling de luxe whisky).

It happened over a planned briefing lunch with Tom Browne, a well-known cartoonist of the time, when – we can assume – no reference was made to the original John Walker's facial features; for the exercise was all about capturing his pioneering spirit to give the product a compelling advertising device. Stirred by George's enthusiasm, the artist instantly picked up the challenge and quickly sketched a top-hatted, caped figure on the back of a menu. He presented it with a smile and a look of triumph. He had given birth to the Striding Man.

Thus Johnnie Walker the logo went on to stride across the world. And although his appearance and outfits regularly changed over the years as he was subtly updated by several other leading artists, few would deny that his original creation was something of a marketing masterstroke; on a par, perhaps, with Coca-Cola's famous fat italics.

Within twenty years the Johnnie Walker image was universally associated with the first truly global brand, sold in over 120 countries around the world, and especially America. The product also won another prestigious stamp – for among the devoted following it built up at home in Britain was none other than King George V himself. He liked Johnnie Walker whisky so much that in 1933 he granted a Royal Warrant to the company, which has remained an official purveyor of whisky to the Royal Household to the present day.

It was, in fact, Alexander Walker II who brought about most of these big follow-up business successes. After stepping into the blending role, as a highly astute businessman he took up responsibility for further development of the company and was eventually regarded as a colossus of the whisky industry and a forceful spokesman on its behalf. He was knighted for his efforts in 1920.

Sir Alexander retired in 1940, but his office still stands in John Finnie Street, Kilmarnock, which remains the centre for the blending and bottling of Johnnie Walker; a leading global name by any measure. Now produced by Diageo plc, the giant food and drinks multinational, it was – at time of writing – running neck-and-neck with Dewar's for the title of top-selling Scotch whisky brand in the United States.

Wherever he is now, the original John Walker is no doubt quite pleased that he decided to put a little nip – like a bright red hunting jacket – into the grey business of general provisions.

# Alexander Bain (1811–77)

*The man who gave us the fax*

Ticker-tape parades through the streets of New York – fêting conquering heroes, VIPs or celebrities with a snowstorm of paper tape from every available window – have long represented a uniquely American expression of released euphoria, bringing out all the New World's glamour and confidence. These days, of course, while hi-tech communication has overtaken the stock market's old paper culture, the effect is preserved by jettisoning large amounts of regular shredded waste paper onto the parade route.

But who would ever guess that the original ticker-stuff itself, although part of a technology developed by others, originated in the brain of a humble crofter's son called Alexander Bain, born in 1811 on the remote northern edge of Scotland?

One of six brothers and six sisters packed into one of the occasional stone cottages that dot the peaty countryside around Watten, Caithness, a few miles north of Wick, he was not a conventionally clever lad. Indeed, when he walked a few miles to school at Backlass he did so only to sit and dream, and his academic slate recorded that apparently bleak fact. What it did not register was that the boy's apparent absence from the mainstream consciousness of schooling was, paradoxically, a sign that his was an extremely fertile mind, which, in later life, was to bombard the modern world with an impressive series of innovative ideas.

One of these was ticker tape – the system that speeded up telegraphic message-sending with an unimaginable leap. Another, which had a huge impact on the business life of the world in general, and of America in particular, was the facsimile – or fax – machine.

Most people assume this was a relatively recent development, certainly a device of the twentieth century, and in its modern guise as a smoothly designed telephonic device generally available to business and private purchasers, that is certainly true. But the fax machine as conceived by Bain, is a nineteenth-century idea that actually pre-dates fellow-Scot Alexander Graham Bell's telephone by thirty-three years. Bain was the first to describe the principle of scanning a picture or text line by line, and to develop a way of receiving the image by means of a 'chemical telegraph'. Despite his unhappy experience with formal schooling, he followed his vocational feelings with real success – 'instinct is untaught ability', he once said – and received a patent for his early fax concept in 1843, when he was thirty-two and styling himself, in what was then a newfangled term 'electrical engineer'.

For it was the then-new discovery of the powers of electricity that had, aptly, sparked his imagination. Having proved a lacklustre scholar and an even less capable shepherd – when he tried his hand at that job in the summer months – he was drawn instinctively to news of a penny lecture on 'Light, heat and the electric fluid' taking place in neighbouring Thurso in 1830. He walked twenty-one miles through the snow from Wick to hear it and, when he emerged, he was hooked. 'It set me thinking,' he said.

Because he had also shown interest in the craft of clockmaking – as a child he once made a model clock using heather for cogwheels and spring – his father had helped him become apprenticed to a clockmaker in Wick and, from there, he went to London and then Edinburgh to practise the trade. The workshop he had in Edinburgh's Hanover Street, between 1844 and 1847, now bears a plaque marking not only his incumbency but also the centenary (in 1940) of his development and patenting of the invention that combined both his intense interests: the original electric clock.

He also invented an earth battery, a mode of measuring ships' speed by vanes revolving in the water, various types of automatic telegraph, insulation for electric cables, an electric fire alarm, and a system of synchronising clocks between Glasgow and Edinburgh rail stations.

He greatly improved the speed of telegraph transmission by using punched paper tape to send messages: from 40 words a minute to about 300. The perforated tape is nicknamed 'ticker tape' because of the ticking sound the telegraph made when dealing with it.

Positively revelling in electricity's multitude of possibilities, in 1852 Alexander Bain expressed his enthusiasm for it thus:

> For many years I have devoted myself to rendering electricity practically
> useful, and have been extensively engaged, not only in this country,

but in America and on the Continent, in the construction and working of the Electric Telegraph; while at the same time the employment of electricity in the measurement of time has also engaged my attention.

But it was his 'electrochemical telegraph', which we would call the fax machine, that was destined (eventually) to create the biggest impact of all his brainwaves.

How did it work? The principle was simple. At each end of a telegraph wire was a sending and receiving machine. The sender used a detector to scan an image or text line by line, point by point and, as it swept over the page left to right, the transmitting needle picked up impulses where there was text, but no impulse where there was a gap. The two signals travelled over a telegraph wire to the receiver, which applied them to chemically treated paper which made marks corresponding to the signals from the sending needle – so reproducing the transmitted text or image.

Though he never actually transmitted anything himself in this fashion and the idea took an inordinately long time to reach the shops, Bain is widely acknowledged as the father of the facsimile – even by most of the many clever developers who came along behind him to refine the concept. His invention was improved in turn by Frederick Collier Blakewell (1847), Giovani Caselli (1865), G. Little (1867), Senlecq de Ardres (1877), Shelford Bidwell (1881), N.S. Amstutz (1892), Buss (1902), Arthur Korn (1904), Edouard Belin (1907), Diekmann (1917), Western Union (1924), American Telephone & Telegram Company (1924/1925), NEC (1927), Wise (1938), the Xerox Corporation (& RCA) (1950/1961), the firm of Rudolf Hell (1965), Magnafax-Xerox (1966) and Ricoh (1970). In 1971 the first prototype of the laserfax appeared and, during the 1980s, the modern facsimile, or fax, spread worldwide.

The general idea was put to commercial work long before that, however. In 1865 the first commercial service began between Lyons and Paris, and in 1895 America made such a system meaningful in media communication with the advent of the Telediagraph, developed by another clockmaker, Ernest A. Hummel, of St Paul, Minnesota. The first of his machines was installed in the *New York Herald* office in 1898, and by the following year there were versions in the offices of the *Boston Herald*, *Chicago Times Herald*, *Philadelphia Inquirer* and *St Louis Republic*.

At first it was all about words; but pictures had to come. An important factor was the reproducability of images thus sent, and by the 1920s the quality of facsimile transmission was beginning to allow that – although the time taken to transmit a photograph could run to several hours. The nut was clearly cracked, however, and refinement to high levels of efficiency, quality and sophistication was only a matter of time. Eventually, newspapers would be sending whole pages off to other lands for editionalised printing.

But for Alexander Bain, it was all too late. Unfortunately, his grasp of business advantage had not matched his hands-on flair for electro-technology. He won few financial rewards for his troubles and died a disappointed man in the Home for Incurables at Kirkintilloch, near Glasgow, in 1877.

# James Dewar (1842–1923)

*Man with a cool idea*

What would a picnic or a long car trip or a walk in the hills be without James Dewar's cool invention? He it was, an industrial chemist from Scotland's central belt, who brought us the marvel of the vacuum flask that keeps our drinks warm or cold for impressively – and conveniently – long periods of time.

But this breakthrough, which has proved such a boon to the home, the campsite and even the armed forces, was almost accidental; for Dewar – who experimented on the liquefaction of gases like hydrogen, nitrogen and oxygen – had initially designed the vacuum flask to store his gases at temperatures low enough to keep them liquid.

This was 1892, and he was not thinking about the idea's domestic application until one of his assistants, a glass-blower called Reinhold Burger, noticed that it kept liquids warm as well as cold. Not surprisingly, the commercial possibilities of this were soon apparent and it wasn't long before two fellow-German glass blowers had formed a company to manufacture and market the first vacuum flasks for domestic use – in 1904. They held a contest to name the product and a Munich resident submitted 'thermos' (from the Greek word 'therme' meaning 'heat') so giving that widely familiar name to the producing company as well . . . Thermos GmbH.

Although the Germans had taken the initiative, they proved not over-jealous of their rights, and by 1907 had sold the Thermos trademark to companies in three countries – the American Thermos Bottle Company of Brooklyn, New York; the Thermos Bottle Co. Ltd of Montreal, Canada; and Thermos Ltd of Tottenham, England.

So the idea had come home again, to the quiet satisfaction (one assumes) of James Dewar who had by now been knighted for his achievements, which also included helping to invent the smokeless explosive cordite and liquefying and solidifying hydrogen.

His innovative product found fame not just in the home but in the most daring of highly publicised famous expeditions, including

Shackleton's to the South Pole and Peary's to the Arctic. It even became airborne with the Wright Brothers and Count Zeppelin.

And when the Second World War broke out in 1939, the American Thermos Bottle Company played an important role, with over 98 per cent of its output being allocated for military use in the field. After this enforced deprivation, the war ended with Thermos products being more in demand than ever with the people.

But how does the ever-popular invention work? It consists of two flasks, one inside the other, separated by a vacuum that reduces the transfer of heat, preventing a temperature change. The walls are of glass because it is a poor conductor of heat; its surfaces are usually lined with a reflective, silvery metal to reduce the transfer of heat by radiation. All of this rests on a shock-absorbing spring within a metal or plastic container, and the air between the flask and the container provides further insulation.

Born in Kincardine-on-Forth, halfway between Glasgow and Edinburgh, in 1842, Dewar was a student and lecturer at Edinburgh University before moving south to England to develop his work with low-temperature phenomena at the University of Cambridge. He later became professor of chemistry at the Royal Institution in London.

He died in 1923 after a career of great distinction and esoteric achievement much admired by his peers in the world of chemistry; but it is by the great mass of the public that he will long be even more appreciated for inventing the humble vessel that has made domestic life all over the world considerably easier.

# Robert Louis Stevenson (1850–94)

*The travelling storyteller*

Robert Louis Stevenson disguised his greatness well. Anyone looking at him superficially would see a long, gangly, rather uncared-for bohemian figure haunted by the looming terminator that was his lifelong 'consumptive' illness. They would do well not to write him off, however, for this near-invisibility made him a keen observer of people – when, for instance, he colourfully described his fellow-passengers on his grim steerage voyage across the Atlantic. And there were always signs that betrayed the intellectual value of the man who would become the greatest of storytellers. The cultured Scots voice, for instance, commanded an impressive vocabulary, and from their dark, unwell sockets his sharp brown eyes shone with vivid intelligence.

It seems odd to record today, when he is held in such high esteem for his gigantic literary impact, that he was forever disappointing people who wanted him to be 'respectable'. From an early age, when growing up as a sickly only child in his well-off family's Georgian house, which still stands in Edinburgh's Howard Place, he was groomed to follow his father Thomas into lighthouse design and engineering. Though he tried, he found the calling of little interest and could only offer the saddened Thomas the half-hearted pursuit of a law degree at Edinburgh University. A formal photograph taken of Robert Louis Stevenson in wig and gown after admission to the bar in 1875 must have been of some consolation to his father and mother Maggie – but that was where the pursuit ended.

He was determined to become a writer, and knew he would need experiences in many parts as essential grist to his literary mill. Some 'respectable friends' he left behind would see him as a velvet-clad dandy and an impulsive, aimless vagabond; but there was a kinder way to look at it: that he was driven to be peripatetic by three understandable and irresistible forces – his writer's curiosity; his need to find better climes for his delicate health; and his burning desire to be with the one he loved.

Although he never lost his deep affection for Edinburgh and its 'windy parallelograms' and made much reference to Scotland in his work wherever he found himself writing, he lodged at various stages in his life in England, France, Switzerland, America, Australia and the South Pacific. Naturally enough, then, it was with travelogues that his publishing career began, in 1878 when he was twenty-eight. As a schoolboy, he had grown to love purposeless rambling tours in Europe, and one such post-graduation trip down the French River Oisé inspired his first full-length book, *An Inland Voyage*. The critics liked it, and his next effort was even more warmly received: the melancholic *Travels with a Donkey* (1879), based on the emotional diversion of a walking tour undertaken after he had fallen in love with the most inconvenient of people: Fanny Vandegrift Osbourne, a married American woman ten years his senior, whom he had met in the artists' village colony of Grez-sur-Loing before she returned to the USA.

The attraction seemed too unlikely to be mutual, so did she wish to encourage him or otherwise? Whatever it said, a cablegram she sent from California in August 1879 had an electrifying effect on him. Within days, he was a steerage passenger aboard a steamer of dubious seaworthiness setting off from the Scottish port of Greenock bound for America: a turbulent experience that informed his book, *The Amateur Emigrant,* in which he offered such evocative observations of fellow-passengers:

> The more you saw of Alick, the more, it must be owned, you learned to despise him. His natural talents were of no use either to himself or others; for his character had degenerated like his face, and become pulpy and pretentious. Even his power of persuasion, which was certainly very surprising, stood in some danger of being lost or neutralised by over-confidence. He lied in an aggressive, brazen manner, like a pert criminal in the dock; and he was so vain of his own cleverness that he could not refrain from boasting, ten minutes after, of the very trick by which he had deceived you.

Eleven days later, a sick and near-penniless Stevenson landed in New York. From there he set off on a cheap and anything-but-cheerful 3,000-mile train trip to California, whose two miserable weeks prompted the second part of his 'emigrant' book, *Across the Plains*; but when he arrived in what was then the fast-rising frontier town of San Francisco, it was love at first sight. He felt moved to capture the American spirit in verse:

See the great new nation
New spirit and new scope
Rise there from the sea's round shoulder
A splendid sun of hope

His love for Fanny Osbourne was of much more immediate import, however, and how the emaciated, apparently impoverished writer persuaded this well-rounded assertive woman to leave a properly employed, if flighty, husband is as big a mystery as the telegram message that sent Robert Louis Stevenson dashing across the ocean in the first place. She may well have had serious doubts, but he was greeted with delight, laughter and tears – also by her eleven-year-old son Lloyd – and she wrote to her lawyer friend Edward Rearden: 'It is almost more than amusing to meet again the only person in the world who really cares anything for me.'

In leaving Scotland so suddenly, Stevenson had certainly shocked his parents, but the estrangement proved temporary. When they heard of his dire circumstances they cabled him some life-saving money, and things looked up again for Robert Louis Stevenson when Fanny finally obtained her divorce and married him on 19 May 1880 in San Francisco. His parents had also been concerned about his interest in a married woman. But there was a surprising end-twist to that when, after a honeymoon at an abandoned silver mine site in the Napa Valley – which yielded his work *The Silverado Squatters* – the newlyweds set sail for Britain, where Fanny was introduced to the Stevensons at their later Edinburgh home in Heriot Row. She set about winning them as she had Robert Louis Stevenson, and was soon well liked by both mother and father.

Thomas Stevenson's death in 1887 seemed to end a super-productive seven-year period for his son, in which he wrote – while travelling a lot for his health's sake – some of his best-known work, including *A Child's Garden of Verses* (1886), *Kidnapped* (1886), *The Strange Case of Dr Jekyll and Mr Hyde* (1886) and the still-much-loved classic *Treasure Island* (1883), which was conceived at Braemar in his home country after he drew a map to amuse his stepson Lloyd. The evocation of a pirate adventure tale to go with the sketch seemed a natural next step, and soon the resulting ripping yarn was being serialised in the boys' magazine *Young Folks*, before becoming one of the most popular books of the time among all age groups. Even Prime Minister William Gladstone was said to have read it avidly, of which revelation Robert Louis Stevenson commented: 'He would do better to attend to the imperial affairs of England.'

Still shocked by his father's death and in search of the ideal climate to promote his health, in the summer of 1888 the author decided to 'play big', as he told a friend: 'I have found a yacht, and we are going the full pitch for seven months. If I cannot get my health back . . . 'tis madness; but of course, there is the hope . . .' And so the Stevenson 'clan' – including his wife, stepson and widowed mother – set off for the Pacific islands on the chartered yacht *Casco*, sailing south-west from San Francisco. He would never see Europe again. In Honolulu, he finished *The Master of Ballantrae* (1889) and, after three cruises in these gentler climes, which seemed to promise him better health, the Stevenson party decided to settle in Western Samoa.

It was to a very handsome home, called Vailima, that he and Fanny chose to retreat, where he became known as Tusitala – 'the teller of tales' – by the natives, who saw him as a good friend as he helped them fight against the injustices of some of the British governors. Ironically, while feeling more robust than he had for years, it was here that Robert Louis Stevenson died – in front of his shaving mirror – only four years after his arrival. It was the end of his long, draining battle with tuberculosis. He was only forty-four, and lying unfinished on his desk were two novels – *St Ives* and *Weir of Hermiston*, which, although a fragment, is generally acknowledged to be a masterpiece of passion and justice set a world away, in the beloved, cold, northern city of his birth.

In his very full life of travels and travails, Robert Louis Stevenson often thought of his own impending end, so it is not surprising that he found the time to pen his own epitaph, which is now engraved on a tablet at his grave on Mount Vaea in Samoa:

Under the wide and starry sky,
Dig the grave and let me lie.
Glad did I live and gladly die,
And I laid me down with a will.

This be the verse you grave for me:
Here he lies where he longed to be;
Home is the sailor, home from sea,
And the hunter home from the hill.

# Arthur Conan Doyle (1859–1930)

*Creator of Sherlock Holmes*

> The chief piece in Beeton's Christmas Annual is a detective story by Mr A. Conan Doyle, A Study in Scarlet. This is as entrancing a tale of ingenuity in tracing out crime as has been written since the time of Edgar Allan Poe. The author shows genius. He has not trodden in the well-worn paths of literature, but has shown how the true detective should work by observation and deduction. His book is bound to have many readers.

Thus *The Scotsman*'s book review section introduced its readers on 19 December 1887, not just to the literary genius of doctor-writer Arthur Conan Doyle but to his 'true detective', by whom all other detectives were henceforth to be judged – the cultivated sleuth in the deerstalker hat who was as clever, coolly calculating and uncannily infallible as he was thoroughly English.

But Conan Doyle was born in Scotland – in Edinburgh's Picardy Place, to be precise, in 1859 – and so also, by extension, was at least the idea behind the character of Sherlock Holmes. But which of them is perceived to be the more important Scot in the great scheme of things?

As it is possible to argue convincingly that in global terms the fictional pipe-smoking consulting detective, chemist, violin player, boxer and swordsman has become bigger and better known than his creator, it is understandable (if not too pleasing to a Scot) to suspect that there are more fans of the detective than of his creator – and the number of visitors who still seek out the Holmes' non-existent 'home' at 221b Baker Street, London, provides some support for that idea.

But surely the author gets the main recognition in his home city? Not as clearly as you might expect. It comes as a surprise to find that the handsome if literal statue erected outside Conan Doyle's birth house – now ambushed by one of the Scottish capital's busiest intersections – depicts the invented detective rather than the real-life writer.

Wherever Conan Doyle is now, however, it may be of some consolation to him to know that the statue is at least dedicated to him, as can be deduced by simply observing (as Holmes might put it) the inscription written upon it . . .

In memory of
SIR ARTHUR CONAN DOYLE
Born on 22 May 1859 close to this spot.

Donated to the City of Edinburgh by Edinburgh and Lothians
branch of the Federation of Master Builders on the Federation's
150th anniversary.

Unveiled on 24 June, 1991, by Professor D. Chisholm, President,
The Royal College of Surgeons, Edinburgh.

The author's spirit might also be consoled by the conspicuous name of the nearby pub across the flow of traffic from which the statue's gaze seems to be turned – it is the Arthur Conan Doyle. And he might also be pleased to know that – after being threatened with demolition in favour of an American fast-food outlet – Liberton Bank House, where he grew up in later childhood on the south side of the city, was at time of writing earmarked for preservation by being transformed into a special school.

The city is, in fact, rich in landmarks relevant to the life of the author – from 23 George Square, where he lived as a university student, through Lauriston Gardens, where a murder takes place in *A Study in Scarlet*, to the adjoining Lonsdale Terrace, where No. 15 was his last Edinburgh residence.

While technically Scottish, as one of ten children in a financially stretched family with Irish Catholic roots, he was a man of many parts – sustained through his youth not so much by his alcoholic civil servant father as by his long-suffering, hard-working mother and a couple of wealthy uncles who paid for a Catholic boarding-school education south of the Border.

He also spent a year on the Continent before returning to Scotland to enter Edinburgh University in 1876 for the 'long, weary grind' of a medical student. In view of his later literary success, you have to wonder if he was cut out for what he called 'the art of curing'. The creative urge in him – inherited perhaps from his political-cartoonist grandfather and even his amateur-painter father – constantly pulled at his sleeve. He had always had a love of books, which fed his desire to write; and several of the characters he would meet at Edinburgh's famed School of Medicine were more diligently studied than the course work itself, and mentally absorbed for future reference.

The character of Sherlock Holmes is believed to have been based on that of Dr Joseph Bell, one of the medical school teachers who was thirty-nine when a seventeen-year-old Doyle first met him and was deeply impressed by him. In describing him later, the author almost seemed to be describing Holmes: 'He was a thin, wiry, dark man, with a high-nosed acute face, penetrating grey eyes, angular shoulders.' Dr Bell 'would sit in his receiving room with a face like a Red Indian, and diagnose the people as they came in, before they even opened their mouths. He would tell them details of their past life; and hardly would he ever make a mistake.'

And an 'elementary' deduction is often made that Holmes' faithful foil, Dr Watson, was based on Dr Patrick Heron Watson, who was made President of the Royal College of Surgeons some ten years before the publication of *A Study in Scarlet*.

But Conan Doyle was a doer as well as a dreamer and successfully graduated to be a (rather unconventional) doctor who, in typically adventurous fashion, started practising aboard a whaler and an African cargo steamer. It was when he settled down to practise in London and Southsea that he began to push his other talents into the public consciousness. In Southsea in early March 1886, he began work on *A Study in Scarlet*, his first story featuring Sherlock Holmes, which was finished by late April.

Though it was twice rejected by unenlightened publishers that summer, he did not have to suffer the endless humiliations that are traditionally heaped on new authors; for by October it was accepted by Ward Lock – with a payment of £25 for the complete copyright – to be the main feature in the following year's *Beeton's Christmas Annual*.

That might have been that, for such an item would normally enjoy only a single print run in the 'annual' context before being quietly forgotten. But – encouraged no doubt by the favourable reviews the piece received – the publisher decided to issue it as a separate book the following year. It was this inspired decision that would bring to the world its most-loved detective.

In the wake of more good reviews, American interest was stirred – first with the syndicator and publisher S.S. McClure, and then with Joseph M. Stoddart, who commissioned works by him (and Oscar Wilde) for *Lippincott's Magazine*, which proved such a success that

Sherlock Holmes was now assured of a continuing future. There were to be more and more stories, from 'A Scandal in Bohemia' and 'The Crooked Man' to 'The Adventure of the Blue Carbuncle' and the memorable *Hound of the Baskervilles*.

Indeed, while the moustached, gentlemanly Doyle was to write other works of real note, such as *The Lost World* and *The White Company*, the series of short stories that he began for *Strand Magazine* in 1891 spawned something of a one-man Holmes industry that featured the famous detective in no fewer than fifty-six such shorter stories and two more long ones.

How he managed to accommodate all of these in his incredibly busy life was another question. For the good twice-married doctor was also a big traveller, lecturer and sportsman (into football, cricket, golf and skiing) as well as would-be politician (who twice failed to win an MP's seat in Scotland) and champion of unusual causes (such as a campaign to repeal a 200-year-old witchcraft act being used to persecute spiritualist mediums). He even found time to establish and run a field hospital in the Boer War at the turn of the twentieth century, for which admirable initiative he was knighted in 1902.

Conan Doyle's own Holmes industry went on until three years before he died in 1930 after a heart attack. But as we all know, the great detective did not die with his creator but went on to live a burgeoning life of his own . . . celebrated in (often new) words and pictures wherever in the world thinking people were intrigued by a cerebral challenge.

Were? We should say 'are'. For it is a logical conclusion, bearing in mind all the available evidence, as Holmes might say, that the incomparable Victorian detective is likely to be with us for a very long time to come.

# James Matthew Barrie (1860–1937)

*Magician with words*

To stand in the old wash-house in the garden of J.M. Barrie's modest, small-windowed birth house is to sense the happy, creative forces that were ignited there along with the coals of the brick-rimmed iron clothes boiler. It's a tiny, cosy, hedge-fringed place a few steps from the house, and you can imagine, on a cold Scottish day, the tepid warmth lingering within the pores of its (now) prettily whitewashed stone walls.

There are, and presumably were, a few baskets and stools to sit on, so it was the ideal place for childhood friends to keep warm and entertain each other. And that is just what the young James Barrie used it for . . . putting on little plays from the age of seven, and charging admission fees of marbles or spinning tops to his already-growing fan base who relished his flights of fantasy, which often ended up with a dramatic struggle between actors trying to push each other into the boiler.

In his childhood days, of course, the Barries' friends and neighbours in Kirriemuir, the 'little red town' nestling in the agricultural hinterland of the coastal county of Angus, would not have seen the plain, foursquare house at 9 Brechin Road as modest. It was, in fact, larger than average, with its two storeys and resident human engine-room of James' two strong parents, successful handloom weaver David and his wife Margaret Ogilvy, who inspired the boy with her love of literature.

Compared to the gigantic international name that he became, however, J.M. Barrie's origins were indeed humble. The shy, often-lonely writer may never have driven into America on a golden chariot, but the impact of his work on that land, and specifically on Hollywood – and so the world – has been massive. At time of writing, for instance, Johnny Depp was starring as Barrie in the movie *Finding Neverland*, about the shy author's life and times. But films spawned from his *Peter Pan* and Neverland have emanated regularly from the

US studios ever since the play about the boy who never grew up had its premiere in the Duke of York Theatre in London over a century ago. It was a hit from the very start. So much so that the hansom cab drivers who queued outside expecting to pick up theatre-goers at the usual time of around 11.30 p.m. could not understand why they were kept waiting for so long. They learned later that it was all about standing ovations and curtain calls.

But while its instant success may have taken the then 44-year-old Barrie somewhat by surprise, it was no fluke. James Matthew Barrie was supremely well equipped to be an author and playwright. And that was not all down to the childish fun in the wash-house – his inspiration for the Wendy House in Peter Pan – which is only one of several Barrie-connected houses in Kirriemuir that give rise to some confusion among visitors.

There is also a picturesque cottage with a small but eye-catching window, which calls itself 'A Window in Thrums', after one of his works of fiction. Many people think of it as Barrie's birthplace, though he was never known to even step inside it. Neither did it even feature in the book. It is pretty, however, and worth noting if only for its dubious and mysteriously rooted claims.

More likely to have been the 'real' window in Thrums – where the work was penned – is 'Strathview', his other Kirriemuir residence at 1 Forfar Road. This deceptively large end-terrace house was where he moved to at the age of twelve – when a clerical job lured his father back to the town after a short spell in nearby Forfar – and where he decided to become an author. Born in 1860, the Barries' seventh surviving child out of ten may have lived there as part of the family for only a year before joining his brother Alexander in Dumfries, but the three-bedroom house was a place to which he would often return to for peace and inspiration, even when he was a famous figure in London.

Duncan and Sheila Philip, relatively recent owners of Strathview, were convinced that that the Thrums idea came from its upstairs window. 'I can just imagine Barrie rounding the top of Bellies Brae and catching a glimpse of his mother by the drawing room window, watching the local characters walk by,' Duncan said.

And Sheila added: 'There is definitely a warm, peaceful atmosphere throughout the house, and, of all the rooms, that feeling is strongest in the garret where Barrie worked as an author and wrote at least two novels.'

Not many people can say their mother was educated at the same school as the author of *Peter Pan*; but mine was – albeit a good couple of generations later! That was Forfar Academy, and a fine school it must have been, too, if I may judge by her enquiring mind. Barrie had that, plus his time at Glasgow Academy and Dumfries Academy, which also delivered the same kind of good old Scots education incomparably endorsed by fellow-pupil and brother Alexander becoming nothing less than Chief Inspector of Schools for Scotland.

But James was well equipped to become an author and playwright not only by virtue of this fine education, crowned by an MA degree taken at the University of Edinburgh, but also by his journalistic training – he first worked for the *Nottingham Journal* before moving to London as a freelance writer – and his own fertile imagination and intensely focused motivation. From a very early age, he had no doubts about what he wanted to do. When his adventure magazines failed to arrive on time, he would make up the following episodes himself and read them to his much-loved mother. 'From the day on which I first tasted blood in the garret my mind was made up,' he wrote. 'There could be no hum-dreadful-drum profession for me: literature was my game.'

There was another vital factor, at least with regard to the genesis of *Peter Pan*. When James was only six, his brother David, his mother's favourite, died, at the age of thirteen. And while James tried in vain to become his replacement for her, he also realised that 'I had not made her forget . . . when I became a man, he was still a boy of 13.'

The brother who never grew up was surely one of the seeds of his most famous story. But it also owed something to Barrie's befriending in London of the five boys of neighbours Arthur and Sylvia Llewelyn-Davies for whom he spun fantastic Pan-style tales, while the children themselves were the inspiration for *The Lost Boys*.

The final piece of the jigsaw was, of course, Barrie's own way of looking at life. It seems *Peter Pan* was largely autobiographical, as he himself never really wanted to grow up. 'The horror of my boyhood was that I knew a time would come when I must give up the games, and how it was to be done I saw not,' he once wrote, 'I felt I must continue playing in secret.'

Though the theatre was to become his adult playground, and his success in the medium was record-breaking – with no fewer than five London stagings, including *The Admirable Crichton* and *Quality Street* in 1902–03 – adulthood and its requirements certainly revealed his shortcomings. Not long after his first full-length play *Walker London* was staged in London in the early 1890s, he had met and married the beautiful young actress Mary Ansell. But for all his love of children, the couple had none and divorced in 1909 at the height of his fame and productivity. This has inevitably led to speculation about his sexuality and his relationships with The Boys. But one of them said later: 'I don't think Uncle Jim ever experienced what one might call a stirring in the undergrowth for anyone – man, woman or child.'

J.M. Barrie's literary output was mountainous. He wrote not only memorable novels such as *The Little Minister* (1891), *A Window in Thrums* (1889) and *Sentimental Tommy* (1896), but most of his work was as a playwright, and well remembered among his stage productions are *Quality Street* (1901), *The Admirable Crichton* (1902), *What Every Woman Knows* (1908), *Dear Brutus* (1917), *Mary Rose* (1920) and *The Boy David* (1936). But his *Peter Pan, or The Boy who Would Not Grow Up* (1904) has always been the epicentre of his celebrity.

This perceptive, complex and magical childhood fantasy caught the imagination like no other production before or since. And while the talent, time and attention he gave to it – and his entire prodigious literary output – may have inhibited his growth as a human being, they certainly won rewards for him in many other ways.

As he came to the end of his life, the quiet handloom weaver's son was loaded with honours – including a baronetcy (in 1913), the Order of Merit, the Chancellorship of Edinburgh University, and the Rectorship of St Andrews University, where he delivered a moving address on 'courage' in 1922. 'You come of a race of men the very wind of whose name has swept to the ultimate seas,' he told the students, and the sound of it was poetry.

This exciting mastery of words was silenced when Sir James Matthew Barrie died in 1937 at seventy-seven. But just like his famous immortal hero, he seems destined to live forever, at least in our collective memory.

# Harry Lauder (1870–1950)

*Darling of the diaspora*

A curious thing about those Scots who can't wait to leave Scotland is that, once away, they can think of little else, with a tear in their eye, but their native land. It was this phenomenon that made the legendary entertainer Harry Lauder so celebrated all over the world, or at least all over the Scottish diaspora – from Australia and Canada through Indonesia and China to Malaysia and the Philippines – in the early years of last century.

In global terms he was Big with a capital B, especially in America, which he toured no fewer than twenty-two times from 1908; and wherever he went he was greeted, if not mobbed, by welcoming crowds. But in human terms he was small – a dynamic, kilted, five-foot-three-inch package of cheeky Caledonian pride who, although he died over half a century ago, still figures large in Scotland's folk memory, thanks to his magical talent for playing on patriotic heartstrings at home or abroad.

This he did through the feisty, affectionate performance of sentimental Scottish songs, woven through with perfectly timed, self-deprecating banter; and although he was a big winner who became very rich, it has to be said that some fellow-countrymen did not appreciate this non-drinker's portrayal of the drunken, penny-pinching Scot contained in his bonneted, kilted caricature with its famous crooked walking stick. They felt it thrust Scotland's emerging image as a modern, civilised place back to somewhere it was urgently trying to leave. And as for penny-pinching, few can match Scots for generosity – so why did he peddle such an odd view of his own culture that has persisted to this day?

Perhaps the answer lay in his background. Born in 1870 in Edinburgh's sandy suburb of Portobello, Henry MacLennan Lauder was one of eight children who, after the death of his father – a master potter – worked as a pit boy in a coalmine near Hamilton. Though not exactly poor, he grew up in a lifestyle where pennies had to be watched in order to survive, but were occasionally squandered by the less strong on payday. So, misguided or not, his view of the typical Scot was largely subjective and, as such, perhaps forgivable. And no matter how rich he became – as the world's highest-paid stage performer, commanding $1,000 a night plus expenses – he could not forget his early pit-boy days, when he cheered himself up with a song to soften the hard edges of the dark life underground.

He cheered up his co-workers too, and soon they were making requests for 'another wee sang, Harry!' Encouraged by them to enter local talent contests, he did amateur singing on the weekends, and won prize money doing it. He eventually came second in a contest that gave him the chance to sing in small music halls. And so he was on his way – first with a concert party to Belfast, then on to international fame. But not before finding time to marry his sweetheart Nancy, daughter of the local colliery manager, who inspired him to write 'Roamin' in the Gloamin'' and 'I Love a Lassie'.

At first, his music-hall routine had been based on the simple performance of comic songs, but he soon developed a distinctive act as amusing introducer, composer and performer of his own such Scottish songs. Few of his footlight fans seemed to worry about his cartoon Scot, and as his shows became more and more talked-about at home, his fame spread first across the British Isles and then all across the Empire. His tunes were so popular that everyone seemed to know at least their choruses. He recorded hundreds of selections for many labels, and as the first British recording artist ever to sell a million records, he became (and remains) the highest-selling Scottish recording artist ever . . . still celebrated today through the singing of many of his songs.

But in the days before everyone had record players and access to easy air travel, he put tremendous energy into bringing his live performances to the people at home or abroad. Often his tours would keep him away from Britain for over two years.

The writer H.V. Morton met him on a rare moment back in Scotland in 1928 and described him as 'small, sturdy and smooth of face', adding:

> He wore hexagonal glasses and smoked a six-inch briar pipe. His Glengarry was worn at a jaunty angle and, as he walked, the almost ankle-length Inverness cape which he wore exposed a bit of a MacLeod kilt. The superior person will perhaps sniff if I suggest that no man

since Sir Walter Scott has warmed the world's heart to Scotland more
surely that Sir Harry Lauder. His genius is a thing apart.

He was certainly a master of the pithy phrase that not only made
you smile but made you think. 'Happiness,' he once said, ' is one of
the few things in this world that doubles every time you share it with
someone else.'

In thus entertaining the world, he did several tours of Australia,
where he liked to visit a brother who had emigrated there. Indeed,
he and his wife were there with their son John when the Empire
mobilised for the First World War. John was the Lauders' only child,
born in 1891 and planning a career in law after being educated at
the City of London School and Cambridge University. However, as
he sat with his parents at lunch in a Melbourne hotel in August 1914,
he was called up to fight for his country through a telegram handed
to him by a hall porter. It read: 'Mobilise. Return.'

'You know your duty, son,' said the 44-year-old father in answer to
the enquiring eyes of his 23-year-old son; but there was to be good
reason for the sad trepidation in his voice. A year and a half later,
it was another telegram – delivered on the first day of January 1917
to his hotel room in London, where he was playing the Shaftesbury
Theatre – that told Harry some dreadful news just as he was expecting
his son home:

Capt. John Lauder killed in action, December 28.
Official. War Office.

Captain John Lauder of the 8th Argyll and Sutherland Highland
Regiment was killed at Poiziers in France in late December 1916,
the victim of a sniper's bullet. His distraught father wrote later: 'I
felt that for me everything had come to an end with the reading of
that dire message. It seemed to me that for me the board of life was
black and blank. For me there was no past and there could be no
future. Everything had been swept away, erased, by one sweep of the
hand of a cruel fate.'

But the show had to go on. As he said, 'Carry on! were the last
words of my boy to his men, but he would mean them for me too.' To
the rapturous applause of an openly weeping audience – the like of
which he had never seen before – Lauder returned from Scotland to
the London stage three nights later with an act that featured a truly
painful item for him: a song about the boys coming home.

Despite – or perhaps because of – this heartbreaking personal tragedy, he resolved to get more deeply involved in war work. Unable to serve as a soldier because of his age, he sought a green light to entertain Allied soldiers in Europe, and got it. 'It's the least I can do for memory of John,' he said, as he became the first performer ever to entertain frontline troops (British and American) among the bullets of the battlefield. Travelling with a small, specially built piano tied to a military vehicle, he sang and joked his way across war-ravaged France – ending each of his shows with his theme tune, written in honour of John, 'Keep Right On to the End of the Road' – to the rare delight of his conflict-weary audiences.

But that was by no means his only contribution to the war effort. It was said that the patriotic Lauder was worth a battalion to that cause as he worked tirelessly to recruit soldiers – pulling in more than 12,000 during the remainder of the war – and to raise huge sums for war charities, including the Harry Lauder Million Pound Fund for war wounded. He even created a pipe band to stir the blood of the young and encourage them to join up. And when in the USA, he used his celebrity to urge his American fans to lobby their president and politicians to enter the conflict. Did he affect the ultimate course of events? We shall never know, but . . .

For all of this – even before his repeat performance in the Second World War at the request of his admirer Winston Churchill, who called him 'Scotland's greatest ever ambassador' – Harry Lauder was made the 'first knight of the music hall' in 1919 under the ceremonial sword of King George V.

Among his many other honours were the Freedom of the City of Edinburgh in 1927 (the year his wife died) and – posthumously – the naming of a modern bypass near his birthplace of Portobello as Sir Harry Lauder Road. His other achievements included the writing of several books, among them four volumes of memoirs, and his appearance in numerous movies.

The curtain came down on Sir Harry Lauder's last performance in Glasgow's Gorbals in 1947, and three years later he died in Lanarkshire at the age of seventy-nine. He was buried after the most memorable funeral ever to be seen in closed-for-the-day Hamilton – where Pathé, the cinema news service, reported that among the grieving, street-lining crowds were wreaths not only from Mr & Mrs Winston Churchill, but also from the Queen.

The end of Sir Harry's road was a long way from a 'wee sang' in a coalmine.

# Alexander Fleming (1881–1955)

*The 'accidental' lifesaver*

There was something of the absent-minded boffin about the shy, short, bow-tied Alexander Fleming. The 47-year-old Scottish professor of bacteriology was not the most organised of people and, being happy to live with some faith in serendipity – 'one sometimes finds what one is not looking for' – he was not overly surprised when he returned to his laboratory at London's St Mary's Hospital after a two-week vacation in September, 1928, to find some mould had colonised his working equipment. But he was intrigued when he noticed something unusual about its behaviour.

He had left a culture dish smeared with staphylococcus bacteria (which turns wounds septic) exposed in a dark corner of his workbench. Spores had drifted in through the window and taken root on the dish, and around the resulting mould there was a clear absence of staphylococcal colonies. The realisation that these had been killed or at least inhibited by the mould was Fleming's 'eureka' moment – and a catalytic point in the treatment of bacterial infections. Surely the first antibiotic had been discovered? Surely the principle could now be developed to benefit all humankind?

Fleming immediately saw such possibilities for his discovery, which he called penicillin because the substance had been produced by the fungal mould *Penicillium notatum*. But his excitement was to be short-lived, for when he presented his findings to the Medical Research Club in 1929 its members could raise little or no interest. A similar response greeted his report on penicillin and its potential uses in the *British Journal of Experimental Pathology*. Other scientists tried in vain to replicate Fleming's result, not realising that an accidental conjunction of temperatures, helped by the open window, had been the key – so much so that when in later years he found himself in a modern, air-conditioned lab in America, he remarked that 'I would never have made my discovery in these conditions'.

In any case, paradoxically, interest in penicillin began to fade in the years immediately after its discovery – as it was ineffective on animals when given by mouth, and proved apparently impossible to produce in volume. Growing and refining it was clearly a complex challenge, which would be better suited to chemists or scientists, and their help would not be forthcoming until the imperatives of the Second World War revitalised interest – on a massive scale, particularly in America – as such a new anti-bacterial would surely prove vital to the successful treatment of wounded soldiers.

Known as 'Alec' to his seven siblings, Alexander Fleming was born into a family working an 800-acre sheep farm near Dalry in Ayrshire, south-west Scotland, in 1881. He was a bright pupil at Kilmarnock High School and in his spare time loved to roam the glens, rivers and woods of the countryside – 'where we unconsciously learned a great deal from nature' – with his brothers and sisters. After his father died and his eldest brother took over the farm, the fourteen-year-old Alec joined three Fleming brothers (one a medical student) and one sister living together in London. He went to the Polytechnic School in Regent Street, and started his working life in a shipping firm. Not being enthralled by the prospect of a career in that field, he decided to study medicine and eventually entered St Mary's Hospital in London, where he proceeded to live out his expected quiet life as a respectable, anonymous bacteriologist. Until penicillin crashed into his life.

Which is not to say he had not been enterprising up to then. He had pioneered the introduction to Britain of Salvarsan, a killer of the micro-organism that causes syphilis, and while serving in the Royal Army Medical Corps in the First World War, began work that would to lead to his discovery in 1922 of lysozyme – a bacteria-killing protein found in tears. But penicillin was the Big One, and in 1929 he got a hint of its effectiveness in humans when his assistant's infection was relieved through washing out the sinus with a penicillin broth.

Fleming was no chemist who could properly isolate the substance, however, and he must have been pleased when, prompted by the war requirement about a decade later, a few Oxford University scientists began intensive research based on his original report – and were encouraged in May 1940, after injecting eight mice with a lethal dose of streptococci, and four of them also with penicillin. The latter four survived.

Thus emboldened, they began to scale up production – using bed-pans, milk churns and bathtubs – with a view to experimenting with penicillin on humans. Their first patient, a 43-year-old policeman, died from staphylococcal infection, which he had at first appeared to be defeating under a four-day penicillin course; but a fifteen-year-old boy suffering from streptococcal septicaemia made a full recovery.

So the era of antibiotics had begun in earnest . . . in February 1941. But although they could thus show penicillin's ability to kill infectious bacteria, the Oxford scientists could not produce the quantities needed for large-scale clinical trials on humans. They looked across the Atlantic for help, and on 9 July 1941, two of them, Dr Howard Florey and Norman Heatley, set out for the USA with a small package of penicillin that would be the seed of a new miracle.

So, with the help of Heatley and a mouldy cantaloupe, it fell to America's scientists and pharmaceutical industry to meet the challenge of large-scale production. And by November of that year Dr Andrew J. Moyer, at his lab in Peoria, Arizona, to which the British team had been sent – as its scientists were already working on fermentation methods to accelerate fungal culture growth rates – had succeeded in increasing the yields of penicillin tenfold.

Its first tests for military use took place in the spring of 1943, with studies on American soldiers with chronic bacterial infections, and by autumn it was being used in combat zones, where it was limited to US and Allied military and to patients with life-threatening infections. Flight crews of the Eighth Air Force stationed in Britain were the first to benefit from it directly and, although there was strict rationing during the war, the armed forces received 85 per cent of America's production – 231 billion units in 1943 and, as production systems improved, 1,633 billion in 1944 and 7,952 billion in 1945. Finally mass-produced by the American drugs industry and given to all soldiers before active service, penicillin became the war's 'wonder drug' and saved the lives of thousands of wounded men.

Fleming was knighted for his work in 1944. The following year he shared with Florey and Ernst Chain – a chemist who had worked on medicinal properties of penicillin – the Nobel Prize for medicine 'for the discovery of penicillin and its curative effect in various infectious diseases'. And in 1990, Oxford University gave an unprecedented honorary doctorate to Norman Heatley for his work on the drug. Dr Moyer from the Peoria Lab was inducted into the Inventors' Hall of Fame and both the British and Peoria laboratories were designated as International Historic Chemical Landmarks.

Of his honour, Heatley, ninety-two and still living in Oxford at time of writing, said: 'This is an enormous privilege since I am not medically qualified . . . I was a third-rate scientist whose only merit was to be in the right place at the right time.'

Despite being the only member of the Oxford team still alive, he was certainly not about to upstage the equally diffident Scot whose 'accidental' achievement created the world's most effective life-saving drug that would conquer some of mankind's most ancient scourges. Sir Alexander Fleming died in 1955 and was buried in St Paul's Cathedral, London.

# John Logie Baird (1888–1946)

*The original man of vision*

Margaret Baird glowed with pride when she talked about her famous husband, but her disappointment with mysterious powers-that-be was equally plain to see. She could not understand why, in an age that scattered honours on people of relatively minor achievement, there had been no acknowledgement of the globally significant pioneering television work of John Logie Baird. 'I feel terribly sad that Logie wasn't properly honoured by his country,' she said, a decade before she died in 1996 at eighty-nine.

She had lived half a century beyond her husband and had come to see many of the changes in society he had foretold – not least the idea that every sitting room would one day have a TV set: a prediction so alarming to a 1920s reporter that he fled from Baird's presence thinking he was a dangerous lunatic.

But in a world that was now taking TV for granted, Mrs Baird clearly had fun making people gasp by saying, just by the way: 'Television? Oh, yes, my husband invented it.'

John Logie Baird always thought about sixty years ahead of his time, she explained to Dorothy-Grace Elder, who interviewed her for the *Scotsman Magazine*. 'Britain could have had colour TV in the Thirties if people had listened to him. And he went into video in 1928, recording moving images on wax discs.'

The pioneering genius was born in Helensburgh, a son of the manse – which is now a private house bearing a plaque that reads: 'John Logie Baird, inventor of Television, was born in this house on August 13, 1888'. There is also a monument to him tucked away in a local park.

It was in England, though, that he did most of his important work, having moved there after studying electrical engineering at Glasgow University and trying his hand at being a sales representative. Specifically, it was in his attic workshop in London's Frith Street that he made the first television transmission of a moving image on 30 October 1925 – a hugely exciting advance on his earlier transmission of the static shadow of a Maltese Cross across ten feet in his laboratory in Hastings.

When Baird received a screen image of a doll's head on that October night – 'not as a mere smudge of black and white but as a real image with detail' – he ran across the street to hire an office boy as a live model to front the camera.

'I placed him before the transmitter and went into the next room to see what the screen would show,' he recalled in an interview in the USA six years later.

> It was entirely blank and no effort of tuning would produce any results. Puzzled and disappointed, I went back to the transmitter and there the cause of the failure became at once evident. The boy, scared by the intense white light, had backed away from the transmitter.
>
> In the excitement of the moment I gave him half a crown and this time he kept his head in the right position. Going again into the next room, this time I saw his head quite clearly. It is curious that the first person in the world to have been seen by television should have required a bribe to accept that distinction.

Three months later, Baird gave two demonstrations of 'true television' – to the press and to members of the Royal Institution. 'We saw the transmission by television of living human faces, the proper gradation of light and shade and all movements of the head, of the lips and mouth and of a cigarette and its smoke were faithfully portrayed on a screen in the theatre,' wrote Dr Alexander Russell of Faraday House later. 'Naturally, the results are far from perfect. The image cannot be compared with that of a good kinematograph film. The likeness, however, was unmistakable and all the motions are reproduced with absolute fidelity. This is the first time that we have seen real television and Mr Baird is the first to have accomplished this marvellous feat.'

Despite the system's development eventually parting company from him, it can't be denied that this first heady breakthrough belonged to Baird. His mechanical set-up was pitched against the formidable resources of the giant Marconi company and, despite working in an attic on a shoestring, begging £10 batteries from friends, 'he won' – his widow claimed quite categorically – 'he was the first. And he was determined to get that first for Britain and for Scotland.'

But while Baird continued experimenting with his mechanical system, his rivals were looking into electronic systems, and he was devastated when, after working on ideas and trial programmes with the BBC 'for ages', the corporation – under fellow-Scot but old adversary Lord Reith – chose Marconi to take its TV plans forward. 'My husband was appalled,' said Mrs Baird, a South African-born concert pianist who had two children with John Logie Baird. 'But with typical courage, he plunged deeper into colour TV work.'

Meanwhile, news of his achievement had crossed the Atlantic and he began to pin his hopes on the more entrepreneurial spirit of America. Taking a business trip to assess possibilities, he was amazed to receive a hero's welcome – complete with pipe band – when he arrived in New York in 1931. He felt there was more chance of his developing television in the USA, and said so in a radio broadcast:

> The whole atmosphere of New York is very different from that of Europe. It is an atmosphere of 'go ahead' vigour, welcoming of novelty and enterprise. The people here are, to use a New York expression, 'all out for progress', whereas in Europe we are inclined to look with distrust and suspicion on anything new . . .
>
> Throughout the world the highest scientific thought is being devoted to television. Vast strides have been made and will be made in this new art. I myself look forward to seeing at no distant day, television theatres supersede the talkies, and the home television become as common as the home radio is today.

But after he returned to Britain a promising deal he had concluded for a jointly operated television station with Donald Flamm – owner of New York's WMCA radio station – was barred by the Federal Radio Commission in Washington on several spurious grounds, one of which was that Baird's company was foreign and, as such, should have no part in American broadcasting.

It could all have been so different if the commission had been more magnanimous. Baird, whose heart and health would have certainly appreciated a move to sunny California or Florida, could have followed in the footsteps of telephone inventor Alexander Graham Bell (see page 80), whose Scottish ingenuity was welcomed even before he became one of America's developmental heroes. As it was, Britain's cold, damp, wartime climate – in more ways than one – so weakened the television inventor that he died in 1946 at the cruelly early age of fifty-seven.

A genius, a world-beater, and a true prophet without honour in his own land.

# Robert Watson-Watt (1892–1973)

*Opener of the eye in the sky*

Of all the defence mechanisms, brainwaves and acts of defiance that kept Britain free of Nazi occupation during the Second World War, the most important had to be Radio Detection and Ranging – or radar for short. Along with Winston Churchill, it arrived just in time to save the country in its darkest hour. But unlike Churchill, its brilliant inventor never seemed to get full credit for his amazing achievement, whose peacetime application remains vitally important today – keeping, as it does, aviation and shipping running like clockwork.

Bespectacled and ruddy-cheeked, the studious-looking Scot was not everyone's picture of a war hero. But his lack of fame then, and even now, was and is more to do with the culture of secrecy that surrounded breakthroughs like his at times of international tension. And Robert Watson-Watt's achievement did not go entirely unacknowledged, as he was quietly knighted during the war to which he contributed so effectively.

A direct descendant of James Watt, the famous steam pioneer, Watson-Watt was born in 1892 in the cathedral 'city' of Brechin – actually a small town eight miles inland from Scotland's north-east coast – and studied engineering, before teaching physics, at Dundee's University College, which was part of St Andrews University at the time.

When he found his next challenge down in England he approached it rather warily, as studying the weather in the Meteorological Office of the new Royal Aircraft Establishment at Farnborough in Kent was a far cry from the heavy engineering he was mentally geared up to. But he found himself becoming intrigued by the possibilities of applying radio to predict the approach of bad weather, which airmen could then be warned about.

His interest in the reflection of radio waves quickly grew, and when only twenty-eight, he took out a patent concerning radio location by means of short-wave radio. He worked on improvements to relevant systems throughout the 1920s and, as his endeavours came to the notice of the British government, he was asked in 1935 if, based on such a principle, he could give some thought to developing a 'death ray' capable of taking out enemy aircraft. His answer was an emphatic 'No', but he offered a considerable consolation: the suggestion that such a 'ray' idea could perhaps be applied to the problem of locating approaching enemy aircraft.

As radio waves always travel at the speed of light, he explained, the position of any large object from which they bounced could be easily worked out. Not surprisingly, great interest was expressed in such a proposition and, before the year was out, Watson-Watt was perfecting a system that could follow an aircraft – as a blip on a screen – by the radio-wave reflection it sent back.

This was the birth of radar, right on time to catch the war clouds gathering over Europe, and as its military significance was immediately appreciated, further research and development had to go underground. Successful trials of the new system were carried out in total secrecy on a remote Suffolk airfield and, as Watson-Watt's team worked on under his guidance, five radio location stations were set up along the south coast of England. And soon, with war becoming a distinct possibility and radar now having an effective range of seventy-five miles, the government made plans for another twenty stations to act as an insurance policy against enemy invasion from across the English Channel

Watson-Watt's work was thus Britain's stunning trump card when the conflict did begin . . . and Luftwaffe planes finally did drone over the horizon in frightening waves. Radar came into its own particularly during the Battle of Britain, by alerting defending RAF fighters to the position of attacking enemy planes in all weathers and as easily by night as by day. So with 'the few' numerically disadvantaged British pilots showing memorably selfless courage that maximised their remarkable technical advantage, the apparently unequal battle turned – much to the Germans' surprise – in Britain's favour. Radar also helped to knock out scores of German aircraft when a badly stung Hitler switched his tactics to night bombing.

The ingenious inventor of radar must have felt very sorry, however, that the United States had not managed to similarly benefit from such a system when waves of Japanese planes attacked Pearl Harbor in 1941. Although he had visited America to help its technical teams complete its radar system, and although that was in place in time – and showed the enemy planes approaching – its warning was tragically ignored through a misreading of the big blip on the screen as a flight of American B-17s due in from the mainland.

Nevertheless, Sir Robert Watson-Watt must have been more than reasonably satisfied with his world-changing achievement when he died in 1973 in Inverness, the northern Scottish town to which he had retired. Quietly . . .

# Sean Connery (1930–   )

*Bottom drawer to superstar*

Writing on the British side of the Atlantic, it is not always easy to judge the degree of impact that this or that important Scot has had on America. On occasion, therefore, a San Francisco-born-and-resident contact has been called in to make a judgement out of ten. Thus we know that Sir Sean Connery couldn't have made bigger waves in the USA, for – after our contact's circle of friends had been sounded – the figure that came back was ten-out-of-ten.

Something for native Scots to bask in the reflection of? Well, perhaps surprisingly, yes.

There are few people of his generation living in Sir Sean's Edinburgh today who won't claim to have some memory of, or connection with, 'Big Tam' – as the over-familiar call him, affecting to have known him before he chose to use his middle name – and some might even be telling the truth. The fact is that Scotland in general, and Edinburgh in particular, is uncharacteristically proud of its super-famous film-star son. Why uncharacteristically? Because it has long been a dour, inexplicable Scottish trait to pour scorn on the Scots who have done well beyond the country's borders. So why, having done miles better than most, is Sir Sean still so favoured at home? He is admired by politicians who seek his endorsement; by bank clerks who see in him the man they'd love to be; and of course by women, among whom you can number hotel chamber maids who compete with each other just to enter his room and breathe his (shaken, not stirred) after-shave.

What's his secret? I believe that, as a mature role-player, he is unusually comfortable being a two-in-one person – a passionate Rangers-supporting Scot and a world movie icon – and sees no conflict between the parts. If some Scots' traditional resentment of such figures is largely born of a fear that they and the old country's culture will be abandoned by the Talented One as he or she flies over the horizon, Connery has never done that. Despite all his years and layers of global success, he has always returned to express a burning love for his homeland. This may have led him down some tricky alleyways (such as support for the Scottish Nationalist Party, an allegiance said to have delayed his knighthood) but its obvious sincerity has been appreciated. And when he finally arose to accept the honour from the Queen in 2000, he looked like the King of Scotland: no one can wear a kilt with such presence and aplomb.

Some, of course, are not satisfied with that and argue that, if he feels so much for Caledonia, why doesn't he live there? Americans might equally argue that, if he thrives on the largesse of Hollywood, why doesn't he make his home in America? These are obviously taxing questions, in more ways than one, for a man who has lived in Spain and was latterly resident in the Bahamas, though he has run an office in Culver City, California, for his erstwhile film production company, sentimentally named Fountainbridge Films.

Fountainbridge is, of course, the name of the street in west Edinburgh where, at No. 176, he grew up as one of two brothers born of working-class (but conspicuously handsome) parents. His father, Joseph, was a truck driver and his mother, Euphemia, a charwoman. Their crowded family apartment had only two rooms and no interior toilet, and the baby Sean slept in the bottom drawer of his parents' wardrobe. Their home has long been demolished but, perhaps a hundred steps from where it used to be, there is a plaque on a high garden wall in his honour. Sir Sean is reported to have said, on seeing it, that 'they might have waited till I was dead'. But it is hardly a fitting marker for so big a presence on the world stage. One can imagine that if the Scottish capital were an American city, it would be comprehensively promoted with signs and posters as 'Connery's Town'. This one-foot-square colour-tinted plate sits on the wall opposite the entrance to the old Fountain Brewery and is almost too high – at something like nine feet – to read. 'You would have to be ten foot tall to see it,' he has said. Certainly, the camera-festooned Chicago couple at the spot when this writer went to check it out were having a hard stretch to register the words:

Commemorating the Century of Cinema 1996

SEAN CONNERY

Born Fountainbridge

25th August 1930

Oscar-winning actor

International Film Star

The Scottish Film Council

A more fitting tribute by far would be the proposed Connery Filmhouse, possible new home of the Edinburgh International Film Festival. Sir Sean was on hand to see the model of architect Richard Murphy's £20 million vision unveiled in the city in September 2004, and he obviously approved – with one reservation, expressed to Tim Cornwell of *The Scotsman*: 'It's very flattering, but there's one thing wrong. I think if it's using Connery, it's better with the whole name.'

While this impressive flight of modern fancy was only at the design stage, it bore not just Connery's name but his picture – in the form of a miniature from *The Name of the Rose*, one of his most remembered films, released in 1986.

Neither can it ever be forgotten, of course, that Connery skyrocketed to international fame in the 1960s as the suave, confident secret agent 007 in six movies of Ian Fleming's Bond stories. Portraying such an English hero could never have been an easy matter for a simple lad with an Edinburgh accent, but he – and his amazingly expressive eyebrows – rose to the challenge to the satisfaction not just of the public who said a big yes to *Dr No* (1962), but of the producers. So over the next decade, more Bonds came thick and fast: *From Russia, With Love* (1963), *Goldfinger* (1964), *Thunderball* (1965), *You Only Live Twice* (1967) and *Diamonds are Forever* (1971). Eventually feeling in danger of being typecast, however, he branched out with an Agatha Christie whodunnit, *Murder on the Orient Express* (1974), John Huston's adaptation of Rudyard Kipling's *The Man Who Would Be King* (1975), the medieval romance *Robin and Marian* (1976) and Peter Hyams' sci-fi film, *Outland* (1981). He resurfaced as a noticeably older Bond in the 1983 adventure, *Never Say Never Again*.

The maturing Connery's 1990s featured such great films as *The Hunt for Red October* (1990, as a Russian submarine commander); and 1993's *Rising Sun* (as an expert in all things Japanese); *Dragonheart* (1996); and the successful contemporary action dramas *Just Cause* (1995) and *The Rock* (1996). In 1999, he starred in and produced *Entrapment*, a love story-thriller, co-starring Catherine Zeta-Jones. The year 2000 brought what many have said to be one of his best films, *Finding Forrester*, and in 2003 he made the acclaimed *League of Extraordinary Gentlemen*, while 2004 saw the making of *Josiah's Canon*, in which he played a Holocaust survivor planning a bank heist in Switzerland. But it was as a representative of the other side of the law – an Irish cop – that he gave his most memorable, Oscar-winning performance in *The Untouchables* (1987).

In all, he has made around seventy films in a non-stop tour de force of a career that the poor boy from Fountainbridge can be more than satisfied with, as he looks back at his magical life from his Bahamian poolside. He has been twice married, to remarkable women: to actress Diane Cilento (with whom he has an actor son, Jason) from 1962 to 1973, and latterly, for almost thirty years, to artist Micheline Roquebrune. It could have turned out a lot differently . . .

Life did not look too promising for lads like him who left school at fourteen in the 1940s. There were jobs, nevertheless, and the young Sean tried his hand at many of them. It is almost the stuff of legend that he began his working life as a milkman, and those who witnessed his deliveries can still dine out on the memories. But the wide world beckoned and at sixteen he enlisted in the Royal Navy. Like many young men in that service, he opted for a tattoo but unusually, he did not live to regret it, as his tattoos reflect two of his big lifelong loves – Scotland and his family. One reads 'Mum and Dad', the other 'Scotland Forever'.

His naval career was abruptly cut short, after three years, by a stomach ulcer. When he came back to Edinburgh he went like a dose of salts through one job after another: bricklayer, lifeguard and French polisher (in which role he is reputed to have held no fewer than five appointments with cabinet-making firms). He was a steel worker for eight weeks, and a male model at Edinburgh College of Art. He sampled cement mixing, he cleaned the printing machines for the *Edinburgh Evening News*, and he was a lifeguard at the now-defunct open-air Portobello swimming pool – where his looks and physique were much admired by the girls from the nearby Duncan's chocolate factory.

No matter what you worked at in Edinburgh in those days, you were almost bound to have bumped into 'Big Tam', or at least someone who knew him. 'I used to watch him and his super-fit colleagues doing their press-ups at the pool,' recalls an old contemporary, 'and one day much later I recognised him retrospectively, as it were, when he appeared in a television production, and I thought: "I've seen you before".'

Indeed, Sean spent much of his free time bodybuilding, and it was to that pastime that he owed the eventual breakthrough into acting. The hobby brought him into a bid for the 1952 Mr Universe title in London. He took third place and was duly noticed.

But Sean Connery was no overnight success. Like many a hopeful Scot before him, he did not find the streets of London paved with gold. 'I spent a lot of time alone,' he told an interviewer. 'I was living in a basement eating minestrone, which would last me three days. In the winter I would cycle up to Chelsea library – because it was warm there – and read and read.' He did some modelling before getting his chorus part in the London stage production of *South Pacific*. He played some bit parts and, as his hard work began to pay off, won some praise for his performance in the TV play *Requiem for a Heavyweight*. And from those modest beginnings, he was to start building the track that would take him all the way to becoming an international film icon.

There followed a series of films – *Hell Drivers* with Sid James and *Time Lock*, but, before these were released in late 1957, Sean would sign a long-term deal with 20th Century Fox, worth £120 a week. It produced little work, however – his accent was seen as a problem – and he had to make do with a small part as a sailor in Terence Young's *Action Of The Tiger*.

Unable to offer him anything more, Fox now loaned Connery out for *Another Time, Another Place*, with a fading Lana Turner playing a newspaperwoman seduced by Sean's war correspondent in London during the Blitz. Sadly, the movie was a failure, but Terence Young had not forgotten the Scot's screen presence, and neither had another very important person who met him during the making of the movie – Cubby Broccoli.

Four years later, Connery's name kept coming up when Broccoli and Harry Salzman were preparing to bring Ian Fleming's Bond novels to the screen, with Young as director. Rex Harrison, David Niven and Cary Grant had all said 'No' to the part and Connery should have had a clear field; but reservations kept being expressed about his accent and rough edges. It couldn't be denied that Harrison, Niven and Grant were more in the posh, private school image that Fleming had presumably meant for his hero – also a Scot, but educated under the tall tower of very expensive Fettes, Alma Mater of Tony Blair. Connery had only ever delivered milk to that school.

Nevertheless, the self-made Broccoli – said to be from the Italian family who developed the vegetable of that name by crossing a cauliflower and a pea – was not unsympathetic to simple roots. And he had a brainwave that would settle all doubts. Among the Scot's more recent films had been a silly Disney fantasy about leprechauns called *Darby O'Gill and the Little People* in which he played a burly farmhand who won a fist fight with a village bully.

Aware that he was no judge of masculine appeal, Broccoli obtained a copy of that film and called his wife Dana, who later recalled the catalytic moment that was to be the making of Sean Connery: 'One day Cubby called me and said: "Could you come down and look at this film at the Goldwyn Studios? I think I've found the guy but I don't know if he has sex appeal." I went and watched the film. I saw that face and the way he moved and talked, and I said: "Cubby, he's fabulous!" He was just perfect. He had star material right there.'

Despite United Artists sending a telegram that read 'See if you can do better', Connery was offered the part and accepted. So in November 1961, he signed up as James Bond in a deal that would hold him for six years. And not even author Ian Fleming demurred. 'When I first met Fleming, there was no dissension between us on how to see Bond,' the actor told interviewer Sheldon Lane in 1965. 'I saw him as a complete sensualist – senses highly tuned, awake to everything, quite amoral. I particularly like him because he thrives on conflict.'

There was acknowledgement that some smoothing-out would have to be done, and *Dr No* director Young – a quintessential Englishmen with many Bond-like qualities himself – took Connery under his tutoring wing, teaching him how to walk, talk and even how to eat and dress. Connery knew he was ready to become Bond when Young took him to his own tailor to have a suit made in London's Savile Row. Thus transformed into a Young-style gentleman, it was a new man with new confidence who went out on his first outing as James Bond, for which he received an upfront fee of £5,000. And the rest, as they say, is history. As it happened, he did not lose all his Scottish edges on screen – and proved that they could be compelling to the point of winning him *People* magazine's title of 'sexiest man alive' while incidentally propelling him towards being one of the world's most adored and bankable stars, commanding millions per movie.

In the spring of 2006, he finally called it a day, vowing to make no more films. But now, in his mid seventies, he could reflect with some satisfaction that it hadn't been a bad career for the baby from the bottom drawer in Fountainbridge.

# Jim Clark (1936–68)

*Conqueror of the Brickyard*

In any overview of the life and times of Jim Clark, racing driver extraordinary, we are told he was a man who could hold his fame like some fellow-Scots can hold their whisky; a man of world-scale achievement, which could only be matched by the depth of his niceness and modesty. He certainly had smiling eyes and a shy, likeable face, which in many ways belied the macho world of speed in which he lived (and prematurely died). This picture of a gifted gentleman is confirmed by quotes from many contemporaries, not least his friend and equally famous Scottish rival, Sir Jackie Stewart, who said of him (in an interview with David Frost): 'He was the best racing driver I ever raced against . . . he was smooth, he was clean, he was honest, he was courteous, he was dignified, on and off the track . . . a master.'

This writer also had reason to be impressed by Jim Clark. Having dealings in different offices in the same building in London's Fleet Street, we once passed on the stairs as he dashed down to the street. As a fan, I felt I knew him and said spontaneously, 'Hi, Jim' – to which he smilingly replied, not knowing me at all: 'Hi there, how are you?' Despite having interviewed a number of well-known people in-depth over the decades, I treasure that small, superficial moment as a piquant brush with the life of an immortal great.

But America also had reason to be impressed by this polite young racer, who numbered among his many achievements two Formula I world championship titles. For in 1965, only a few years into his track career, he set the US motor-racing world back on its heels by registering a stunning triumph in the Indianapolis 500, jewel in the crown of the once all-American race calendar. Not only did US drivers have a wake-up call; the rear-engined design of Clark's winning Lotus began to change the style of their race-cars from that moment on.

So who was this little Scottish upstart who so upset the Brickyard?

Jim Clark was born into a farming family at Kilmany near Cupar in Fife – north of the Scottish capital of Edinburgh – in 1936. He was the only son among five children, and his early enthusiasm for sheep rearing allowed his parents the hope that he would follow his father into a farm career; but when he caught the speed bug, it was not to be. After a family move to the Borders – where the town of Duns now has a museum room devoted to him – he became intrigued by sports car racing there and, on joining the Borders Reivers team, chalked up some impressive local victories in a Jaguar. Thus encouraged, he was soon off to the Brands Hatch track in England where, in late 1958, he raced a Lotus Elite so well that he made a big impression on Colin Chapman, who just beat him to the flag. Chapman was, of course, the prime mover at the Lotus racing operation and wasted no time in inviting Clark to test a Lotus Formula II car.

The lad did not disappoint, and so his short but potent career was exclusively with the Lotus team, for which he drove from the Dutch Grand Prix in 1960 until his untimely death in 1968. In all, he won 33 Grand Prix pole positions and 25 victories in just 77 starts. He was only three years into his driving career when he won seven out of the ten races in 1963 – to gain his first world championship title. And he repeated that world-beating performance in 1965, when he again won the championship. That was the year he also won the Indianapolis 500, much to the chagrin of his rivals.

His appearances in the Indy races of 1963 (when he came second) and 1964 (led, but retired) had put the cat among the racing pigeons. The drivers of the big front-engined roadsters initially laughed at the 'funny' European rear-engined Lotuses, but by the start of the 1964 race as many as twenty-one of the sixty-one entered cars were rear-engined.

In the event, Clark became the first driver to top 160 m.p.h. at the Brickyard and won the 1965 Indy 500 after leading for no fewer than 190 out of the 200 laps. America in general, and intense rivals like Parnelli Jones in particular, gasped with surprise – and admiration – for a world champion driver who was apparently without equal.

Meanwhile, however, a second Scots star was rising fast. Jackie Stewart had already served notice in Europe that he was about to challenge all the established great drivers of the day, and when he and his famous English team-mate Graham Hill got moving at the following year's chaotic Indy 500, Jim Clark did not have it all his own way. Described by one newspaper as 'the most fantastic, confused and incredible 500', the race's result is still a matter of controversy today among motor-racing aficionados. The complexities that arose after a sixteen-car tangle that stopped the race for over an hour resulted in Hill being declared the surprise winner – though Clark thought he had won, and Stewart probably would have won if his engine had not blown up.

Just before that point, he had taken the lead from Clark, who had spun twice, and it looked – in his own words – 'as if we were about to give them a double Scotch'. But it was not to be even a single Scotch. While Clark's crew continued to flash the P-1 sign to him, the race ended with Hill being declared winner and – despite protests that he had been incorrectly scored with an extra lap – he went home to England with the winner's cheque for $156,297.

Just how much Stewart received for his official sixth place, I don't know, but on his return to Scotland, I had occasion to be sitting with him (and his editor for a magazine column) in Glasgow's Lorne Hotel, when a waiter came up to congratulate him on his exciting performance. He smiled and said: 'At least my bank manager's happy with me at last!'

Soon, of course, the 'double Scotch' effect became apparent to all, as – the Lotus having become temporarily uncompetitive after an engine rule change – Clark's career fortunes began to level out while Stewart's rose. Ironically, it was just after a South African Grand Prix win had marked a brighter start to his 1968 season that Jim Clark tragically lost his life when his Lotus left the track and crashed into trees in a Formula II race at Hockenheim. He was thirty-two.

Many people still say his natural talent was such that, had he lived, he would have broken every record in the book. But that ignores the fact that he would have had to contend with Stewart, who quickly took on his friend's mantle and went on to do what he might have done. The new Scot on the scene, a garage-owner's son from Dumbarton, won his first of three world titles in 1969 and the other two in 1971 and 1973. And in all, he won 27 of the 101 races he competed in.

But Clark and Stewart are not the only two Scots to have had an impact on the motor-racing life of America . . .

Dario Franchitti may have an Italian-sounding name, but he comes from the little town of Bathgate, in the Scottish central belt between Glasgow and Edinburgh, and cites many Scottish cultural references in his published biographies – he admires fellow-Scot Sean Connery; rates Edinburgh and Glasgow respectively as first and second before

San Francisco in his choice of top cities; keeps a house in Dalgety Bay, Scotland; and was married – to film star Ashley Judd – at the old home of Andrew Carnegie, Skibo Castle near Dornoch, Sutherland, in 2001.

Franchitti began his career in karting, becoming the Scottish Junior Champion at the age of eleven. By 1994, he was having significant success in Formula III racing. He moved to the USA to become involved in the Championship Auto Racing Teams (CART) competitions, and almost clinched the championship in 1999. His transition to the Indy Racing League (IRL) IndyCar Series in 2003 was one of the most highly anticipated in the league and only spoiled by a back injury sustained in a motorcycle accident. He was literally back on track in 2004 and 2005 with the successful Andretti Green Racing team, and at time of writing it seemed only a matter of time before the 31-year-old took the Indy 500 chequered flag.

Now based in Nashville, Tennessee, Dario is frequently put forward in Europe as a potential Formula I driver, and he calls Jackie Stewart the person to have most influenced his life, after only his father George and mother Marina. Watch this space . . .

# Tom Farmer (1940–  )

*Kwik way to a billion*

Anyone who can get an American corporate giant to deposit more than one and a half billion dollars into his bank account has to be a serious player on the world's business stage. But the recipient in this case – the Scots entrepreneur Sir Tom Farmer – owed much of it, metaphorically at least, back to the United States. For he admits gracefully and gratefully that he got the inspiration for his world-famous Kwik-Fit enterprise from the time he lived in California; and, in the end, after it grew to be the biggest automotive repair chain in the world, the learning feeling was entirely mutual and reciprocal.

It was no surprise to Scots watching its rapid growth from home that Sir Tom's huge company eventually attracted the attention of a diversifying Ford around the turn of the millennium. The surprise was that, up to then, there had never been a direct involvement from that side of the Atlantic in its thirty-year history. The whole culture of his company, not least the happy-zappy name – which became a household word throughout Europe and much of the world – was a Scottish tribute to the American way of doing things, and as such a supreme example of cultural cross-pollenisation in business.

How did it happen? The youngest of a brood of seven children, Tom Farmer was born in Leith – the Scottish capital's port area – in 1940, and, like his shipbuilder father, was interested in ships; but when a medical test proved him colour-blind, he failed in his first ambition to become a merchant seaman. Keen to get going in life, however, he left Holy Cross School at fourteen to become a store boy with a tyre company – where, while sweeping the floor, his entrepreneurial instincts saw him studying out of the corner of his eye just how such a business worked. For he already knew he wanted to do something like that for himself. And today, as he sits in the smart surroundings of his clean-lined modern office which fills a handsome old Edinburgh house, the maturing Sir Tom, now engaged in yet another ambitious car-oriented scheme, recalls being quite a dynamic youth who dabbled in ventures such as cooker cleaning, a service which he advertised with the eye-catching spelling 'Kookers Kleaned'. It was to come back and help him . . .

Hanging on the office wall behind him is a painting of a modest corner premises in the city's Buccleuch Street near the university. This was the former grocer's shop where, when he was in his early twenties in the mid-1960s, he started his first serious business, Tyre and Accessory Supplies. Drawing on that early tyre-firm experience, he bought tyres at a discount and offered the refreshingly new service of fitting them for customers outside the relatively quiet shop he rented for what sounds today like an absurd figure: £5 a week.

He was still only twenty-eight when, six years after opening it, he sold that company to the English-owned Albany Tyre Service. And when he then suggested to his young wife Anne that they take their two little children to California 'to retire' on the considerable fortune the sale had yielded, 'she just said, "fine"'.

They went to live in Orinda, in Marin County, outside San Francisco, where Tom had a sister, but the couple of years they spent there felt like a vacation, as they went out of their way to see and savour all the local sights and experiences. It turned out, however, that what Tom was savouring most of all was the American way of doing business. And when he had been there, done that as a tourist, 'my inactivity became a real problem . . . it didn't suit me . . . and I started to look around for interesting ideas'.

It did not take him long to see several. 'This was around the time when the idea of specialisation was beginning to spawn a number of uniquely dedicated companies in the US,' he recalls.

> Becoming more and more popular were establishments that – unlike conventional garages that dealt with the total automotive repair repertoire – did just transmissions, or just exhausts, or just engines, or a small group of products like tyres and batteries. There were even firms that resprayed – and dried – the body of your car in one working day.
>
> This was all fascinating to me. Rather like the drive-in-and-out convenience of the fast-food chains like McDonald's and Kentucky Fried Chicken, what they had was speed, instant reactions and value for money. I sensed something important was happening and I went to visit as many of them as I could, to look around, make friends and ask questions.
>
> I was attracted by the whole idea of specialisation, as I had previously been touching on that with tyres and car accessories,

so to some extent I was topping up what I already knew. But there were other factors that impressed me, such as the Americans' level of customer service – something the British were not too good at in the Seventies – and the respect they expressed for good employees through good remuneration. All in all, I was intrigued by the thought of bringing all that back to Scotland.

Sir Tom is a tidy man in his sixties, with neat, well-balanced features, a friendly smile, thinning brown hair, and a liking for dark business suits. He drives a top-of-the-range Mercedes and his office is always pristine. But for the rest, he has few pretensions, still speaking with a gentle Scottish accent and being happy to deal personally with customers – often to their surprise, for he is something of a legend in Scotland. One night, when he was working late and the staff had gone home, a difficult client telephoned his previous HQ and demanded to speak to the manager.

'This is Tom Farmer,' came the reply.

'Aye,' said the disbelieving caller, 'and I'm Sean Connery.'

Sir Tom's considerable achievements may have been recognised by the Queen with the bestowal of a knighthood in 1997, but the one-time store boy has developed few social or intellectual pretensions. 'We all have different qualities to offer society,' he says. 'When we were born God gave some people high intellect. He gave some high energy, and He gave some a good dose of common sense.'

Where would he put himself? 'High energy and common sense,' he responds without hesitation. 'What these two qualities give you is the ability – when you see an opportunity – to reach out and do something about it immediately.'

If that means he is denying himself intellectual talents, Sir Tom can nevertheless be quite philosophical and back that up with strong evidence of late-night reading. Explaining his decision to return to Scotland from the USA after a couple of years, for instance, he quotes Alfred Lord Tennyson from 'Hands All Round': 'That man's the best cosmopolite who loves his country best'.

And so, like the good cosmopolite and incurable entrepreneur that he is, Tom Farmer took not just his family back to Scotland in the early 1970s but also a lot of America's spirit, in the form of many new and exciting ideas.

Indeed, he had three favourite ones, all based on the specialisation principle, and he was determined to try them all. There was the super-quick paint-spraying venture ('a straight copy of the American idea') that got so busy that the supply of skilled painters could not keep up with the forty-cars-a-day demand. There was World of Sound, focusing on car radios and stereos. And there was that other little idea specialising in high-speed, while-you-wait fitting of exhaust pipes, brakes and tyres. He was sure it had great promise but what it really needed was a slick, easy-to-remember name.

That was when his Kooker Kleaning past came back to him. 'I was not too well at the time,' he recalls. 'Just lying in bed with 'flu, thinking and thinking . . . then, as I remembered the cooker idea, it came to me in an Archimedes moment – Eureka! Kwik-Fit was born. It was just the perfect name. It explained so clearly what we would be trying to do.'

Soon, he had called together many of his old gang of fitters from Buccleuch Street and the rest is history. Starting with one local station in Edinburgh in 1971, the chain just 'growed and growed like Topsy' at a speed he himself had not anticipated. At a time when you often had to make appointments a week ahead with conventional garages, the while-you-wait-and-watch convenience and American-inspired cheerful customer service caught on quickly. While people all over Britain, from schoolchildren to grandmothers, knew the company's catchy televised slogan 'You can't get better than a Kwik-Fit fitter', the company's station-count had topped the 400 mark within 17 years – not just planting Farmer flags in Scotland and England but also on mainland Europe, in Holland and Belgium, where there were no fewer than 50.

A cosmopolite he may have been, but the port-raised Farmer was anything but insular: a charge that is often set against British business people. Despite his fast-rising wings and growing fame, the dapper entrepreneur kept his smart black shoes tied firmly on the ground over all the years in which his company grew out further and further, to France and North Africa; then on to Thailand and even the Pacific Islands. 'Why did I do it?' he asks himself. 'Well, on my travels to Amsterdam or Paris or further afield, I couldn't help noticing that there were an awful lot of cars in the streets of these cities, and to me these represented business, of course.'

When Kwik-Fit had finished expanding, it had over 2,500 outlets and 11,000 employees across the world. So phenomenal was its growth that £100 invested at its birth in the early 1970s would have been worth £23,000 at the time of its sale to Ford.

That time was 1999, and there were many reasons for Ford's bold buying strategy (which kept on Sir Tom as Kwik-Fit chairman for the transition period). The idea was not just about taking over a now-famous brand name and growing it to be even bigger in the States. 'Ford wanted to cement its position in Europe in the light automotive repair industry,' says Sir Tom, 'and ours was the biggest organisation of that type in the world.'

In Kwik-Fit the American giant saw development potential for its embryonic policy in the 'after-market' business – which meant building strong permanent bonds between itself and its car customers: an after-care programme in which a Ford purchaser would have his or her car, and its parts requirements, looked after through the organisation for life, and so would – presumably – always came back to Ford for the next purchase.

As Kwik-Fit had already diversified into parts, mobile fitting and insurance, its acquisition represented for Ford a ready-made basis on which to build. 'When Ford executives came to see me for the early discussions it was clear that they were most interested in developing the parts business,' says Sir Tom. 'It is, after all, extremely lucrative – when you consider that a £10,000 car is probably worth £25,000 when you break down and sell all its parts separately.'

Indeed, while the gigantic $1.6 billion price paid made many people gasp, Ford's muscle and positive after-market business plan behind the final stage of Kwik-Fit's global spread seemed to make sense to most business commentators; so it was with some surprise that, only a couple of years later, they learned that reverse gear was suddenly being engaged with a back-to-basics philosophy, and that the project was to be stopped in its tracks.

'Profit margins had been squeezed at Ford over that period,' explains Sir Tom, 'and there had been top management changes: people coming in with different ideas.'

So in mid-2002, Ford announced that, despite having originally hoped to raise about £800 million from divesting itself of the Scottish car-repair empire, it had agreed to sell it for £330 million – about a quarter of the 1999 purchase price – to the European private equity group CVC Capital Partners. The car giant retained a 19 per cent stake in Kwik-Fit, allowing it to benefit from future growth.

As the beneficiary of all these corporate machinations in what was clearly a massive personal coup, Sir Tom ironically found himself explaining on Ford's behalf that, while it had bought Kwik-Fit in more buoyant times and had had 'grand plans' for the chain, 'circumstances have changed throughout the world and it has decided it wants to concentrate on its core business'.

In view of this awesome financial success and his company's general track record of super-fast growth, some people (and not a few Scots) have called Sir Tom lucky. And he might agree, although he remembers how 'we worked like Trojans' and how young employees were selected for their high energy and communicating personalities which complemented their bosses' sense of mission and also pleased the customer.

Yet Sir Tom does not think of himself as driven, especially not these days, when he is 'taking time to smell the flowers'. He denies being a 'workaholic' and likes to add that 'people should work to live, not live to work'.

Though he can still skip up the stairs of his smart new office, urgency is no longer a big consideration, a fact perhaps reflected in the less-than-kwik title of his new co-ownership enterprise – Tyres 'n' Wheels Farmer Autocare – which he runs alongside several vast property projects. You sense that he wouldn't worry too much if Autocare's growth pace turned out to be considerably slower than Kwik-Fit's.

For Sir Tom, working to live means sheer enjoyment of his daily endeavours. And he has never found them tiresome or boring or (excuse the expression) exhausting. 'It's been wonderful,' he says, with genuine surprise.

> What happened with me was quite exceptional. Sometimes I have found myself wondering if it's all a dream. But I wouldn't want to be pointed at as some kind of template for success. I would hate people to be saying to each other: 'There's Tom Farmer – you haven't done well with your life if it doesn't measure up to his.'
>
> Success is relative. I was reminded of that by my son John when I complained about some Joe Bloggs having reached his 'comfort level'. John said: 'Why shouldn't he enjoy his life?' And he was right. Not everybody needs to be a Tom Farmer – and if they were, there would be no one to work for me!

The Farmer formula for success, however, would be a hard one to beat. 'There's a great benefit in being second first, or maybe I mean first second,' he says.

> In being able to look at how other people do things, and take what they're doing and adapt it and change it for your own market. The

pioneers of this world are not necessarily always the most successful. I was able to see a lot of things that were happening and I always had quite an inquisitive mind. I remember a tour of America with my son in which we just talked to people in big retailers like Sears, Roebuck & Co. We'd always pick up something and come back to Scotland and adapt it accordingly.

What then happened turned the tables a bit. We set up a number of training schools in a programme called, very simply, the Kwik-Fit Way. Then we found American companies starting to make visits to Edinburgh to spend time with us, to see how we were doing it, as did other companies from all over the world. What were we doing that was new? Why were we so successful? What was the secret sauce we had? It was actually very simple. We were just doing what many good US firms were doing . . . only changing it a little to try to do better.

The US widened my whole thinking . . . I built tremendous relationships with tyre companies like the Big O and Discount Tires . . . I made more friends in America than anywhere else in the business.

Sir Tom likes to feel that, despite Ford's change of heart, his remarkable company had a big impact on US corporate life – without ever having been there.

It would just be returning the compliment to America, he feels.

# Tony Blair (1953–    )

*The presidents' vital friend*

From the top of the little front lawn of 5 Paisley Terrace you get a spectacular view across the glittering River Forth estuary and its islands into the Kingdom of Fife beyond. Tony Blair may have been only nineteen months old when he left this modest 1930s bungalow in Edinburgh's elevated Willowbrae district, but even then, playing in the garden or gazing out the front window, he must have had a sweeping sense of space and the limitless possibilities that lay before him.

Grand thoughts perhaps, and it has to be said that the underwhelming impact of the house itself seems hardly worthy of them, with even its owners admitting its need for 'love and attention' when it was offered for sale with a starting price of £155,000 in late 2004.

But it was in this unremarkable two-bedroom semi-detached house, similar to all the others in the neighbourhood, that his parents, Leo and Hazel, lived when Anthony Charles Lynton Blair was born on 6 May 1953, at Edinburgh's Queen Mary Maternity Home. At the end of the following year the family left for Australia, where Leo – a Conservative tax inspector who studied hard to become a lawyer – had been offered a lecturing job. It lasted five years, after which they returned to the UK to live in the English cathedral city of Durham, though Tony picked up his Scottish roots again when he spent 1966 to 1971 at one of the capital's most prestigious private schools, the Disney-towered Fettes College.

Having followed the professional (if not political) example of his father and gone on to study law at Oxford University, he became a practising trial lawyer after graduation in 1975, and simultaneously developed an interest in national politics – an interest abruptly heightened when he was elected Labour MP for Sedgefield, near Durham, three years after marrying fellow trial lawyer Cherie Booth in 1980. They had four children together, the latest christened Leo after the PM's father.

Blair served as Labour's trade and industry spokesman before being made Shadow Secretary of State for Energy. In 1989 he moved to the employment brief, and when his leader and mentor, fellow-Scot John Smith, died unexpectedly in 1994, Blair's fresh face seemed to promise considerable consolation as he took over the mantle.

It was to be an interesting journey. Though he had thought long and hard before choosing left-wing philosophy over the mores of his own relatively privileged background, he decided to draw on the latter to play the power game differently from his predecessors. He was the first Labour leader to see that, if it wanted to win its first taste of government since 1979, his party would have to shed much of its traditional socialist baggage and embrace a degree of free enterprise, while still keeping the old guard on-side.

It was a difficult balancing act, but he pulled it off. 'Ours is a philosophy, not of the past, not some relic of a museum, but of the future,' he told applauding supporters at a local Labour club at the end of his first campaign. And having espoused a refreshing political centralism and coined the seductive slogan 'New Labour, New Britain', he was on his way to real power.

It seemed people from every walk of life liked his boundless energy and easy, articulate command of argument. By the end of his first year as leader, the party had gained a strong lead in the opinion polls and its membership had risen by 150,000. So no one was surprised when, with its emphatic election in 1997, Blair became, at forty-three, the youngest British prime minister in 185 years. Nor was there much surprise when, in May 2001, he again swept to victory in the general election with a stunning 167-seat advantage in the House of Commons, the largest second-term majority in British history.

So Blair's administration had not only the numerical muscle but also the public mandate to carry out some pretty radical changes. It was a huge bank of political goodwill that seemed impossible to spend, as his government charged through an impressive agenda that included . . .

Granting the Bank of England the right to set interest rates without government consultation; signing the EU's Social Chapter, aimed at harmonising European social policies; setting up an elected post of Mayor of London at the head of a new capital-wide authority; reforming the House of Lords, upper chamber of Parliament; implementing a £42 billion investment programme in health and education; orchestrating the 1998 Good Friday peace accord between

Northern Ireland's Republicans and Unionists; devolving local legislative and executive power to assemblies in Wales and Scotland; and on the foreign policy front generally aligning with the USA rather than Europe.

In short, it did many good things that won much approval. But the last two points were rather more sensitive and controversial. Indeed, Blair's enthusiasm for both Scots and Americans was to see him spending much of his political capital.

On the Scottish front, not only did he turn something of a blind eye to the rapidly escalating cost of the brand new parliament building in Edinburgh, but at any given time his UK political appointees included an inordinate number of high-profile Scots – Gordon Brown as Chancellor, George Robertson as Defence Secretary, Robin Cook as Foreign Secretary, Alistair Darling as Transport Minister, John Reid as Health Minister. Even the UK Parliament's Speaker, Michael Martin, was from Glasgow – not to mention Labour Party Chairman Ian McCartney – and as his long honeymoon period began at last to fade, one could sense a growing English resentment at so many Scots (now with their own parliament, after all) having such big bites of the UK cherry.

Added to which, some senior cabinet Scots proved less than faithful as Blair's enthusiastic development of the 'special relationship' with the USA (first mooted by Churchill to keep the post-war Soviets at bay) brought real troubles down on his head. The turn of international events made him look increasingly embattled.

At first, it had all looked pretty positive. From the moment President Bill Clinton first visited the newly elected Blair at Downing Street in May 1997, there was an extra-special personal quality about the relationship between two men with so much power and so much ambition that would benefit from mutual help – the president in his second term seeking his place in history, the premier beginning his first term and determined to win a second. Together they would tackle the Northern Ireland problem, Iraq, Kosovo and . . . what Blair did not expect to have to deal with just after his first landslide victory was Clinton's sexual indiscretions, when his improper relationship with White House intern Monica Lewinsky threatened to bring him down through an impeachment process.

A good deal of Blair's credibility was spent on that when, at a Washington press conference ostensibly about Iraq weapons inspections, he found himself defending Clinton's 'pretty impressive record' and urging everyone 'to focus upon the issues we were elected to focus upon'.

It was almost a relief when, at the end of that year, 1998, the two countries got down to the serious business of launching joint air strikes aimed at degrading Iraq's ability to produce weapons of mass destruction, and employing military strategies during the 1999 Kosovo crisis to force then-Serbian president Slobodan Milošević's troops to withdraw.

But the president's second term expired at the end of 2000, and no sooner had the two natural bedfellows bid each other a fond farewell than a new American challenge came Blair's way, with the highly disputed election of George W. Bush. Though they came from opposite sides of the political spectrum, it was seen as important by each that the Blair–Bush alliance should be just as strong as the Blair–Clinton one. And if there were any doubts about that, they were blown away by the explosive force of Osama Bin Laden's attack on New York's twin towers on September 11, 2001.

In the subsequent 'war against terrorism' British troops joined US and other allied forces in a war that failed to find Bin Laden but overthrew the Taliban regime of Afghanistan. And in a move thought by many to be a step too far, Blair further cemented Britain's position as America's closest European ally, with his unswerving support of a war against Iraq in the spring of 2003. Both leaders having accused Iraqi President Saddam Hussein of developing chemical and biological weapons in violation of UN Security Council resolutions, they embarked on a risky strategy of convincing their respective peoples that, as weapons inspections had failed, military action was justified.

The Security Council refused to sanction force, but Bush and Blair pushed on regardless of that – and fierce opposition from disillusioned supporters, shocked political colleagues and record numbers of anti-war protestors, including over a million in London. American and British forces began attacking Iraq in March 2003, flattening much of Baghdad, ousting Saddam's regime within a few weeks, and eventually capturing the tyrant himself, who had exchanged his many golden palaces for a hole in the ground. But the challenge of stabilising and rebuilding the country had been clearly underestimated, as unyielding insurgent activity repeatedly blew apart any attempt to calm things down, particularly the aborted election plan of January 2005.

Even left-wingers could have forgiven Blair his political allegiance and personal warmth towards Bush, the repeated displays of buddy-style hospitality as each hosted the other at his office or home on the range, as it were. Even the exaggerated suspicion of Iraqi WMD justifying the war could be forgotten by others. But what could never be forgiven by most voters was the flouting of the Security Council. This, they argued, made the war illegal, and while Bush sailed through into a second term at the end of 2004, the once-'Teflon' Tony never really recovered from the charge.

Though he broke Clement Attlee's record as the UK's longest continuously serving Labour prime minister in August 2003, Blair's popularity slumped amid allegations that he had misled the public about the Iraqi weapons threat, and there was little surprise that, when he was elected for the third time in May 2005, it was with a paper-thin majority.

Sooner rather than later, it seemed, the Blair family would be leaving 10 Downing Street and moving into the elegant £3.6 million home in London's Connaught Square purchased during the busy years in anticipation of less-busy times.

An unhappy end to a remarkable journey. But all things considered, still a far cry from 5 Paisley Terrace.